Voice of an Exile

Voice of an Exile

Reflections on Islam

Nasr Abu Zaid with Esther R. Nelson

PRAEGER

Westport, Connecticut
London

Library of Congress Cataloging-in-Publication Data

Abu Zayd, Nasr Hamid.
  Voice of an exile : reflections on Islam / Nasr Abu Zaid with Esther R. Nelson.
    p. cm.
  Includes bibliographical references and index.
  ISBN 0–275–98250–5 (alk. paper)
    1. Abu Zayd, Nasr Hamid. 2. Scholars, Muslim—Egypt—Biography. 3. Intellectuals—
  Egypt—Biography. 4. Islamic renewal—Egypt. 5. Islamic modernism—Egypt. I. Title.
  BP80.A295A3 2004
  297′.092—dc22
  [B]   2003062427

British Library Cataloguing in Publication Data is available.

Library of Congress Catalog Card Number: 2003062427
ISBN: 0–275–98250–5

First published in 2004

Praeger Publishers, 88 Post Road West, Westport, CT 06881
An imprint of Greenwood Publishing Group, Inc.
www.praeger.com

Printed in the United States of America

♾️™

The paper used in this book complies with the
Permanent Paper Standard issued by the National
Information Standards Organization (Z39.48–1984).

10 9 8 7 6 5 4 3 2 1

*To Cliff, who like Nasr, is Sensei
of the sensei—Teacher of the teacher*

Contents

Preface

I first became acquainted with Nasr Abu Zaid after reading Mary Anne Weaver's article "Revolution by Stealth" in *The New Yorker* (June 8, 1998). I was immediately drawn to his story. Islamists forced Nasr from Cairo University, his alma mater and the institution where he currently taught, charging him with heresy. His crime? Nasr had stated in his writings that history and culture must be taken into account when interpreting the Qur'an. In addition, Nasr argued for a metaphoric interpretation of the Qur'an rather than an inflexible, literal understanding of that sacred text.

In June 1995, the Cairo Court of Appeals found "that Abu Z[a]id's writings in and of themselves proved him to be an apostate."[1] Islamists threatened his life. He no longer was able to teach. Guards, armed with machine guns, surrounded his home. Islamist lawyers attempted to separate him from his wife, Dr. Ebtehal Younes, also a professor at Cairo University, on the grounds that a Muslim woman cannot be married to a non-Muslim. Nasr, having been declared an apostate, could no longer be considered a Muslim. Subsequently both of them fled to the Netherlands, and since then Nasr has been teaching Arabic and Islamic Studies at Leiden University.

In 2000, my husband began working for an oil company in Saudi Arabia. Since then, I've split my time between Saudi Arabia and the United States. When I'm in the States, I teach religious studies in the School of World Studies at Virginia Commonwealth University in Richmond. In February 2002, I discovered Nasr all over again in an

interview article, written by Daniel del Castillo, on the back page of
The Chronicle of Higher Education (February 8, 2002), titled "An
Exiled Scholar of Islam." Again, I felt myself drawn to his story. In this
interview, Nasr states, "We have a problem in the Arab world of intellectuals only talking to intellectuals." And "the basic issue behind terrorism [is the] absence of any public sphere for exchanging ideas."

Excitedly, I showed the interview article to my department chairman, Dr. Cliff Edwards. "It seems to me," he stated matter-of-factly,
"that if someone were flying through Amsterdam on her way to the
Middle East, she could easily stop off and interview Nasr Abu Zaid."
Yes, yes, of course. That's exactly what I would do. But would he agree
to meet with me? If so, what would I say? How would I explain what
it was that drew (and continues to draw) me to his story?

I grew up in Buenos Aires, Argentina, the daughter of evangelical,
fundamentalist missionaries. My parents spent their lifetimes fighting
heresy. Convinced they were commissioned by God Himself, they had
devoted their lives to God's service. Their job was to "Go . . . into all
the world, and preach the gospel to every creature," fully assured that
"He that believeth and is baptized shall be saved; but he that believeth
not shall be damned."[2] My parents never wielded enough power to
issue death threats. It's hard to imagine them ever carrying out such
edicts. Nonetheless, they easily and comfortably took God on their side,
understood Truth through a specific interpretation of a specific text, and
were not at all bashful about condemning to hell those who understood
and believed differently from them.

What always seemed odd to me was that today's heresy, over
time, could (and often would) become tomorrow's Truth. In the meantime, those who manage to have themselves declared apostate and
branded as heretics are stripped of their dignity, discriminated against,
discredited—and sometimes have to run for their lives. I could never
quite buy into the fundamentalist rhetoric that my parents defended.
However, fundamentalism as a system knows no ideological boundaries. No wonder I felt so drawn to Nasr's story.

I am grateful to Dr. Cliff Edwards, my department chairman, for
encouraging me to get in touch with Nasr. Without Cliff's gentle prod-
ding and steadfast encouragement, this book would not have taken off.
Nor could this book have come into being without the efforts of
Suzanne I. Staszak-Silva, senior editor of Greenwood Publishing
Group. I'm grateful for Suzanne's expertise and cheerful readiness to
attend to the innumerable details involved with bringing a book to
publication. Most of the text took shape after I spread out my materials

on my sister Betty's kitchen table in Redwood, Virginia, and began to peck away at the keys of a laptop computer. Not only did Betty ignore the clutter in her kitchen, she provided a cozy home for me in the midst of my gypsylike existence. A kinder and more loving sister would be hard to find. In addition, Nasr's patience seemed endless as he tirelessly unfolded Islamic doctrine to me while simultaneously weaving that doctrine into his own life experience. Throughout the text, Nasr demonstrates that personal experience cannot be separated from scholarly achievement. Experience provides the stuff from which scholarship sprouts.

My first meeting with Nasr happened in a coffee shop underneath Leiden's train station in May 2002. As we chatted over coffee and tea, I noticed the sleeves on Nasr's navy blue suit jacket inching higher and higher. Eventually, a good six inches of white shirt on each arm lay exposed. I couldn't help but think that here was a man ready to roll up his sleeves and get to work. And that's exactly what happened. But even more noteworthy was that as we continued to talk underneath the rumbling of commuter trains, I felt Nasr's warmth, compassion, and generosity flowing from what I can best describe as the heart of a born teacher.

I suggested that Nasr write a book about himself, not merely focusing on the events that led to his exile (although that would be included), but also showing the path that carried him along his scholarly journey. How did he come to see and interpret the Qur'an from a perspective that today is at odds with mainstream understanding?

"I would love to write such a book in English," Nasr assured me. "I speak English so much better than I'm able to write it. This is a problem for me."

"That's where I come in," I said. "I'll help you craft your story. My degree is in English—writing and rhetoric."

What follows is the product of our combined efforts. Above all, we want to convey to our reading audience that Islam, like all major world religions, expresses itself in a wide variety of ways. There is no single Islam. We also believe dialogue among Muslims (as well as with non-Muslims) regarding the various expressions of Islam to be an essential ingredient in promoting understanding both within and outside Islam. If our work contributes toward that end, we will count ourselves as having been successful.

Esther R. Nelson

1 Exiled

I left Egypt—my home—in 1995. Ever since then, I've been a professor of Arabic and Islamic Studies at Leiden University in the Netherlands, a well-known institution established in 1575. Leiden is located south of Amsterdam, a thirty-minute train ride from the center of the city. During the day, I'm busy supervising students, digging away at my research through my writing, debating with my colleagues, attending conferences, and speaking to the public through community events and functions. It's what we scholars do in our attempt to create and disseminate knowledge.

At night, though, I dream of Egypt. I was born in Egypt. The waters of the Nile flow through my veins. Egypt has shaped me. To this day, I remain thoroughly Egyptian. Born on July 10, 1943, in Quhafa, a small village near Tanta in the Nile Delta, to ordinary, poor, hardworking parents, I learned early on about the concept of justice. Justice lies at the heart of the Qur'an. I've worked on and developed this idea of justice in my scholarship—especially as it applies to social issues. But I'm getting ahead of myself.

I live in exile. Some of the facts surrounding the case which led to my exile are widely known. Other facts have not been as well publicized. This is what happened: In May 1992, I applied to the Department of Arabic at Cairo University for promotion to full professor. I submitted my publications (eleven papers and two books) to the University Tenure and Promotion Committee. This committee gave the material to a subcommittee of three professors to evaluate. Those professors were Dr. Abd al-Sabur Shahin, professor in the College of Dar al-Ulum and a fundamentalist preacher in the Amr ibn al-As Mosque in Old Cairo; Dr. Mahmud Ali Makki, professor of Andalusian Studies at Cairo University; and Dr. Awni Abd al-Ra'uf, professor of linguistics at 'Ayn Shams University. The job of the University Tenure and Promotion Committee was to write a report, based on the report from the subcommittee, and then to send it, with their recommendation, to the dean of the faculty.

Seven months later, December 3, 1992—four months longer than the usual period of time to decide such things—I learned that the committee had rejected my bid for promotion. Later on, I found that I had narrowly missed being promoted by a vote of 7 to 6, not the unanimous verdict that the official report claimed. Professors in the Department of Arabic Studies, colleagues of mine, had submitted a favorable report on my behalf that stressed the breadth of my knowledge, my scientific contributions to the field of Islamic Studies, and my use of modern methodology when doing research. The departmental report emphasized my use of *ijtihâd*, independent reasoning. Many Muslims today consider "the gates of *ijtihâd*" closed. Those gates have been shut in traditional Islam since the thirteenth century. This means that scholars today must rely on insights garnered before the thirteenth century as they attempt to bring the Qur'an to bear on the *umma*, the Muslim community. There is no place, nor space, to come to new insights regarding the Qur'an through application of modern scholarship to the sacred text. Of the three experts consulted by the committee, two gave a positive report on my work. Shahin did not. According to him, my writing demonstrated an "atrophy of religious conscience" while engaging in "intellectual terrorism." He likened my work to "cultural AIDS" and a "Marxian-secularist attempt to destroy Egypt's Muslim society."[1]

There were specific things about my scholarship that Shahin took issue with. Among them was my contention that many different copies of the *mushaf*, a word literally meaning "book," circulated during the time of the Prophet. The *mushaf* contains the Qur'an, although when we speak about the Qur'an, we understand that the Qur'an is not limited to the *mushaf*. The Qur'an can reside in the memory of the reciter. So when Muslims speak about the Qur'an, we refer to that which can be memorized and orally transmitted. When we speak about the *mushaf*, we refer to the book in which the Qur'an is written. When the Prophet Muhammad died (632), there were many copies of the *mushaf* circulating among his followers. People wanted their own copy. In spite of this, oral transmission of the Qur'an was (and in many ways still is) the primary means of passing on the sacred text to succeeding generations. The early copies of the *mushaf* were written using Arabic letters. At that time, there were no vowels signs. It didn't matter a whole lot because the text was merely an aid to the memory of the reciter.

'Uthmân ibn 'Affân, the third caliph, was instrumental in bringing about a standardized Qur'anic text. Muhammad, before his death, had begun the task of getting the revelation into textual form. Scribes used materials such as rocks and palm leaves for that purpose, so the written text was already in existence when 'Uthmân came along. There were, however, different ways of reciting and reading the Qur'an because of the varieties of dialects spoken by the Prophet's followers. The Prophet had no qualms about these variations. How could a standardized dialect be enforced, anyway?

During 'Uthmân's caliphate, soldiers from various backgrounds were thrust together in close quarters. As they recited the Qur'an according to the particular version they had learned, they noticed some differences—differences that stemmed from the variety of dialects represented. They began to accuse each other of making changes in the sacred text. Because of this dispute, 'Uthmân decided to standardize the Qur'an. A committee gathered together, produced the Ottomanic *mushaf*, and subsequently decided that all other copies of the Qur'an should be burned. A dispute erupted—people were loath to give up their personal copies, but the decision to standardize the Qur'an had been made.

This is history. There were different *mushaf*s circulating during the Prophet's time along with a variety of ways of reciting the text, not different Qur'ans. This was not new information for Shahin, a man who earned his Ph.D. doing work on the history of the Qur'an. I quoted publicly from his work, showing where he himself makes mention of the variety of *mushaf*s in circulation among families in the earliest Muslim communities. Why was he going against his own scholarship and taking me to task on this issue?

Shahin also balked at my scholarship that argues for a human dimension of the Qur'an. Orthodox Islam has always insisted that the Qur'an is God's eternal, uncreated speech. Because it always existed, it was never created. The fact that the Qur'an was revealed to Muhammad in the context of seventh-century Arabia should have no bearing on how we interpret the text. The text should be read literally and applied uniformly across time and place. As a result of this understanding, Islam has no tradition of using textual criticism—a practice long employed by Hebrew and biblical scholars. Nonetheless, there have been Islamic scholars who have challenged the orthodoxy. The rationalist school known as the Mu'tazilites emerged in the ninth century under the Abbasid Empire (750–935). They argued that the Qur'an, having come into existence at a specific time and in a specific place, was indeed created. There's a difference, they insisted, between God's essence—something eternal and beyond human understanding—and God's Word, which is created and accessible to reason. Even though the Mu'tazilites were marginalized after only two decades, their thinking has remained alive and has carried down through the generations. I believe that in order to make sense of the Qur'an, we need to understand the text metaphorically rather than literally. I also believe that it is essential to interpret the text by taking into account the cultural context in which it was received.

To be sure, my scholarship is controversial. I bear the guilt of trafficking in ideas. But isn't that what the academy is all about? Ideas, debate, teaching, research. The climate in Egypt today is one of intellectual stagnation when it comes to the study of religion. Lack of any public space to exchange and debate ideas has resulted in a siege mentality. To offer new explanations or interpretations of religion becomes a blasphemous act. In universities throughout the Muslim world, no Islamic scholarship exists. You'll find plenty of preaching, but no comparative study. I use nontraditional research methods as I delve into the field of Islamic Studies. That alone is enough to label me apostate.

A verbal war erupted between the Islamists, who balked at the conclusions I reached as a result of my scientific, methodological research regarding the Qur'an, and the intellectual freethinkers, who were appalled at Cairo University just rolling over and playing dead while people they described as bullies—the Islamists—swayed academic decisions. As a result of this "bullying," I was denied my promotion to full professor.

What's at the core of this clash? Two ways of thinking. The Islamists cling to the immutability of the past. This attachment to the past appeals to those who find change and development threatening. Intellectual free-thinkers such as I do not consider our Islamic heritage sacred in and of itself. Islamic Studies has always emerged from human thought about religion. As culture develops and moves forward, our thinking needs to develop and go forward in relationship to the Qur'an as well. Modern methods of scholarship can help us know how to apply the Qur'an in useful and meaningful ways to our ever-changing world. My quarrel has never been with religion, but with the religious thought (which is human thought) coming from, in this particular case, the Islamists.

In spite of this clash of ideologies, I'm convinced that Shahin allowed his personal animosity toward me to cloud an objective, scholarly assessment of my work. He was the one individual on the subcommittee who voted against me. I think I know why.

In the introductory pages of my book *Critique of Islamic Discourse*,[2] I draw attention to the relationship between political Islamist discourse in Egypt and the socioeconomic scandal brought about by Islamic investment companies. Islamists had published a number of *fatwas* (formal legal opinions on matters of Islamic law) condemning the current Egyptian banking system as religiously illegal because it operates on a fixed interest rate. This is usury, they said, and therefore prohibited in Islam.

Islamic investment companies sprang up as alternative institutions to the usurious practice of Westernized banks. These investment companies, among them al-Rayyan Islamic Investment Company—the one Shahin was associated with—claimed they structured themselves according to Islamic principles. Because of the *fatwas*, many Egyptian people put their savings into these investment companies. These companies were at the center of a huge public scandal in 1988. Hundreds of thousands of people, trusting the companies' representatives and attracted by the religious emblems designed to appeal to Egyptians' religious sensibilities, lost their life savings. Shahin, the religious adviser to al-Rayyan Islamic Investment Company, stood accused of misappropriating the savings of the faithful.

I believe Shahin became incensed after reading the introductory pages of *Critique of Islamic Discourse*, one of the two books I had submitted to the University Tenure and Promotion Committee. In his report, he made no comment on the bulk of my scholarship, nor did he address my methodology. When the professors of my department read the report that rejected my bid for full professor, they protested by writing a letter to the dean. They argued that Shahin had not kept abreast of scholarly research, nor had he familiarized himself with theoretical developments such as semiotics. The professors also believed

Public denunciation

NIS-Yale 1975

that Shahin either had not read or had failed to appreciate my work as a whole. They thought that his report went beyond the scope of the Tenure and Promotion Committee's job, which was to investigate the scholarship of the candidate up for promotion, without any other consideration. Shahin, they concluded, was passing judgment on my faith rather than on my academic credentials.

Within the academy, matters came to a head when all the documents—the report of the committee rejecting my appointment, the favorable report reflecting departmental opinion about me, and the faculty's endorsement of this opinion—were placed in the hands of Ma'mun Salama, rector of Cairo University. The position of rector of a university is a political appointment. Eager to keep his job, as well as to keep things on an even keel and not provoke the Islamists in the university, Salama found it easier to deny my promotion than to address the core issue—manipulation of the academy by a political group. Salama thought I could reapply for full professor some months down the road and get promoted in the second go-round. Provoking the Islamists by attempting a compromise was just too dangerous. Unfortunately, Salama behaved in an academically irresponsible manner. His failure to take a stand grossly compromised the integrity of the academy. This, to me, is an extremely serious issue.

Besides his job as professor at Cairo University, Shahin is a preacher in Amr ibn al-As Mosque in Old Cairo. On Friday, April 2, 1993, not long after I was officially denied my promotion, Shahin, from the pulpit of this mosque, declared me an apostate. The following Friday, April 9, preachers in mosques all over the country followed Shahin's lead, including the preacher in a small mosque in Quhafa, my home village. The preacher in that mosque and I grew up together. We learned and memorized the Qur'an in the traditional school known as *kuttâb*. My friend believed Shahin's allegation that I was an apostate. Why else would a man of his caliber speak out so forcefully? The university's decision to deny my promotion gave the apostasy label even more weight.

Denounced in public

Once I had been declared an apostate from the pulpit, Muhammad Samida Abd al-Samad, an Islamist lawyer, along with six of his colleagues, brought a case against me before the Personal Affair Department of the Giza Court of the First Instance on June 10, 1993. They wanted to separate me from my wife, Dr. Ebtehal Younes, an associate professor of French at Cairo University, on the grounds that I was an apostate.

Shari'a consists of laws derived from the Qur'an and the *sunna* (Prophetic tradition). The *sunna* contains the *hadith*—the sayings of the Prophet—and other documented teachings of the Prophet not found in the Qur'an. Islamists claim that *shari'a* law is divinely ordained and immutable—valid for all times and all places. I, along with others, believe that *shari'a* law is a human interpretation of principles found within the Qur'an and Islamic history. Islam is flexible, and when we apply reasoning to the sacred texts, we promote individual and public well-being by steering Qur'anic interpretation in the direction of the Word of God.

In Egypt, *shari'a* court was abolished during Gamal Abdel Nasser's regime (1952–1970) in favor of a judicial system based on secular principles. The one exception to this secularization was family law. So my case went before the Personal Affair Court through use of a ninth-century principle called *hisba*. *Hisba* allows any Muslim to sue before a court of law if he or she believes Islam is being harmed. The person who sues need not be personally involved in the case.

This is how *hisba* worked in my case: In Islam, a Muslim woman may not marry outside her faith. I stood accused of being an apostate—outside the pale of Islam. Therefore, I was being sued for separation, not by my wife but by a group of Islamists charging me with apostasy. Our marital status, of course, did not really concern them. Their intent was to have me declared an apostate by the court. Their one chance to do this was to use the *hisba* loophole. (Even though this loophole was responsible for my ultimate conviction of apostasy, due largely to the work of my lawyer, Mona Zulficar, a law was passed in 2000 that closed the *hisba* loophole. Because this loophole no longer exists, the courts have rejected hearing the cases of several liberal thinkers and artists. Mona has told me, "We have unfairly lost the battle, but we are winning the war.")

Abd al-Sauad and his entourage charged me with publishing material that reputable scholars declared put me outside Islam. If the court were to find my writings blasphemous, not only would my marriage be officially dissolved, but proceedings could begin to have me fired from my teaching post at the university. The editor of the moderate Islamic weekly *al-Liwâ' al-Islâmî* (The Islamic Banner), a newspaper financed by Egypt's ruling party, published an editorial (April 15, 1993) that railed against "the heretic Abu Zaid" as someone who endangered the spirituality of his students and urged the rector of Cairo University to fire me.

The intellectual community throughout the Arab and Muslim world was up in arms. How could this be happening? What about freedom of thought within the academy? How could a person's faith be a matter of public discussion and up for judgment before the courts? The Egyptian Organization for Human Rights urged the government to provide police protection for Ebtehal and me. Muslim extremists had gunned down and killed Farag Foda, an Egyptian secularist, in 1992. Later (1994), they tried to snuff out the life of Naguib Mahfouz, a Nobel laureate in literature, by stabbing him in the neck—an act that, ironically, left him unable to use his hand to write. Things were spinning out of control—at least that's how it seemed to me.

Ever since the Islamists had succeeded in sticking the label of apostate on me, preachers in mosques all across Egypt had clamored for my death, at the same time declaring I had no right, as an apostate, to remain married to a Muslim woman. Ebtehal and I were confined to our apartment. Government guards, armed with automatic assault weapons, were stationed around the block where we lived. Ebtehal and I feared for our lives.

I felt some relief when the Giza First Instant Court ruled in my favor in January 1994. That relief, though, was short-lived. The ruling was appealed through the use of a 1971 constitutional amendment that makes shari'a law "the principle source" of Egyptian law. (This amendment came as a result of Anwar Sadat's concession to Islamists. Sadat ruled Egypt from 1970 until his assassination in 1981.) The court accused me of denying "the existence of certain creatures such as angels and devils referred to in the Qur'an." It stated that I "described certain images in the Qur'an about heaven and hell as mythical," that I believed "the text of the Holy Qur'an [to be] human," and that I had "advocated the use of intellect to replace the concepts derived from the literal reading of the text of the Qur'an by modern, more human and progressive concepts, [particularly] the texts related to inheritance, women, the Christians and the Jews [ahl adh-dhimma] and women slaves."[3]

On June 14, 1995, just two weeks after Cairo University decided to promote me to full professor in spite of all the controversy surrounding me and my work, the Cairo Court of Appeals ruled that my writings proved I was indeed an apostate. Since Islamic law prohibits the marriage of a believer to an apostate, the courts declared my marriage to Ebtehal null and void. As if that were not enough, a fatwa issued by Ayman al-Zawahri from al-Jihad, the underground terrorist group responsible for assassinating Anwar Sadat, decreed that it was an Islamic duty that I be killed. A week later a group of scholars, known as the Front of al-Azhar Scholars, in an effort to force my repentance, called on the government to carry out the legal punishment for apostasy—death.

Islamists—including Shahin—were thrilled with the court's ruling. On June 16, 1995, while delivering his sermon at the Amr ibn al-As Mosque, he had this to say about the ruling of the Appeals Court: "The Court has issued its ruling after having examined the case over a period of two years, and has become convinced that the man [Abu Zaid] is an apostate who should be separated from his wife."[4]

On July 3, 1995, the Committee on Academic Freedom of the Middle East Studies Association of North America wrote a letter to President Hosni Mubarak. They were concerned. The ruling, they said, placed "drastic limits on the freedom of research and publication of our colleagues in Egypt," and was "incompatible with international norms of academic freedom and human rights."[5]

Even support such as this was not enough to reverse the ruling against me. When Mubarak came to power after Sadat's assassination, he signed a law which guaranteed immunity to the public prosecutor and his deputies. Egyptian intellectuals are generally happy that the judiciary system enjoys an independence offered by this immunity. I am more interested in having the system run its course with my case, not having Mubarak—or or anybody else—intervene.

On the evening of July 23, 1995, Ebtehal and I were on a plane, on our way to Spain. Ebtehal had made plans to be in Madrid for the month of September after having been awarded a professional fellowship. She had initially intended to go alone, but because of all the turmoil around us, we decided to go earlier and to go together. I remember telling her, "I don't want to go back to Egypt—back to the siege." That's all it took. By October 25, 1995, we were in Leiden, the Netherlands.

On August 5, 1996, the Egyptian Supreme Court upheld the June 14, 1995, Appeals Court's decision. The reasons for my conviction follow:

1. Describing certain things mentioned in the Qur'an such as the throne of God, angels, devils, jinn, paradise, and hell as myths of the past.
2. Calling the Qur'an a cultural product, thereby denying its pre-existence in the preserved Tablet.

3. Calling the Qur'an a linguistic text. (The implication is that the Prophet lied about receiving revelations from God.)
4. Calling the Qur'anic sciences . . . "reactionary heritage," and saying that the *shari'a* is the cause of Muslims' backwardness and decline.
5. Saying that a belief in the supernatural reflects a mind submerged in myth.
6. Calling Islam an Arabic religion, thus denying its universality.
7. Asserting that the final version of the Qur'an was established in the Qurayshi idiom in order to assert the supremacy of the Quraysh tribe. (Prophet Muhammad was from the Quraysh tribe.)
8. Denying the authenticity of the *sunna*.
9. Calling for emancipation from the authority of religious texts.
10. Contending that submitting to religious text is a form of slavery.[6]

There was no doubt about it in the collective mind of the courts. I was guilty of *kufr*, therefore, considered an infidel or an apostate.

Egyptian intellectuals groaned, knowing that the Supreme Court's decision was irrevocable. As a result of this decision, many intellectuals consider August 5, 1996, to be the darkest day in Egyptian history. A spokesman for the Egyptian Organization for Human Rights said the decision was "a big shock to us . . . a damaging blow to Egypt...and a slap in the face of civil society, a restriction on freedom of opinion and belief, and a license to murder." And Fahmi Huwaydi, a popular Egyptian columnist, called the Appeals Court verdict "symptomatic of a breakdown in society. Nobody debates anymore, only two channels are left, guns and judges."[7]

The conservative writer Dr. Muhammad 'Amara, known for his commitment to freedom of thought, acknowledged that my case was an intellectual one, not a legal one. If my work was to be challenged, it ought to be done through debate, not taken to the courts. He noted that the Qur'an does not prescribe punishment for apostasy. Death for such an offense is based on the *hâdith*, documented traditions of the Prophet's teachings and actions, which states, "He who changes his religion, and deserts the Muslim community, must be killed." Deserting the community, according to teachings which were later ascribed to Muhammad, was seen as tantamount to treason. "Faith," said 'Amara, "is a matter of assent and certainty in the heart."[8] The Qur'an asserts, "There shall be no compulsion in religion" (Sura 2:257).

A retired judge, Sa'îd al-Ashmawy, a prominent Egyptian Islamic scholar, noted:

> [F]or me, the most frightening thing about the Abu Z[a]id precedent is that the courts have no jurisdiction to judge whether a person is a believer or not—they can judge only concrete issues, not ideas. But in Abu Z[a]id's trial it was ideas that were on trial. This is the first time that the courts have ruled someone an apostate in modern history. We're returning to the Inquisition.[9]

Never do I want to give the impression that I am against Islam. Far from it. Nor do I want to give the impression that I am a new Salman Rushdie. I am not. One of my worst fears is that Westerners will consider me only as a critic of Islam. That's not the whole picture at all. I'm a teacher, a scholar, an intellectual, and a researcher. I see my role as a producer of concepts. I treat the Qur'an as a text given by God to the Prophet Muhammad. That text came to us in a human language, Arabic. As a result of my work, I have been critical of Islamic religious discourse. I show how social, political, and economic institutions use religious discourse to get hold of power. My work threatens some of those who wield that power. Nonetheless, I identify myself as a Muslim. I was born a Muslim, I was raised a Muslim, and I live as a Muslim. God willing, I will die a Muslim.

Those people who look for ways to discredit me and my work say that my "books don't amount to anything. Let him say whatever he wants,"[10] they insist, dismissing my ideas with a wave of their hand. And that's true—I am at liberty to write what I think. But look at the downside. I'm free to say and write whatever I want outside the university, but where freedom of thought is absolutely essential, I have been silenced. I can write all the books I want to, even propagate what some folks call heresy, but under no circumstances am I permitted to teach. That's considered much too dangerous. What kind of freedom is it that doesn't allow me to transform my ideas into any sort of power? Silencing is at the heart of my case. Expelling me from the university is a way of silencing me.

During the early summer of 1995, just after the courts declared our marriage over, I received a phone call from a woman whose daughter was in elementary school. The woman was extremely respectful. She said, "My daughter is just in elementary school but she is so upset about the verdict, forcing your separation from your wife, she would like to talk with you. May we stop by and see you?" Our apartment at this time was filled with people who supported us in our current trouble. We lived far outside of Cairo, but the woman told me her daughter could not be consoled. She wanted to visit with me. She could not imagine that a court verdict could enforce the separation of a husband from his wife against their will—all under the guise of religion. How could this be possible? In Egypt, the family is considered sacred. Separation and divorce are not light matters.

Even though she was quite young, this girl took her religion seriously. She insisted on wearing the *hijâb*, the traditional head covering of Muslim women. So, even though we lived quite a distance from them, the woman and her daughter came to visit. I was happy to receive them. What was significant to me about this visit and others like it was the fact that these folks, like so many people in Egypt, knew little, if anything, about my academic writing and scholarly pursuits. They had difficulty getting a handle on the crimes I supposedly had committed, but I'll not forget their support, their love, and their compassion toward Ebtehal and me. These visits were a source of strength and comfort.

I also found the response of many Egyptian women, interviewed by journalists, refreshing and quite telling. Many women frankly stated that they didn't understand the crime of Nasr Abu Zaid. Why this punishment? Why insist on divorce? Why destroy a family? It made no sense to them. They were particularly concerned about the fate of the children. Most people were unaware that we were childless. Nonetheless, their concern underscored the high esteem Egyptian people have for the family.

I remember one woman in particular. She was illiterate, but her thinking was sharp. She said, "Suppose this man really did say all these terrible things about God and the Qur'an. Suppose he is an apostate. I hear that his wife is a good Muslim." The argument, of course, is that we (Muslims) cannot let a Muslim woman be married to a non-Muslim. I, having been declared an apostate, could no longer be considered a Muslim.

The woman continued, "If Abu Zaid's wife is a good Muslim and she wants to live with him, why don't you leave them alone? Maybe she will be able to convince him to be a good man." This illiterate woman's understanding showed me that in spite of the patriarchal nature of Egyptian society, Egyptian women can and do resist living passive lives. Their resistance carries with it the possibility of shaking those patriarchal foundations, paving the way for a more just society.

At the same time, jokes and cartoons abounded in popular magazines and journals. One such cartoon showed a man sitting with his wife. The man's thought balloon reads, "I would like to know how Abu Zaid did it."

I understand from several of my friends that a one-act play, titled *Good Morning, Egypt,* appeared on the scene as well, mocking the process that declared me an apostate and separated me from Ebtehal. (I never saw the play and have been unable to locate the playwright. What I relay is what I remember from my friends' account.)

The title, *Good Morning, Egypt,* reflects the way Egyptians respond to you if they think you are talking nonsense. It's an attempt to get you to wake up and not behave as though you are still asleep. The title is really saying, "Wake up, Egypt." The play is not just about me. Parts of the play deal with politics in Egypt and the problem of housing, poking fun at different aspects of Egyptian society.

The first section of the play, though, is about me. It begins by projecting newspaper clippings titled "The Case against Abu Zaid" onto a screen, along with a display of all the covers of my books. An extremely angry woman then appears on stage. The cause of her anger is her upstairs neighbor, who sets out wet laundry that drips down on the woman's clothes. When the woman's husband returns home, she asks, "Can't you do something about this madwoman upstairs?"

"What can I do?" he asks.

"You are a lawyer. You have an office. Can't you just accuse her husband of apostasy like they did Abu Zaid, and ask them to separate?" the woman says.

The husband/lawyer succeeds in making a case. The court decides the upstairs couple should be separated. But who will leave the one-bedroom apartment? Egypt has a severe housing shortage. It wouldn't do to throw one of them out in the street. So they divide the apartment down the middle and a policeman watches their every move to ensure that there is no physical contact between them. After all, they are separated, and separation is understood within the framework of sex. This is all part of the spoof.

The audience then sees the couple in the same bed—a bed that separates easily into halves. A policeman stands guard over the couple. They're stuck living with one another because of the severe housing shortage in Cairo. The government cannot provide another living space for either of the individuals caught in this enforced separation, so the policeman keeps watch over the bed. God forbid the couple should have sex. As the policeman nods off, the bed that had separated down the middle comes together. The policeman's eyes start to open. The bed separates and the policeman starts to fall asleep again. This happens several times before the couple decides to grab hold of the cop and throw him out the window.

Actually, I think I gave the idea of this play to the playwright because Ebtehal and I made a joke about this very thing in the middle of the court case against us. Ebtehal and I said that we would never separate. "There is a problem," I noted. "Who will leave the apartment?" This happens all the time in Egypt when a couple divorces. Each person lays claim to the apartment. According to the law, the wife is allowed to stay put. But I said, "I am not going to leave the apartment to Ebtehal." Ebtehal responded with, "I am not going to give the apartment to Nasr. The government should give us each another place to live." So I feel that in a real way, Ebtehal and I wrote this play.

Egyptian society is definitely a traditional society. When it comes to the family, well, this is sacred ground.

I have a very dear friend—an actress—who visited Ebtehal and me at home sometime after the final verdict in our case. She was wailing, her grief and sadness apparent. "Oh, my God, what are they doing to you? They are destroying you. My poor friend."

Get a grip—that's what I really wanted to tell her. "Yes, they are trying to destroy me," I agreed with her, "but in fact, I am destroying them. I'm here. I never spoke a word." I did not defend myself in court. I refused to defend myself against charges of apostasy because I do not allow anyone, no matter whom, no matter what authority, to judge my faith.

My friend's demeanor changed. She no longer wailed or moped about.

"Don't ever think that I will allow myself to be victimized," I said. "I don't go around crying about things such as this. Doing so is not healthy, and I would like to have a healthy life."

What happened to me—the accusation, the conviction of apostasy, my enforced divorce, being deprived of my place at Cairo University, my exile—was hard on me. Through it all, I refused to play the role of a victim. I am not a victim. Neither am I Superman. But I refuse to be dragged too deeply into the muck and mire of the corrupt system that put me through the wringer. I love life and insist on living it to the fullest.

Interestingly enough, several years ago, Shahin wrote a book titled *My Father, Adam*.[11] This book tried to reconcile Darwinism with the

Qur'an. Shahin attempted to prove that Adam was not the first man.
The whole subject had been settled long ago. Shahin produced nothing new. I didn't think highly of his work. Shahin tried to come off as
a liberal thinker, but he made mistakes no undergraduate student
would make while developing a thesis. At any rate, the book brought
him accusations of heresy. The irony of the whole case wasn't wasted
on the Egyptian people. The thinking was "OK, Shahin, you once set
the fire, and now that same fire burns you."

A journalist called me, asking what I thought of this turn of events.
I think he was expecting me to say, "Wonderful, Shahin is getting a
taste of his own medicine," or something along those lines.

I think I surprised him. "No, I am not happy at all about this. What
we are witnessing is a fire in our house, a fire in our culture. We cannot kill a man for a stupid book."

"Are you supporting Shahin?" the journalist asked.

"Yes, definitely I am," I said. "I will defend his right to write what
he thinks."

Shahin didn't seem too happy about what I said. The Egyptian
people wanted to know what he made of my statement "We cannot
kill a man for a stupid book."

One of the journalists told me Shahin said, "What do you want
me to do? Should I go around saying, 'Thank you, Abu Zaid, you are
my hero'?"

How could I be happy about the system going after Shahin in the
same way it came after me? I believe that if you are not able to defend your enemy in a situation such as this, you cannot defend yourself. When we defend our opponents, the Islamists, we are really
defending ourselves. I'm not talking about defending their interests, but
I cannot support the principles of freedom and exclude the Islamists.
Some will tell you that when the Islamists talk about freedom, they
mean freedom only for themselves. That's true. But that doesn't mean
we should make the same mistake.

Nevertheless, Shahin's name is not popular in our household. He
was vicious as he pushed for our divorce during the trial. He offered
to bring Ebtehal another husband—he would pay for it all. I find it hard
to forgive such arrogance. If I have an opportunity, I will do my best
to insult him—not for my sake, but for Ebtehal's. Imagine! Offering to
bring Ebtehal a man to marry her. He's vulgar. I have to wonder. The
whole country. The president. The rector of Cairo University. The prime
minister. They all are aware that Shahin is as crooked as the day is

long. Egypt's culture considers marriage and family sacred. How could Shahin get away with treating the institution so disrespectfully?

Corruption. Corruption permeates everything about Egypt. It makes me terribly worried about the future of my country. Shahin, believe it or not, is a TV star. A corrupt society supporting a corrupt man. Because of the investment scandal in which he was implicated, people know he is a thief. People are lackadaisical about that. So what? they ask. I think if you are unable to confront a thief with his theft, there must be some skeleton in your own closet. It's the stuff corruption is made of.

Edward Said, professor of English and comparative literature at Columbia University until his death in 2003, delivered the commencement address at the American University in Cairo on June 17, 1999. During his speech, he wondered if the university "can survive as a real university if its governance and teaching mission become the objects of scrutiny and direct interference not of its teachers but of powers outside the university." He continued, "We must always view the academy as a place to voyage in, owning none of it but at home everywhere in it. There can be no forbidden knowledge if the modern university is to maintain its place, its mission, its power to educate." Said added, "[T]he whole notion of academic freedom underwent a significant downgrading during the past three decades. It became possible for one to be free in the university only if one completely avoided anything that might attract unwelcome attention or suspicion."[12]

I don't know whether Said had my case in mind when he made this speech. His words, though, certainly apply.

By this time, Ebtehal and I had long since made our decision to leave Egypt. We arrived in the Netherlands on October 25, 1995, and I've been a professor of Arabic and Islamic Studies at Leiden University ever since. I'm grateful to Leiden University and the Dutch government for opening their collective arms to us. I've made some solid and lasting friendships as a result of my exile. I've supervised students—many of whom have made great strides in furthering Islamic scholarship.

Egypt, though, is the mother who has nurtured me. It is Egypt who calls to me at night in my dreams. It is Egypt to whom I long to return.

2 My Early Years

I am firmly convinced that life experience is at the heart of this thing we call knowledge. Our experiences are what give knowledge its shape. Knowledge is not an independent entity. It does not exist apart from our understanding and interpretation of facts or events. That interpretation, to a large degree, comes from our own individual experiences. For that reason, two people may witness the same event, yet give two different accounts of it. One reason for writing this book is to show how connected and interrelated my life experiences are with my academic scholarship.

I came into the world short, round, and heavy. I've been battling my weight for my entire life. My father was also heavy—no doubt I inherited this proclivity for poundage from him. As in most societies, my weight made me vulnerable to ridicule from other children while growing up. I wasn't nearly as agile as they, so I learned early on to compensate for this lack of agility. I took up reading as a hobby. I enjoyed reading, and I soon realized that reading was the one activity at which I could excel.

Quhafa, a small village located in the Nile Delta area of northern Egypt, is the place I call home. Tanta, a mere ten-minute walk from Quhafa (when I was a child), is the capital of this district. (Quhafa is one of many villages in the area, each of which has its own local administration.) In spite of being so close to Tanta, most folks were reluctant to travel to the big city where cars sped through the streets, giving the place a boisterousness that Quhafa lacked. Quhafa had no cars, no electricity, and no running water when I was growing up. Gradually, though, our village grew, expanding until it became part of Tanta. A branch of the Nile snaked around our small village, so we enjoyed lush green fields and lovely trees. Students would often venture outside to study. I attended the *kuttâb*, a traditional school, where I learned the Qur'an, reading, writing, and simple math. By my eighth birthday, I had memorized the entire Qur'an.

Although my father started out in life as a farmer, he soon discovered that the piece of land he owned was too small to sustain his growing family. So he sold the land and became a grocer. His grocery store, one of the two in our village, stood on one of the corners of the only crossroads in Quhafa. As far back as I can remember, he had problems with his health. In retrospect, I believe he suffered from some kind of heart disease. None of us realized this at the time. He died in 1957. I was fourteen years old.

My mother's family had deep roots in the village. Her father was a professional reciter of the Qur'an, thereby giving the family an elevated status within the community. My mother was a beautiful, somewhat pampered, woman. One of her most striking features was her soft, smooth skin. She was her father's favorite child and therefore stayed indoors for most of her childhood. Being sequestered in this fashion was considered a privilege, a favor showered upon beloved children by doting parents. My aunts—my mother's sisters—told me, "Your mother was the closest to our father, so we had to do all the dirty jobs while she sat around like a queen."

As a result of her "regal" status, she never learned how to navigate in and around the small village of Quhafa. When she married, the villagers carried her to my father's house. When she wanted to visit her family, a five-minute walk from her new home, she could not go alone. She didn't know how. I remember how proud I felt when I accompanied her on these visits, showing her the way.

Quhafa always seemed to me like one huge family. Everybody knew everybody else—as well as their business. There were two mosques—one was an official government mosque, and the other one was what we called our local mosque. The public cemetery sprawled by the side of one of the main roads. Our village appropriated several saints whose shrines have taken root in the village. A popular saint throughout the entire region, Sayyid Ahamad al-Badawî, was enshrined in Tanta even though he originally came from Morocco. No matter. Tanta claimed him as its own. (*Sayyid* is an Arabic title meaning "belonging to the Prophet's family." In English, the word becomes just Mister.) Every year, we celebrated the birthdays of our favorite saints with weeklong festivals.

Quhafa had a mayor, of course, appointed to that position because of his wealth. He lived in luxury compared with most of the people. With the exception of the mayor's house, the villagers' homes stood tightly crammed together. Our house was planted right in the middle of the village. The many small streets that wound around Quhafa reminded me of a maze, except there were no dead ends. Every street connected in some way to every other street. There were two doors in our house. Enter through one door and you would find yourself rubbing elbows with the Abu Zaid clan. Go through the other door and you would meet a completely different family.

As in all agrarian communities, village life in Quhafa revolved around the changing of the seasons as well as the rising and setting of the sun. People returned to their homes at sunset after working the land, and ate their evening meal. When night settled, we used candles and oil lamps to illuminate our homes. After dinner, folks sat outside their houses, chatting with those who happened to pass by.

We celebrated Ramadân—a festival lasting a month—in a big way. Ramadân commemorates Muhammad's receiving the Qur'an from God through the mediation of the angel Gabriel. Muslims throughout the world refrain from eating, drinking, smoking, and having sexual intercourse from sunrise to sunset during this monthlong holiday. Each day, the sun slipping below the horizon ushered in an end to that fast, and the mood in Quhafa became festive.

The men set up huge oil lamps all around our village while the women prepared special food. People often stayed awake until dawn, especially if Ramadân fell during the summer. (Muslims use a lunar calendar; therefore, Ramadân falls several days earlier each year.) Children, delighted with the change of routine, played throughout the night. The Qur'an was recited in the mosques as well as in people's homes, especially in the more affluent homes. The Festival of Eid marks the end of Ramadân. This is a big occasion as well. People decorated the mosque for this special event and an array of sweet-smelling fragrances wafted through the air. Village life in Quhafa was a full and vibrant experience for me.

In spite of my modest surroundings and upbringing, I gradually became aware of my country's rich culture and ancient civilization. Long before the advent of Islam, Egypt was home to the Coptic

Orthodox Church, a church with a strong monastic tradition. When the Romans, intent on expanding their empire, marched into Egypt during the early part of the first millennium (c. 200), they persecuted and then massacred many Copts. Even after Emperor Constantine legalized Christianity (313), persecution of the Copts continued. (Eventually the Christian Church split, an act formalized at the Council of Chalcedon in 451. The Copts then established their own patriarchate in Alexandria even though the "official" separation of the Eastern and Western branches of Christianity didn't happen until 1054.) Saint Anthony, the world's first Christian monk, was a Copt. Saint Pachom, also a Copt, established rules that the monastic tradition follows to this day. Other famous Coptic desert fathers include Saint Makarios, Saint Moses the Black, and Saint Mina the Wondrous. The later desert fathers include Pope Cyril VI and his disciple Bishop Mina Abba Mina. In spite of Roman persecution, by the end of the fourth century, hundreds of monasteries were scattered throughout the Egyptian hills. Many of these monasteries continue to flourish. I believe that Sufism, the mystical expression of Islam, derives much of its substance from the Coptic Christian monastic heritage in Egypt.

Islam, even before the advent of Sufism, concerned itself with issues of social justice. There are many Qur'anic passages that speak directly to the concerns of orphans and the poor, condemning those who accumulate wealth for themselves while turning a blind eye to people in need. For this reason, the Qur'an takes a strong stance against usury. The aim of such a stance was to establish justice in an inequitable society.

Sufism began as a spiritual revolutionary reaction against social and political injustice, especially the uneven distribution of wealth. People within this movement, in order to bring attention to this inequity, used what we call today passive resistance. They fasted. Fasting hits at the heart of self-control. In Arabic, the word for fasting is siyâm. More is involved here than ritual fasting (no eating, no drinking, no smoking, no sexual intercourse between dawn and sunset) during Ramadan. Siyâm involves giving up unnecessary behavior and communication in order to contemplate. Contemplation involves listening to the inner music of the soul, music that reflects the rhythm of the cosmos. To do this effectively, dissociating yourself from the distractions of everyday living becomes essential. Dhu-Nun al-Misrî (796–861), a man from Upper Egypt, was the first Muslim Sufi who developed the practice of zuhd (asceticism) into a philosophical sys-

ambled

tem known as Gnosticism. He was the first Muslim to claim that love is the essence of mystical experience. He visited the temples of the pharaohs and also had contact with Coptic monks.

Muslims, Coptic Christians, and a small Jewish presence blended together in the Egypt I remember as a child. For years, my family hosted a strange old Coptic man who came from Upper Egypt to Quhafa, looking for work. He was a carpenter. I called him Uncle Salama—his name means "Peaceful"—and he really knew how to tell a story. How I enjoyed listening to the tales he brought with him! He never spoke about his background. My father did not press him for information about himself even though my father's friends were uneasy with my father's unconditional hospitality.

"Perhaps Salama is hiding from someone who is after him for revenge," my father speculated. "Maybe he wants to remain anonymous. Why should I force him to reveal what he would rather keep secret? The man is my guest. It is not appropriate to question your guest." When Uncle Salama died, my father disregarded the difference in religion and buried him in the family cemetery.

This is the atmosphere in which I was raised—an atmosphere of compassion, consideration, and sympathy toward the needy regardless of their religious affiliation. I also learned to work hard and take responsibility at an early age.

As far back as I can remember, my father never really enjoyed robust health. Being the oldest male child in the family, it became my duty to help my father keep the grocery store running smoothly. When I turned ten, I would wake early in the morning, take the keys, and open the shop in order to serve the early customers. Around noon, my father ambled into the store and took over the business so I could attend to my schoolwork. My father insisted that I continue with my schooling in spite of his illness, and for that I am grateful. He expected me to excel in my studies. And I did. But my first lessons in life came from a handful of my father's friends who gathered every afternoon in front of our small grocery store just to talk.

These men, my father's friends, talked about everything—heavy subjects such as the political situation in Egypt as well as lighter matters, such as gossip about husbands and wives. Because I was so young, I think they assumed I wouldn't be interested in their conversation. But I was. I listened to everything. Much of their talk had to do with the British occupation of Egypt (1882–1952), the new revolution (1952), the politics of the Muslim Brotherhood, the revolution of 1919 led by Sa'd Zaghlûl, as well as the older revolution when the Egyptian officer Ahmad 'Urâbî went up against Khedive Tawfîq—a revolt that was suppressed by the British. I learned a basic history of Egypt from these men. Today, I consider this experience to be my first real school. After my father died and I had matured somewhat, some of these men, blessed with longevity, became my friends as well.

I also learned about private things. These men spoke in code when discussing sexual matters. When they talked to each other about sex, they would say, "So, yesterday you were traveling, right?" If a man had splashed some fragrant scent on himself, it was a dead giveaway. That meant he had taken a bath, and when a man took a bath in Quhafa, he most certainly had enjoyed a sexual escapade with his wife.

Since our village had no running water, people bathed in metal tubs. I learned that if a woman tossed out sweet-smelling water from a metal tub into the street, that was another sure sign that intercourse had recently taken place in that household. For a child of ten, this was exciting stuff.

While I was tending the shop one morning, the wife of one of my father's friends stopped by. I had seen her throwing out bathwater from a metal tub early that morning. I said to her, "Well, I think Uncle Muhammad [the woman's husband] was traveling yesterday."

The woman gave me a quizzical look. She said, "Traveling? I don't know—I'm not sure." I was toying with her, and when I look back on the incident, I am ashamed of myself.

Later on, I learned that when Uncle Muhammad arrived home from work, his wife asked him, "Were you traveling yesterday?"

"Who told you that?" he demanded.

"The son of Hamed Abu Zaid," she replied.

Uncle Muhammad immediately realized that I had been listening to and—even worse—understanding their afternoon conversations in front of the grocery store. He told my father. My father, not knowing what else to do, gave me the usual punishment doled out by a father in Arab society: He hit me. At the same time, I felt my father took great pride in my budding sexual interest and development. I was eavesdropping at my parents' bedroom door later that day when I heard my father say to my mother, "Can you imagine what this stupid boy did?" As he recounted the traveling story, his tone of voice did not reflect anger, but pride. In my mind's eye, I could see him smiling.

While growing up in Quhafa, I often heard stories about jinns or genies. Jinns are spirits or ghosts that appear to people, usually during the night. I would often wander off by myself in the dark to the outskirts of the village, waiting sometimes for hours, hoping to see a jinn. I never did.

We had jinn experts—people you consulted if you lost something or suspected that a certain item had been stolen. A jinn expert supposedly had special powers to summon the jinn, who would then divulge the information through the mouth of a child. A child is believed to be innocent, whereas an adult is tainted with sin.

One day one of the villagers discovered that an item was missing from his house. I had not gone to school that day due to some problem with my teeth. Since I was the only child available when the man called on the jinn expert for help, the jinn expert decided to use me as the innocent mouthpiece. He covered my head with a cap and then set a cup filled with ink in front of me. After he finished reciting a formula or two, my job was to peer into the cup, look right through the ink, and watch a scene unfold at the bottom of the cup. The jinn expert asked me, "What do you see?"

All rituals have a pattern. This one was no exception. It was understood that the scene at the bottom of the cup showed a jinn setting the stage for a celebration—usually arranging some chairs. Children inevitably said, "Yes, I see him." The expert would always follow up with the question, "What does he look like?"

I saw nothing but ink, the color of midnight, taking up the entire space inside the cup. Was I expected to somehow see through this stuff? The onlookers kept telling me to concentrate, just concentrate. The jinn expert kept asking me, "What do you see?"

Repeatedly I replied, "Nothing." Folks were scandalized. The scene went on for hours.

The angry jinn expert was about to hit me. In desperation, he asked, "How old are you?" I was ten years old at the time. He continued with his probing, "Did you have a dream?" He was trying to ascertain whether or not I had ever had a wet dream. If so, this would have put me into the sinful category of adult. If I were an adult, it was no wonder that I did not see anything at the bottom of the cup of ink.

At the time, I had no idea what he meant. "No, no, what do you mean did I have a dream?" I asked.

The jinn expert, in order to bring an end to this embarrassing episode, proclaimed that I had a very strange nature. "He belongs to the fire," he declared. According to him, some people belonged to fire, and others to dust. And that was the end of it. The attempt to have a jinn speak through me failed and, as a result of this experience, my longing to meet a jinn went up in smoke.

Even so, after my father died, I'd often go to the cemetery at night and sit near his grave. Most of the villagers believed dangerous jinns lived in cemeteries. I'm not sure what I expected to find at the cemetery. I did know I felt lonely and abandoned—much like an orphan. Did I expect my father to somehow reveal himself to me while I sat near his grave? I think I yearned for some communication from him—something I never had with him while growing up in Quhafa.

It wasn't all that long ago that it hit me—most of what I know about my father comes from seeing him through the eyes of his group of friends who hung around his grocery store. Their words—their talk—created an image of him for me. It's the image I carry with me to this day. I don't believe I ever experienced him on a one-to-one basis.

After my father died in 1957, I started to see my mother in a new light. When my father was still alive, her role was that of intermediary, even acting as a protective shield at times. In Egyptian society, a father demands respect. A huge amount of fear usually accompanies that respect. At least, that was so in my case.

Sometimes my father would ask me, "Do you need any school supplies?"

My automatic response was always "No." I'd then go to my mother to tell her what supplies I needed for school.

"But your father just asked you. Why didn't you tell him?" A puzzled look would come over her face. But I could never get past my fear of my father. Keeping him at arm's length seemed the safest thing to do.

When my father's health began to deteriorate severely, he gave the family instructions regarding his funeral. He was adamant about not having a procession of wailing women follow his corpse as villagers carried him to the cemetery. Furthermore, he did not want my mother ever to visit his grave once he had been buried. He had a conservative religious bent and believed that visiting graves served no useful purpose. As it turned out, there were no wailing women in the procession that accompanied his body to the cemetery, but my mother on several occasions after the burial did visit his grave. At first, I took her there. Later on, as she began to experience life more fully, she went alone.

My mother was thirty-five years old when my father died. She had five children living with her at home. My elder sister, Badriyya—her name is the feminine form of "full moon"—had married by this time and lived with her husband's family. She was barely eighteen years old. At fourteen, I was the eldest child in my mother's house. My brother Muhammad, born in 1945, is two years my junior. My sister Karima came along in 1950. Osama (the name means "lion"), named after the son of the adopted son of Prophet Muhammad, was born in 1952. Another sister, Ayat, whose name means "miracles," arrived in 1957, the year my father died.

After my father's death, much of the responsibility of providing for the family fell to my mother. Being the eldest male in the household, some of that responsibility fell on my shoulders as well. I had an older brother who died when he was four or five years old. I jokingly tell people that he and I are not on good terms. If he had lived, so much of that familial responsibility—something I did not hesitate to assume—would have been his. If he had lived, my life, I'm sure, would have been quite different.

But, here I was—not quite fifteen years old, having recently buried my father. My behavior during the funeral proceedings could best be described as stoic. I walked, along with the rest of the villagers, behind my father's coffin to the cemetery. The journey took only ten minutes. After returning home, I did not cry. That came much later. I do remember that our friends and relatives worried about my stiff upper lip.

With my father's passing, I could feel a change happening deep inside of me. I no longer thought of myself as a child. Suddenly, overnight, I had become a man. I had an enormous task ahead of me— one that completely overwhelmed me. How would I ever manage to help feed, clothe, and educate my siblings? My father's medical expenses had drained away any savings we had managed to scrape together over the years. The grocery store had deteriorated along with my father's health, and finally, not long after my father died, gave up the ghost altogether.

I can honestly say that the experience of supporting my family over a period of years transformed my life. As I became deeply involved in the individual lives of each sibling, I discovered the delicious mixture of pain and pleasure that attends the job of parenting. Now that the children are grown, I can look back on the experience and feel a large degree of satisfaction when I think about how my mother and I provided for the family's needs. Focusing on the wider picture (my family) forced me to enlarge my vision. I didn't have the time to gaze at my navel, thinking only of myself and how best to promote my own interests.

Through the often painful and always difficult process of caring and providing for my family, I became sensitive to the suffering that people endure as a result of social injustice. When I began my career as a scholar in Islamic Studies, academic research to me was neither an abstract concept nor just an interesting career choice. My academic research came to life as a result of my own experiences. My passion for social justice did not come out of the blue. I was looking for answers to questions—questions that sprang initially from the difficulties I experienced while trying to make ends meet for my family. At first, my concern didn't go beyond the boundaries of my own family. That concern gradually stretched to Egypt, then to the Arab and Muslim world, and as I immersed myself in reading and research, my concern broadened to include the whole world. How could it not? The whole world (people, animals, plants, and the Earth itself) suffers when inequity takes hold in a society. We are all connected.

Of course, this understanding took years to develop. Immediately after my father's death, I became possessive toward my mother. I was terrified of losing her. She attracted quite a number of suitors. Men began to hang around our house. I knew about traveling. I saw how men flirted with her. I could feel the jealousy welling up inside my chest. I wished that I had had an ugly mother. I felt certain that if she were ugly, that would keep all her suitors at bay. I would then be safe. All these feelings wrapped themselves up in aggressive and angry behavior that I hurled in my mother's direction. Today, I shudder when I think about it.

One day I happened to have a pair of scissors in my hand. I don't recall the particular incident that got me hot under the collar, but I do remember throwing the scissors right at her. She ducked. I'm sure she would have been severely injured had the scissors hit her. She stared at me for a moment before dashing into my bedroom. I was terrified by the calm, but determined, look on her face. She put all of my clothes on a sheet, brought the corners of the sheet together, tied a sturdy knot in the sheet, threw the bundle out the front door, pushed me out after the bundle, and then slammed the door shut behind me. Insolent chap that I was, I didn't take the incident very seriously. I thought that in a couple of hours, she'd calm down, perhaps even cry, and then beg me to return home. Things didn't go the way I expected.

After a couple of hours, people noticed me standing by the front door of my house with a white bundle beside me. "What's happening? Where are you going?" they asked. I had no choice but to tell them what had happened. Night began to settle. More and more people gathered around me, demanding to know what kind of problem would have driven my mother to such a desperate act. They knocked on the front door. She did not answer. "What could possibly be wrong?" folks wondered aloud. "We know she is inside."

The villagers summoned certain men in our extended family to come over and help sort out this problem of my sudden homelessness. These men possessed an enormous amount of authority in our community. My father would submit to them whenever there was a dispute of some sort. When they arrived, one of them shouted, "Ma-Nasr [mother of Nasr], open the door, Ma-Nasr." And she did.

"What happened?" he asked when he was inside. "Why is your son outside?" I could hear the whole conversation quite well.

"Nothing happened," she replied. "He is outside because he does not belong here." This woman, my mother, was playing it cool. I hardly recognized her.

"What do you mean?" the man asked.

"He does not belong to me. If you would like to have him, help yourself; he is not my son." She was strong and determined. She was about to get rid of me without so much as batting an eye.

"No, you cannot do this," the man declared. And then he tried begging. "Please, for my sake, do not do this."

My mother was emphatic. "No, Nasr does not belong with me."

The man became furious. No man in the family had ever said no to him, but here was my mother, a woman, standing her ground, refusing to do what he asked of her.

As if to remind my mother of her duty, he said, "You are not listening to me."

She was bold. "You listen to me. Nasr is my son. He threw a pair of scissors in my direction. Now, he is a boy. I am feeding him. What can we expect from him in a few years? How will he treat me then if he throws scissors at me now—while I am feeding him?"

The man was speechless. My mother continued, "If Nasr would like to return, I have one condition. He must kiss my feet."

She brought our only chair into full view of the villagers who were hanging around. She sat down and stretched out her legs. She astonished everybody. To me, she looked like Queen Cleopatra. I bent down and like a dog, I kissed her feet. She then allowed me back in the house and everybody left. The show was over. It was the most humiliating moment of my whole life. To think that I had kissed her feet in front of all those villagers! At that moment, I hated her. Later that evening, I could hear the muffled sounds of my mother's crying. I began to realize how difficult life must be for her.

The next morning, she was quite pleasant. She didn't seem to hold a grudge against me. And then she spoke—very calmly. "Look, you are my son. You are not my husband. I expect you to behave like a proper son. When you grow up, you will be responsible for this family. Right now, I am the head of this family. I expect you to respect and obey me." Her words cut me to the quick. Much later on, though, I learned to appreciate the strength it must have taken for her to take the stand she did. If she had not taken such a stand, I'm sure that our family life would have spun out of control. The results could very well have been disastrous.

I witnessed a similar situation when I lived in the States in the late 1970s. An Egyptian family had taken me under their wing. The man, a professor of sociology and anthropology, died suddenly. He and his wife, an educated woman who had earned her Ph.D. and worked within the community, had one son. Both mother and son accompanied the body of their husband and father back to Egypt. After forty days (the amount of time required to complete the death ceremony), they returned to the States. I witnessed this fourteen-year-old boy behaving in the exact way I had behaved toward my mother after my father's death. The difference, though, was that this woman, in spite of her education, was unable to act decisively and effectively as my wise, but illiterate, mother had done with me.

I visited this woman and her son from time to time after their return to the States. I was appalled when the son would shout at his mother from upstairs, "Come here!" And his mother would run up the stairs and see to his needs.

One day I said to her, "This boy is not your husband. Your husband died. He is your son." I told her the story of kissing my mother's feet shortly after my father died. She listened, but didn't seem able to connect my story with her own situation.

At one point, the boy attempted to set the house on fire. Someone had told him that he would be able to collect several thousand dollars from the fire insurance policy. His mother called me, begging me for help. Even as we spoke, her son was looking for the most efficient way to set the house ablaze. I went over there and found the boy out of control. I dragged him down to the basement so we could talk privately. At the time, it seemed that the best thing I could do for him was to hit him. I knew I was taking a chance. I knew about the many charges of child abuse thrown at parents in the States when they hit their children as a means of disciplining them. His father used to tell me, "I would love to take this boy to Egypt and just hit him."

Frankly, I was at a loss. I spoke to him about filial responsibility, but all he did was stare at me, not hitting me back—something I really thought this strong young boy would do. Eventually, he broke down and cried. I held him as he sobbed on my shoulder. "You have to understand," I said, "that your father died. You cannot be your father. You are acting like a jerk."

Unfortunately, his mother could never summon the strength to undertake the difficult job of putting her foot down with her son as my mother had done with me, an act that eventually would have freed them both.

When I listened to my mother cry after the kissing of the feet incident, my heart became softer toward her. I, along with the rest of the family, had a rough road ahead of us, but the way had been opened for my mother and me to work together to help the family thrive. I eventually learned to give up the entitlement I felt by virtue of being the eldest male in the household.

My mother loved to sew. She owned her own sewing machine, and while my father was alive, she'd design and make clothes for people. It was her hobby. After my father's death, sewing became her profession. In addition to the income she earned from that, we were able to keep the grocery store afloat for a short while with the help of my cousin Sayyid, the man who eventually married my elder sister, Badriyya.

Sayyid became a frequent presence in our house. He unobtrusively helped fill the huge gap left by my father's death. He became our unofficial guardian—a father figure—someone who kindly and gently helped us get back on our feet after the loss that disrupted our lives. Sayyid is the third of three brothers. When their father died, my father contributed his resources to care for them. Now Sayyid had an opportunity to give back to our family what we had given to his. I have always respected Sayyid. Over the years, I grew to love him as well.

After I graduated from the *kuttâb,* my father's dream was for me to continue my education in a religious institution, eventually becoming a *sheikh,* a leader in the religious community. He admired the

Egyptian scholar and theologian Muhammad 'Abduh (1849–1905), who believed education was essential to bring about a better society. Political revolution was no substitute for the lasting transformation possible through an educated population. 'Abduh, considered to be a pioneer in Islamic thought, became known as the founder of the Egyptian modernist school.

As my father's health deteriorated—when he became aware that he probably would not live more than two or three more years—he took me out of religious education and transferred me into civil education. These were the two educational paths available in Egypt at this time. My father's older brother objected to this move, thinking I should go to high school and eventually university, not enroll in technical school after my secondary education was completed.

"OK," my father shot back at his brother, "if he goes to high school and I die, will you pay for his education? Who will take care of the family?" My father knew that I would need a job where I could earn enough money to help support the family after he died. A technical education provided me with this ability because it gave me a basic education in electronics. The curriculum also exposed me to some geography and a little history.

While I was enrolled in this course of study, I listened one Friday as a *sheikh* from the local mosque denounced magic, using verses taken from the Qur'an dealing with the stars. Originally, he said, some of the stars were husband and wife, but they committed adultery. God cursed them, and as a result, they became stars.

I could be an arrogant youngster. "This is stupid talk," I told him. "Stars were never human beings."

People overhearing this exchange were shocked. After all, I was speaking with a *sheikh*. I was a mere boy. "How dare you speak like this to the *sheikh*?" they asked. I thought they were going to hit me, but instead they reported the incident to my father.

My father asked me about the incident and patiently listened to my explanation of the event. "We studied this in school," I told him. "Stars were never human beings."

"You are right," my father said. "I am not going to punish you, but in the future, please be tactful and polite when you disagree with people." I was surprised, yet so relieved, at his response. Maybe he just didn't have the energy to hit me.

As a young man, enrolled in civil education and studying electronics, I was concerned about separating fact from myth. Myth, to me, meant something false—not true. I did not yet understand that mythology or story contains those values that a culture or society holds dear. Much later in my life, I would come to understand how sacred texts hold life-changing truths within their mythologies. Myth or story teaches us on a different plane than factual information. Discovering and uncovering the meaning of a text eventually became a part of my life's work. But all of this was a long way off.

I began to feel intellectually superior to most of the villagers—just because I had the privilege of continuing with some kind of education. It was the group of my father's friends who brought me down a notch or two. These men avidly devoured the daily newspaper. Not all of them could read, though. Nonetheless, all of them made it a point to keep current with what was happening in the world. My father could read and write. Every day, ritually, his friends would stop by the store and ask, "What is the news today?" My father would tell them the news. I would read the news to them from the newspaper itself. "Come, Nasr," they would say, "bring the newspaper and read to us."

I made a lot of mistakes. I mispronounced the names of world leaders such as Churchill. My father's friends didn't even try to muffle their laughter. "We thought you knew how to read," they'd say. "Looks like you can't read after all." I had no idea what an important role Churchill played on the world's stage at the time.

It became clear to me at that moment that knowing how to read does not automatically make a person knowledgeable, let alone wise. These men—my father's friends—understood the material I was reading to them. I did not. These illiterate men were among my first teachers. I may have been the reader, but they interpreted what I read. They gave meaning to the text.

I graduated from technical school in 1960. Almost immediately, I began to bring enough money into the household to meet our needs. I worked for the Ministry of Communication as an electronic technician, maintaining the communication equipment in a police headquarters. Although my father wanted me to emulate Muhammad 'Abduh, I had long admired Tâhâ Husayn (1889–1973), Muhammad 'Abduh's disciple. I never lost my dream of following in his shadow, so I started studying between working hours, eventually earning my B.A. in Arabic language and literature from Cairo University in 1972.

Tâhâ Husayn, picking up on the theme that 'Abduh began—approaching the Qur'an from a literary perspective—developed 'Abduh's work even further. 'Abduh had concluded that the Qur'an's main purpose was not to teach us about history. No doubt there are some historical incidents recorded in the text, but we should understand the text symbolically, looking for spiritual meaning, not historical facts, in the sacred book. Husayn was convinced that 'Abduh, who wrote in the staid language of a classic, religious scholar, was right on track with his scholarship. Husayn's approach was different, though. He used colorful—even shocking—language to make the case that a literary approach to the Qur'an was essential in order to understand its meaning.

Because I brought home a regular paycheck, I suggested to my mother that it was time for her to quit slaving over her sewing machine. She objected. She wanted to continue making her contribution to the family's coffers. Working every day and sometimes through the night, though, had compromised her health.

Since I was working in al-Mahallala Kubra, a city some thirty kilometers from Tanta, I felt that the family would benefit by moving to al-Mahallala Kubra. This city, famous for its textile industry, is a source of national pride for all Egyptians. I commuted every day, often returning home late at night. My schedule didn't give me adequate time to supervise the children's schoolwork. I wanted to make sure they were keeping up with their lessons. I was better able to stay on top of this when we moved.

My mother and I dreamed of giving every one of my brothers and sisters a good start in life by ensuring they were educated. We accomplished that goal. I feel as if I've been a parent ever since I graduated from technical school. I became concerned, though, that in my zeal to educate my siblings, supporting them as far as they were able to go in school, I would leave myself behind. Worse yet, I feared I might grow envious of them. I did not want to end up resentful and bitter. I vowed to educate them, but along with that vow, I made a promise to myself that I would not neglect my own education. I enjoyed school, and I wanted to continue with my studies in the university, but part of my motivation to go ahead with my studies had to do with my refusal to play a victim's role. I guard against that—always. My mother and I sacrificed much in order to launch my siblings, but I was always aware of the fact that a sacrifice, if not freely given, stinks.

Moving away from Quhafa made it easier for my mother to disengage from her customers. She had built up quite a clientele over the years. My mother's health started to improve once she gave up her business. My relationship with my mother began to change as well— we developed a comfortable friendship. Even so, I still clung to some sense of entitlement. Frankly, I was still quite a spoiled boy.

When I'd come home from work at the end of the day, my mother always had supper prepared for us. If I did not like the food, I insisted on eating something else. She didn't cater to my gastronomical whims, but one evening when the children were in bed for the night, she said, "I would love to serve you fancy, expensive meals. You realize, of course, that it would cost you. When I cook something that you refuse to eat, all your brothers and sisters refuse to eat it as well. I end up throwing it away. It's your money, though, so you decide what you'd like me to do." I got the point. Never again did I complain about the food she served.

After several years, my mother's health began to fail. We had moved to Cairo by this time. My youngest brother, Osama, wanted to marry. I felt he was too young. He had no apartment. I was against the whole thing. Nonetheless, he did marry, and lived with his wife in my mother's apartment. Not wanting to be in the way of the newly-weds, my mother announced, "I would like to visit your brother Muhammad in the village."

I understood that she wanted to give Osama and his bride some space, so I asked, "How long will you be with my brother Muhammad?"

"One month, maybe two," she offered.

After two weeks, she became quite ill. The doctor diagnosed her with a heart valve problem. He recommended that she change her dietary habits, but the moment her doctor told her to refrain from eating certain foods, she demanded them. I'd visit her every week, trying to keep her spirits up.

My brother's wife said, "I cannot refuse her any food she asks for. You must understand my position. If I refuse her, I will be subject to her anger."

I told my mother, "If you do not follow your doctor's advice, you will die."

She became quite angry. "This is none of your business. I would welcome death. And by the way, don't come and visit me again. Even if I die, don't come."

"No, if you die, I should be there. People will be expecting me to be present to receive their condolences." What else could I say to her?

"You are giving me a hard time by telling me what to eat and what not to eat," she wailed.

"Actually, I am not telling you, the doctor is," I offered.

I paid her doctor, Ibrahim Badran, a visit. He was the president of Cairo University at the time. Later he became the minister of health.

Thanks to the efforts of my friend Ahmad Mursy, a close friend of the doctor, the doctor made a courtesy visit to check my mother in the village. I returned to Cairo with both of them.

The doctor told me, "Listen, we could perform a technically simple operation on your mother to fix the valves in her heart. The problem with your mother, it seems to me, is that she has decided to die. We would most likely be clinically successful operating on your mother, but we doctors always say the surgical outcome has much to do with the patient." He glanced at me. He knew I was skeptical of what he was saying.

He continued, "I think your mother has decided to die."

In Egypt at that time, people avoided hospitals if at all possible. The doctor explained that he would be willing to perform the operation, but the hospital stay would be stressful for her. "I examined your mother thoroughly. She is a woman obsessed with cleanliness. She will have a terrible time with people washing and caring for her in the hospital."

My mother did not have the operation. We stopped fighting with her about her diet. I visited her every week at my brother's home. Every week she would ask me for money. When my siblings visited her, she asked for money from them as well. Whenever anyone asked, "Do you need anything?" her standard response was, "Yes, I need money."

One day the mood was light, so I asked her, "Why do you need all this money? Our brother should be providing for all your needs. If he is not doing so, tell me."

"No, no, he is taking very good care of me," she insisted. "When I ask you for money, just give it to me. I brought you up. I protected you. Now that you are grown, you should not question me."

"OK, Mother," I said. "But I need to know if you are going to remarry. If you are collecting this money to establish a new household, let me know, so I can help you. Of course, I must know who the groom will be." She laughed, but continued to ask for money.

The night she died, she called my brother to her side and gave him all the money she had been begging from her children. She said, "This money is for my funeral. I need a respectable burial. I'd like two Qur'an reciters—the famous ones we see on TV—to lead the ceremony at my funeral. I didn't want to burden you with this expense when I died."

My mother died while I was on my way to visit her. Before I stepped out of the car, I knew she was gone. I could see many people milling in and about my brother's house—a sure sign that death had visited this home. I immediately went to the room where she had been laid out. I uncovered her face and kissed her on the cheek. She had lived to see her sixtieth birthday.

My brother came in the room and said, "Here is the money that our mother has been asking for over the past months." My mother had squirreled away five hundred Egyptian pounds—quite a decent sum of money at the time. I didn't know whether to laugh or cry. I ended up doing a little of each.

We honored her request for a respectable funeral. It was the least we could do.

When I reflect on the person my mother had become over the twenty-five years since my father's death and compare her with the woman I knew just before my father died, I have to marvel. Over the years, she developed a strength and confidence that suited her well. She had been forced by her circumstances to engage the world in a way that had been closed off to her when my father was still alive. That engagement transformed her into a different person, and the transformation intrigued me. She radiated an inner beauty— something I found much more attractive than her physical charms.

3 Badriyya, Karima, Ayat, and Shereen

After living in al-Mahallala Kubra for some years while I worked at the police headquarters there, we moved to Cairo. I had enrolled in Cairo University in 1968, when my youngest sister, Ayat, was still in elementary school. Both Karima and Osama had graduated from high school by that time. By 1972, I had earned my undergraduate degree.

Moving was hard on the family, especially on my mother. She had really balked when I first moved the family to al-Mahallala Kubra from Quhafa in 1962. At that time, she actually refused to move. I could understand her reluctance to be uprooted. She had her own house in Quhafa and raised chickens, ducks, and rabbits, producing much of the food we consumed. In al-Mahallala Kubra, we lived in a small apartment and had to buy all our food. It cost more to just live.

My mother stayed alone in Quhafa for a week while the rest of us went on ahead. Then Sayyid's brother, who worked in a department store in al-Mahallala Kubra, paid my mother a visit. (Sayyid, my cousin, was the man who became our unofficial guardian after my father died.) Sayyid's brother told my mother how difficult life had become for us since moving and how badly the children suffered as they attempted to adjust to their new situation. "Nasr, especially, is doing terrible," he said. His report had the desired effect. The next day, my mother boarded a train and joined us in our small apartment in al-Mahallala Kubra.

My mother was just as reluctant to move to Cairo when the time came. Life in Cairo moved at a faster pace than it did in al-Mahallala Kubra. It wasn't easy to navigate the city. It also cost more to live in Cairo. Because I was an excellent student, the university granted me a position as assistant teacher, compensating me with a yearly stipend. We struggled financially—I no longer worked at the police headquarters—but we managed.

Badriyya, my elder sister, had been married briefly to a young man before she married my cousin Sayyid. She was a brilliant, ambitious girl and wanted to continue with school. Because she was a girl, my father decided that she should marry, not pursue an education. In traditional Egyptian society at that time, a girl's education was, at best, optional. The marriage didn't work out. Badriyya's husband was an only child, and his mother resented a new bride getting most of her son's attention. They all lived together in the same house.

The marriage lasted for about a year. During that year, Badriyya begged my father to allow her to divorce her husband, but my father refused. Instead he asked his son-in-law, "Why don't you get your own place?" If his mother made life miserable for the couple, living apart from her could only help matters, my father reasoned. Badriyya's husband was unable to make the break when his mother threatened to commit suicide if he went out on his own with his wife.

Things went from bad to worse. Neighbors approached my father asking, "Why are you letting your daughter suffer? Her husband may be a good man, but her mother-in-law is awful." My father finally agreed to allow Badriyya to divorce her husband.

Many Muslims believe divorce to be a rupture that God allows under some circumstances. Nonetheless, God is never pleased with such a turn of events. My father wanted a smooth transition with this whole divorce thing. Even though in Islam there are rights that a wife can lay claim to when she divorces her husband, my father released his son-in-law from any responsibility toward Badriyya. I overheard my father say, "If my daughter hates him, I will ask him for release, that's all. Then we will all be free." He did as he said, and the divorce became a reality. Shortly after the divorce, Badriyya found herself pregnant. It angered my father no end—not because he wasn't eager to welcome a grandchild, but a grandchild would mean that the two families would continue to have some kind of relationship, and he wanted to put Badriyya's failed marriage behind him.

My father took Badriyya to a Coptic doctor. He asked the doctor to "get rid of the baby." It would have been practically impossible to find a Muslim doctor to perform an abortion. Coptic doctors, he thought, performed abortions at will. The doctor gave Badriyya some medicine and told the family that she would soon abort her pregnancy. It didn't work. The doctor had actually deceived my father, and instead of prescribing an abortifacient, he had prescribed vitamins to keep Badriyya and her child healthy. Nobody bothered to ask Badriyya what she wanted to do about her pregnancy. The decision was my father's alone.

In due time, Badriyya gave birth to a healthy boy. Shortly after his birth, my father took me along to pay the Coptic doctor a visit. "What went wrong?" my father asked the doctor.

"Hamed," he said, addressing my father, "you thought that because I am a Copt, I would have no qualms about killing an unborn child. You were wrong. You don't have the right to kill the child, and neither do I."

Not only was my father pleased with the doctor's response, he took great pride in telling the story to all his friends. "This doctor has more faith in God than I do," he'd say, grinning from ear to ear. Later in my life I was to look back at incidents such as this one, seeing from a removed perspective how Coptic Christians and Muslims lived together in peace—freely interacting with one another.

The child was still a baby when my cousin Sayyid proposed marriage to Badriyya. My father, believing his nephew to be acting merely out of a sense of responsibility, refused to give his blessing to their union. I believe they were in love. My father, though, soon became persuaded that their marriage might be a good thing after all. Unfortunately, the child Badriyya brought to the marriage lived only until he was four or five years old. One day he fell ill and died. Most Egyptian people had no access to health care at that time.

Badriyya died in 1980. She was almost forty years old. The doctors thought her death was due to some kind of heart ailment. I never really knew. I was in the States at the time, on a two-year course of study. When I returned to Egypt several months after her funeral, I found her husband, Sayyid, devastated and still reeling from my sister's death. For me, it was as though she had died the very day I set foot on Egyptian soil after my two-year absence.

Sayyid said, "Your sister has left me lost. She took care of everything. I don't know anything about my house or my children." My cousin's statement seems petty, perhaps even whiny, to our modern sensibilities—sensibilities which have been influenced by feminist theory. Traditional Egyptian society operates with the understanding that men occupy the public domain while women work within the private sphere. My cousin's statement reflected the givens in Egyptian society.

Sayyid approached me one day and told me he had found somebody he planned to marry. He then asked, "Will you support me in this marriage?" Two years had passed since my sister's death. My mother, still grieving for her daughter, refused to attend his wedding. She tried to get me to abandon my plans to attend. "Don't go," she pleaded. If the truth be known, I was hesitant when my cousin announced that he was about to establish another household. I, as well as my mother, was still raw with grief.

"Of course I will support you," I replied. After my father's death, Sayyid helped support our family, both financially and emotionally, for quite some time. How could I turn my back on him when he asked for some familial support? I felt I owed him something. Even though my mother objected, I promised him that I'd be at his wedding ceremony.

When the day arrived, my cousin's new father-in-law made a point of coming over to me and saying, "Thank you very much for coming." He made an attempt to tone down the festivities out of respect for Badriyya.

"No, please," I assured him. "This is the bride's first marriage. She has a right to this joyful celebration." At that moment, I was glad I had gone to the wedding. I felt my presence sent a message to both my family and Sayyid's new family—a message of acceptance.

My mother, after some time, did adjust to her son-in-law's remarriage, a union that eventually produced three children. Like many people, my mother felt that Sayyid's remarriage indicated that he no longer loved Badriyya. Nothing could have been further from the truth.

Of all my siblings, I felt especially close to Karima. When she was fifteen, she could have passed for twenty. She possessed a classic beauty. I felt protective toward her. I saw how young men stared at her. I was already beginning to receive people interested in marrying her. Both my mother and I were concerned about her education. We wanted to arm all of the children with what we called "weapons for living." We had no inheritance to leave them. In fact, we were living hand-to-mouth. To obtain a decent job in order to earn a living, they needed to be educated.

In Egypt, there are financial responsibilities for both families when a couple decides to marry. So even if we thought it might be a good thing for Karima to marry one of her suitors, we would not have been able to come up with the necessary money. I knew Karima had a special suitor because I found some letters. I worried. In Egyptian society, there is this matter of honor. A girl dishonors herself and her family if she engages in sex before marriage. Would Karima be one of those girls?

It terrified me to be responsible for teenage girls. I certainly had made my share of mistakes. I learned valuable lessons from them. Why should my younger sisters not have that same privilege—making mistakes and going on with their lives? This is unheard-of in the Arab world. When Ayat, my youngest sister, was a student at the university, one of my friends came to me and in an angry voice asked, "Did you know that Ayat is seeing someone?"

"No," I replied, "but why are you so angry?"

"Aren't you afraid of what might happen?" he asked.

"No. If I were afraid, I would never have consented for her to be at the university, where boys and girls mix freely. So what? She is seeing somebody." My friend was appalled at what seemed to him to be my indifference.

"Well, you know, the boy she is seeing is one of your students," he said. "Are you telling me that you will just look the other way?"

"I'm telling you that I'm trying to bring up my sister in an appropriate way," I responded.

"Well, suppose she makes a mistake and allows this boy to have intercourse with her? What will you do then? This has to do with honor," he reminded me.

"I will not be very happy about her decision," I told him, "but do you really think that a girl's honor lies within this little piece of skin—the hymen? Certainly, I think it would be a big mistake for her to have intercourse with him. I don't think she will, but if she did, I am not going to kill her."

The boy whom Ayat was seeing came to me one day and asked to speak with me privately. He was one of my favorite students. "I'm in love with your sister," he blurted out.

"So?" That was my gut response. It surprised me.

"Don't you have anything to say to me?" he asked.

"No," I assured him. "If you were to come to me asking to marry Ayat, then I would have something to say, but you are telling me you are in love with her. I don't know if she is in love with you. You are giving me information—information I don't have to make a decision about. You need to be telling Ayat that you love her, not me." I truly believed what I told him. People need to be free to experience their lives. This is how we learn.

In spite of what I knew to be true, my first reaction after finding Karima's love letters was anger. I could have hit her, shut her off from the outside world, and not let her go to school. In Egypt, this would not have been considered aberrant behavior on the part of a father or guardian. It would have been a stupid move on my part, though. I wanted Karima, as well as my other siblings, to have the freedom to choose—to make decisions about their own lives. How would they ever learn if I scripted their lives? Of course, I tried to discourage her from this liaison. I told her, "You will have plenty of time in the future for such things—you need to consider your education." It was the kind of talk parents give their teenage children all the time.

Before long, a man loaded with presents came knocking on my door—the father of Karima's suitor. The man was well known in al-Mahallala Kubra and quite wealthy. I did the polite thing. I welcomed him into my home. He said, "My son, Sayyid, wants to propose marriage to your sister. You are a decent, respectable family. I know you want Karima to finish school. We would be willing to wait until she graduates." He went on to assure me that he would undertake the whole financial responsibility. His son had already graduated and was preparing to do his military service.

My mother thought this marriage might not be such a bad idea. "Why not?" she asked. "The man is rich. His reputation is good. The boy has graduated. Why not?"

I dreamed of a different future for Karima—one that would give her the freedom to make choices, to have more options. If she were to marry as soon as she finished school, her life experience would be quite limited. I wanted more for her. Besides, I was not convinced that if we established an engagement at this particular time, Karima would actually finish school.

I said to the man, "Thank you very much for coming and bringing so many gifts. I cannot accept such generosity. Please understand. I cannot make any commitment right now. My father, God rest his soul, asked me never to arrange marriage for any of his daughters until they finished their education."

Of course, my father never said any such thing. It was just a diplomatic and tactful way to say, "No—you are asking me to go beyond what I feel I can do." I did tell him that after Karima finished her education—and who knows, she might qualify to go to the university—if Sayyid was still interested and Karima agreed, I would be very happy to give my consent for their marriage. At the moment, I was unable to promise him anything.

We ended up keeping the presents. It would have been an insult to the man to return his gifts. Karima continued to see Sayyid. I wasn't able to persuade her to stop seeing him, and I certainly wasn't interested in forcing the issue. She needed room to find her own way—a way that would ultimately help her make wise decisions, decisions in her best interest. I did ask Karima to keep me abreast of their friendship. She did. She told me he waited for her in front of the school. After school, they'd talk for a bit. At least she felt comfortable enough to tell me this much.

When we moved to Cairo, I thought they had forgotten all about each other. Five years had elapsed. Karima had graduated and was working as a secretary at Cairo University. She had joined me in Cairo for a short while before the rest of the family arrived. During this time, she and I hung out together. I introduced her to my friends. We went to the movies and to the theater. It was all quite wonderful.

Then, one day Sayyid appeared in my office at the police headquarters in Giza. Sayyid knew I had been transferred from al-Mahallala Kubra to Giza several years before. I wasn't hard to locate. He was smartly dressed in his military uniform. His visit came as a surprise—not a very pleasant one. It wouldn't do not to be polite, though. "Please, sit down. Have a drink," I said.

"I came to ask you to make good on your promise," he said, getting right to the point. "I'm about to finish my military service and Karima has graduated. You made me a promise."

"Yes, this is true," I said. "I will not go back on a promise, but it's been five years—almost six. Much has happened." I was stalling. What should I do? And then I got an idea. I asked him to come home with me—right then—unannounced. We would sit down together and see if Karima wanted to marry him. "But you must promise that you will accept whatever she says." I was not convinced that this would be a wise union. In my opinion, Sayyid was a spoiled boy—the only son of a wealthy man, dependent on his father for his livelihood. In Egypt, during the 1960s, the ideal model of manhood was one where a person carved out his own future. Today, things are different. It's all about how much wealth you can inherit.

It took an hour to get home. I could feel myself shaking. I reminded myself that this would be Karima's choice. She was mature enough to make her own decision regarding marriage. Even if I didn't like her decision, I would go along with her. When we arrived home, Karima opened the door. Her eyes widened and she gasped. We sat down and drank some tea. I was holding my breath.

"Karima," I began, "I promised Sayyid almost six years ago that if you were still interested in each other after you graduated, I would give my blessing to the wedding. Now, it's up to you. Are you interested?" The moment stretched into what seemed an eternity.

Karima said nothing for a minute or two. Then she said, "Look, Sayyid, we were very young. We were children."

Sayyid stared blankly ahead of him. He had heard enough. He looked over to me and asked, "May I please be excused?"

"You are welcome any time in this house," I offered. Feeling relieved by Karima's response, it wasn't difficult to be hospitable.

"Thank you," he said. "You've kept your word, and now I will go."

I walked with him to the bus stop. When I returned home, I found Karima in tears. I comforted her the best I could. "It's OK. You've made a difficult choice. I know it wasn't easy for you." Internal conflict always seems to accompany difficult decisions.

"I have so many fond memories of our time together," Karima sobbed.

"Yes, of course. These memories become part of who you are. Why would you want to erase them?" I asked.

"What did you expect the outcome to be?" Karima asked.

"I really did not know. If marrying him would have made you happy, I would have moved forward with the wedding. It was really up to you." Even though I had reservations about the marriage, I meant what I told her.

Karima pushed me even further. "What would you have me do in my situation?"

"I would like you to have a family someday with someone who has made a life for himself, not with somebody dependent on his father." I spoke with complete honesty.

Karima worked for two or three more years, experiencing much of the vibrant life that Cairo offered. One day she told me she had found somebody she wanted to marry. I had confidence in her judgment. I never regretted giving her enough freedom to make her own way through life. Sometimes, under the guise of protection, parents can destroy their children's lives. Women in a patriarchal society such as Egypt are especially vulnerable to this kind of exploitation. Certainly Badriyya, my elder sister, suffered as my father, in his attempt to do what he thought best for her, manipulated her life, making decisions for her instead of involving her in the process.

All my younger siblings finished their high school education. Ayat graduated from Cairo University–Department of Japanese Language. Osama studied engineering in college. Muhammad had no interest in going to school any longer than he had to. He had some experience working in my father's grocery store when my father was living. Later on, he worked for a textile company in Tanta. He received promotions along the way, eventually settling into a good position. Both my younger brothers, being men, navigated their adolescence with an independence not generally experienced by Egyptian women. Knowing that Egyptian society puts women at a disadvantage had much to do with my taking special pains to insure that Karima and Ayat had the freedom they needed to experience life on their own terms. Badriyya, my elder sister, the only one of us who never attended high school, read voraciously. She educated herself. It was most unfortunate that she was not able to continue with her education. I believe she would have gone far.

I would be remiss if I failed to mention Shereen, my adopted daughter. I met Shereen shortly after she had been appointed an assistant teacher at Cairo University. At that time, I was an associate professor. We worked together on the examination committee. This is an occasion where the older and younger generations come together in a more relaxed atmosphere, a change of pace from the usual formal academic—dare I say it?—stuffiness. Sometimes, after we had completed our work, we'd go out to lunch or have a drink together.

Ebtehal, at this time, was an assistant professor, having already earned her Ph.D. We were not yet married, but Ebtehal and Shereen were close friends. One day—it seemed to come from right out of the blue—Shereen asked me, "Do you mind if I call you Dad?"

I had a knee-jerk response. "Yes, I mind. You have a father, don't you?"

"No, my father died a long time ago, and I don't think my mother would object if I called you Dad," she assured me. Her mother, a teacher, had raised Shereen single-handedly. "What is your objection to my calling you Dad?" she asked.

"I don't want to take anything that doesn't belong to me," I replied. "We can be friends, of course, but you don't have to call me Dad."

"But I'd like to call you Dad." She was already acting like a daughter, pushing to get her way with me just as my younger sisters had done with me many times.

"Well, OK," I finally conceded. "If you really want to, that's fine. I have so many children, what's one more? But not even my brothers and sisters—people I helped to raise—call me Dad."

Nevertheless, Shereen began to call me Dad. When Ebtehal and I married, Shereen celebrated with us. Ebtehal and I then traveled. Shereen traveled as well, earning her M.A. and Ph.D. degrees along the way. When my case became national news, she published an article supporting me. We remained in close contact even after I had gone into exile.

In 1997, Shereen and I met in Oxford to attend a huge conference. She was a participant on one of the panel discussions. Shereen teaches English literature at Cairo University and accepts speaking invitations from all over the world. Her most recent project has to do with Arab women authors who write in English. I arrived at the airport two hours before her flight was due—that's how eager I was to see her. I wanted to be sure I was there to greet her when she landed. As soon as she arrived, we went to the cafeteria. We spent hours sipping coffee, catching each other up on our lives. I noticed the sky darkening as night began to fall. "We should make our way toward Oxford," I said.

When we arrived at Oxford, our accommodations were not yet ready, so we were forced to check into a nearby hotel. There was only one room available. Shereen noticed me fidgeting. "What's your problem?" she demanded.

"I don't have a problem," I lied. I have a conservative background. Even though Shereen had long ago declared herself to be my daughter, how could I just check into a hotel and stay in the same room overnight with this beautiful young woman?

Shereen was matter-of-fact. "Yes, Dad, you have a problem. We don't have a choice. We need to share this room, that's all there is to it."

"I do have a problem, you're right," I conceded. "I snore."

"Then I'll just put earplugs in my ears," she said. And that was that.

The following morning, the rooms at Oxford were ready and we moved into separate quarters. We spent a delightful week together. Many of my friends, present from all over the globe, looked at us skeptically. "Is she really your daughter? Her name is different from yours."

"Yes," I assured them. "She decided to be my daughter. This is our choice." For many Arabs and Muslims, it takes time to accept the fact that you have a daughter who is not your biological offspring. In addition, many of the men would smile as if to say, "It's OK, I understand." Many folks have difficulty thinking that friendship without sex is possible between women and men.

One day she called me—in ecstasy. "Dad, I am going to get married. We are in love. After our marriage, we are coming to visit you." I spoke with her husband-to-be on the phone. He was a movie director. I knew him by name. But after they had been married a year, he died. "Where should I go? What should I do?" I asked her over the phone. My instinct was to rush to her side, but she came to me instead, staying with Ebtehal and me for a week. As a result of her visit, I realized in a new way how much I had grown to love and care for this human being. She suffered after losing her husband, but she was ready to pick up and keep going.

The morning she left, I told Ebtehal, "That girl is strong. She will do well." And she did—in spite of some difficulties with her husband's family over inheritance.

"They [the family] want me to disappear into thin air," she told me later as we spoke by phone. "I'm not going to do that. I have certain rights." There was no doubt in my mind she'd take care of herself.

When I was appointed to the Clerevinga Chair (2000–2001) at Leiden University, I wanted Shereen to attend the ceremony. "Yes, I am coming," she assured me. I addressed her in my speech as my daughter. Tradition dictates that the family stands together in the reception area after all the speeches have been delivered. She was included, of course.

"Now, I'm officially your daughter," she said. "See, it's right here on paper. You cannot deny it anymore."

I would not even think of denying our bond. Over the years, I've developed a fatherly pride in the person she is—as well as taking pride in her achievements. We recently met in Damascus to attend a conference. The organizing committee had booked Muhammad Munir, a famous singer, to entertain us in the evening after our workshops. I know Munir. We were students together. He began to sing—beautiful words that unfortunately lose something in translation. "Raise your voice in singing/Songs are still possible."

I found myself quite moved by the words and the music. Is it possible? Is it really still possible? Can we still sing? For me, of course, singing here is a metaphor—a symbol of rejoicing in life, happiness, and intellectual freedom. Is singing still possible? Munir repeated the phrase over and over, and before long, I realized that my face was wet. Munir's song had touched me in a deep place, and my tears flowed freely. My thoughts were about Egypt—the Egypt that I love and the Egypt that I hate. Part of my sorrow had to do with the wound Egypt had inflicted on me. Shereen's presence comforted me.

The next day Shereen took part in a panel discussion. I carefully watched her performance. She was under attack. She talked about how censorship these days seems to be coming from the grass roots of society. There is a sense in the Arab world that so many of our problems and so much of our suffering are a direct result of Western influence. The Arab world responds to this sense by censoring. Shereen, in her attempt to show that censorship could never achieve the kind of society many Muslims envision, spoke out against the practice. Folks in the audience were trying to "take her down." She responded articulately and clearly, and used her sense of humor to ease the tense situation. Afterward, I enveloped her in my arms, comforting her the best I could. The discussion had taken its toll on her.

Many young people look to me as a father figure. I love them all. Over the years, though, Shereen has taken her place beside my siblings—the children I raised. I am fortunate indeed to be able to claim her as my daughter.

4 A Reluctant Scholar

As soon as I finished my undergraduate studies at Cairo University in 1972, I was appointed as an assistant teacher in the university's Department of Arabic, Faculty of Letters. I felt honored. These appointments are awarded to those who graduate with high marks. I felt fortunate as well. I had always dreamed of teaching, and that dream was finally being realized. I quit my job at the police headquarters and delved into my responsibilities with a newfound zeal.

The next academic hurdle I faced was choosing a field of research for my graduate studies. The faculty in the Department of Arabic, who had recently become my colleagues, told me they had an urgent need for a specialist in the field of Islamic Studies. They strongly advised me to go in that direction for both my M.A. and Ph.D. theses. I was reluctant to take their advice.

My reluctance to focus on Islamic Studies stemmed from the reading I had done even before enrolling in the university. Since I was well into my twenties when I began my formal university education, I had more reading tucked under my belt than most students have when they matriculate. Through my reading, I became aware of the danger of working within Islamic Studies.

I learned about the case against 'Alî Abdel-Râziq in 1925. He wrote a book titled *Islam and the Foundation of Political Authority*.[1] In his book, he argued for an end to the caliphate system of government. The caliphate, he asserted, is not essential to Islam. It is nothing more than a political system of government used by Muslim people.

Islam, in fact, does not insist on any particular form of government. Muhammad never claimed to be a king or a ruler. Muhammad's role was that of a leader and a prophet in Medina. It was up to the people to decide what form of government they wanted. Abdel-Râzik was walking on thin ice. At that time (1925), Islam and the state were considered to be one entity.

In spite of Turkish authorities abolishing the caliphate in Turkey after World War I (1924), many Arab and Islamic leaders since then have vied for nomination as the new caliph. None was successful. In 1925, Fuad was the king of Egypt. Abdel-Râzik's book did not just undermine the orthodox foundations of Islam, it threatened political interests as well. King Fuad believed that his regime, a regime that included religious rulers, was under attack. The government needed to squelch Abdel-Râziq.

Abdel-Râziq was a judge in a *shari'a* court when he wrote his controversial book. He had graduated from a religious institution. He was a Muslim scholar, intent on bringing an up-to-date perspective to Islam—a perspective that, if implemented, would lead to change. That was the problem. He threatened established power. The orthodoxy (al-Azhar) formed an investigating committee to evaluate and judge Abdel-Râziq's book. In the end, the committee found him guilty of heresy and fired him from his position. No longer could he be a judge. The courts even revoked the grades he had earned when he was a student.

I also read about Tâhâ Husayn. Husayn earned his Ph.D. at the Sorbonne under the supervision of the French sociologist Emile Durkheim (1858–1917). In 1926, Tâhâ Husayn published a book titled *Pre-Islamic Poetry.*[2] In this book, he questioned the authenticity of the entire body of pre-Islamic poetry. Husayn's work took place within the context of a burgeoning intellectual movement associated with the newly established academic institution, the National University. (The National University later became Cairo University.) During the early part of the twentieth century, it was believed that the languages of North Arabia and of South Arabia were two distinct tongues. But when Husayn researched the subject of pre-Islamic poetry, he found poets from Yemen (South Arabia) and poets from the northern part of the peninsula expressing themselves through an identical language. Because pre-Islamic poetry did not reflect the expected linguistic diversity, Husayn came to the conclusion that this poetry was written after the Qur'an had been revealed to Muhammad.

Furthermore, Husayn argued that the Qur'anic story of Abraham's arrival in Mecca with his wife Hagar and newborn child Ishmael—an event taken as historical fact, marking the time Arabia became unified by a common language—was really an oral narrative that existed before the revelation of the Qur'an. (Various versions of the story of Abraham, Hagar, Sarah, Isaac, and Ishmael were well known before the Qur'an.) Husayn maintained that the Qur'anic story had been adapted and then embellished by the Arabs (the original inhabitants of Medina) in response to the Jewish migration from Yemen to Medina. These newcomers (Jews) were strangers, and as is often the case when newcomers appear on the scene, conflict followed. As a way to ease this conflict, the Arabs spun a tale showing that the Jews (and Christians) descend from one ancestor, Abraham. Story is one way to assimilate newcomers into an existing society. In this case, the story was used to bridge the distance between Jews and Arabs. Since the story existed before the Qur'an, the Qur'an used the story to connect itself to other Abrahamic traditions. It's a folk narrative saying that we all belong to one grandfather. Husayn's point was that the story ought not to be understood factually—it was not necessarily history. In addition, the Qur'an used this particular story not only to situate Islam within the Judeo-Christian traditions but also to establish the priority of Islam as a monotheistic religion.

Even though Husayn considered the Qur'an to be the most reliable and authentic source for understanding pre-Islamic social and religious life, his book created quite a stir. The dispute reached the Egyptian Parliament. Husayn stood accused of insulting Islam. Before going to trial, the public attorney questioned him. Being a well-educated and enlightened person, he read Husayn's controversial book, investigated the charges of heresy brought against him, and came to the conclusion that Husayn had no intention of compromising Islam. His was an intellectual, scientific work. His language might be offensive to some, but this was the language of inquiry and science. Husayn's intentions were honorable. The public attorney declared Husayn innocent of any criminal intention against Islam. In spite of this, Husayn endured hardship as his reputation suffered. He was forced to rewrite the book and publish it under a different title. Even so, the new edition was based on the same methodology and rationale as his original work. In the second, enlarged edition of his book, he removed the story of Abraham and Hagar bringing Ishmael to Arabia. He titled this new book *Pre-Islamic Literature*.[3]

According to the more popular story, Abraham had two wives, Sarah and Hagar. Sarah became jealous of Hagar and Hagar's son, Ishmael, in spite of the fact that Sarah had given birth (some years after Hagar) to her own son, Isaac. Because of all the domestic friction, Sarah demanded that Abraham send Hagar and Ishmael away. Abraham took Hagar and Ishmael to an uninhabited area of the Arabian Peninsula, leaving them there with this prayer: "Please God, send people around them to settle." And people did start to arrive because, as the story goes, Ishmael's heels dug into the sand as he cried and flailed his arms. Water gushed from the place where Ishmael had inadvertently been digging. When the water flowed, people gathered about and eventually settled. God answered Abraham's prayer. Ishmael was not Arab, but because Arab people nurtured and sustained him within this newly founded community, it wasn't long before he identified himself with them.

Husayn noted that the Qur'an speaks about Abraham and Ishmael, but just because the Qur'an speaks about them in no way proves that these characters were real flesh-and-blood people. Of course, Husayn was building on the work of the Islamic Reformation Movement—a movement that reached its peak toward the end of the nineteenth century. This movement made a clear distinction between history and religious text. Muhammad 'Abduh (1849–1905), a rational thinker considered to be the father of modern Islamic thought, believed that all the stories in the Qur'an were allegories—not historical accounts of specific events. The Qur'an uses a narrative style, he said, in order to convey spiritual and ethical truths.

When Husayn asserted that the stories in the Qur'an did not necessarily reflect history, texts such as pre-Islamic poetry—poetry Husayn believed was written after the Qur'an—received a status never before granted to such work. Religious text might relay a historical incident, he noted, but the text is not meant to reflect an accurate historical event. Stories have a meaning beyond the text. Husayn created a ruckus. How could anybody claim that the Qur'an was not historically accurate?

There were other cases as well. Even though I had read about them, the general public had no clue about all the upheaval the Department of Arabic in Cairo University had gone through in the recent past.

In 1947, Muhammad Ahmed Khalafallah, an assistant teacher, presented his Ph.D. thesis to the Department of Arabic at Cairo University. Professor Amîn al-Khûlî, an important reformist scholar whose work to date has gone unrecognized, supervised Khalafallah's thesis, which was titled "The Art of Narration in the Qur'an." Al-Khûlî had developed a literary approach to the study of the Qur'an—a direction begun by Muhammad 'Abduh and followed up by Tâhâ Husayn. Al-Khûlî continued the direction of these scholars, further developing the literary approach to the study of the Qur'an. He made it crystal clear that we can come to the sacred text from different angles, such as philosophically and ethically, but to do that, we must first begin by studying the Qur'an as a literary text.

Khalafallah used a literary approach as well to find meaning in the Qur'an. He based his thesis on making a clear distinction between history and story in the Qur'an. After a heated debate, the university rejected Khalafallah's thesis, declaring that such an approach when studying the Qur'an casts doubts on the authenticity and divinity of Islam's sacred text. The university fired Khalafallah and transferred him to a nonteaching position within the Ministry of Education.

Amîn al-Khûlî, a man I consider to be my grandfather, was barred from teaching and supervising Islamic Studies. He could teach only literary criticism and classical Arabic. In 1954, a government decree, initiated by the new military authority called the Free Officers Movement, forced al-Khûlî into retirement along with many other professors. According to the government, this action was part of a revolutionary process intended to remove corruption from Egyptian society and to cleanse the universities. The chair which had been occupied by Amîn al-Khûlî fell vacant. Teaching undergraduates was left to any professor interested in doing so.

I wanted to find out what ultimately happened to Muhammad Ahmed Khalafallah. I strongly identified with Amîn al-Khûlî and believed, along with him, that we were tending a garden, growing scholars, lovingly caring for them as a gardener might tend to roses, but then some crazy wind came along, blowing everything away. I discovered that Khalafallah wrote another thesis three months after his original one had been rejected—something trivial—just to get his degree. I met him. I know him. When my own trouble began, the trouble that eventually led me into exile, he wrote three important articles about my work, explaining how a scientific report should be written. He was eager to explain to the Egyptian people that the accusation of heresy hurled in my direction demonstrated that my accusers knew nothing about how to go about doing scientific inquiry and research.

When I was teaching at Cairo University, I invited Khalafallah to come and speak to my class. This is one of my teaching strategies—inviting professors from outside the university to share their experience and wisdom with my students. He hesitated.

"You are part of the history of Cairo University, whether the university likes it or not," I reminded him. "Even the problems you experienced with your thesis are part of the history of this university. You are an Islamic Studies scholar. I would like my students to meet you. We could have some good discussion."

He finally agreed to come. However, as I was about to leave my apartment to pick him up on the day he was to speak to my students, he phoned me. "Look, Nasr, I am sorry. I am unable to come. I have not been to Cairo University in fifty years, and I just can't do it."

I understood at the time. I understand even better today. I wonder if I could go back and teach at Cairo University after being away for eight years. Many times I feel like an abandoned child. Khalafallah must have felt just as deserted.

So I was aware of all this history in the Department of Arabic Studies when I began my graduate studies at Cairo University. Even though Islamic Studies had always interested me and I had at one time every intention of pursuing a degree in the field, I resolved not to go that route. I felt the risk would be too great. I would work on literary criticism instead. The department, though, exerted considerable pressure on me, insisting that the newly appointed assistant lecturer should be an Islamic Studies scholar.

I objected. People in the department didn't seem to understand. "Why?" they asked.

I said, "You know the problem—the problem of 'Alî Abdel-Râziq, the problem of Tâhâ Husayn, the problem of Muhammad Ahmed Khalafallah."

My professors downplayed my concerns, saying that the problems these men had were personal, just something between professors—an internal affair. They were unaware how deeply I had delved into the history of the department. One of my professors asked, "Why do you think that this will happen to you? Do you think you are going to say something new?"

This, of course, is the usual thinking. If you work within the field of Islamic Studies, the assumption is that you will discover no new knowledge. Islamic scholars, generally speaking, explain what has already been established. Scientific investigation is considered superfluous—even dangerous. Islamic Studies focuses on preaching. Amîn al-Khûlî, Tâhâ Husayn, and others started to bring Islamic Studies into the field of scientific inquiry. I try to do this as well. Most of the Muslim world resists applying scientific methodology to the study of Islam. This is the basic problem. When the subject of Islamic Studies comes up, people think of faith, not investigation. Islamic Studies today, for the most part, brings tried-and-true ideas to the attention of the people through preaching, but does not look at those ideas through a critical lens.

Needless to say, I was provoked with this kind of talk from my professors. "What are you saying?" I asked. "Are you appointing me as a scholar of Islamic Studies just to repeat what has been said already? How is that being respectful to the Qur'an? Are you actually encouraging me not to bring anything new to my field of study? Why, then, should I be a scholar?"

True, I was a bit outspoken. I was also critical of their assumption—the study of Islam creates no new knowledge. The professors scolded me, reminding me that I was just a junior member of the department. Nonetheless, I felt I had to speak my mind. "I'm sorry," I said, "but I think it is my duty as a scholar to bring something new to the field."

To avoid further trouble, I went along with the department's plan for me. I would become a scholar of Islamic Studies. I bent over backward to ensure that I would not work with any of the traditional professors who used to supervise Islamic Studies. That chair had been vacant ever since Amîn al-Khûlî was forced into retirement, so there was nobody within the field to supervise me. I chose Abd al-Azîz al-Ahwânî, an Andalusian Studies expert and professor of classical literature, to supervise my work.

For my M.A. thesis, I decided to study the Mu'tazilite interpretation of the Qur'an, focusing on the concept of metaphor. The Mu'tazilite movement, begun by Wâsil ibn 'Atâ' (d. 748), enjoyed its heyday during the first half of the ninth century. According to the Mu'tazilites, the Qur'an is God's uncreated speech; however, the words, the ink, and the paper used to express that speech came to us in time and space, and therefore the actual text we have today is a created phenomenon. Between 827 and 833, the Abbasid caliph al-Ma'mûn began an inquisition. He announced that any religious judge who resisted the Mu'tazilite thesis of the created Qur'an would lose his job or go to jail. Ahmad ibn Hanbal (780–855), al-Ma'mûn's opponent, held fast to the traditional understanding that the Qur'an was both uncreated and eternal.

Is God's Word found in the content of the message as expressed in human language? Does that message include language as an essential component? The Qur'an states, "If all the trees of the earth were pens, and the sea, replenished by seven more seas, were ink, the words of God could not be finished still" (Sura 31:27). If God's Word cannot be confined, how can the Qur'an, a text limited within space and time, be the only manifestation of the Word of God?

At the same time, the Qur'an refers to itself as *Kalam Allah*, the speech of God—an idea that would equate the Word of God with the Qur'an. The idea of God as speaker raises theological difficulties—difficulties that the Mu'tazilites resolved by interpreting certain passages metaphorically.

The Mu'tazilites were heavily influenced by Greek philosophy and logic, and therefore they applied rational methods of investigation when interpreting the Qur'an. Mu'tazilite theologians disagreed on some points, but they were all in agreement on five fundamental principles— God's justice, God's unity, the "intermediate position" (committing a grave sin does not automatically make one an infidel), God's irreversible threats and promises, and God's commanding the right and prohibiting the wrong—principles best understood as a response to their rivals. Their opponents included those who held to a literal interpretation of the Qur'an and those who believed in unqualified predestination.

After four years of analyzing and comparing Mu'tazilite theology with the discourse of their critics, I understood that at the heart of the battle was this matter of interpretation. How do we find meaning in the text when unambiguous verses (*ayât muhkamât*), considered the backbone of the Qur'an, come up against ambiguous verses (*ayât mutashâbihât*)? There is no argument within Islam that ambiguous verses are to be interpreted in light of the unambiguous texts. The problem? What the Mu'tazilites considered unambiguous, their opponents considered ambiguous, and vice versa. Each side held tenaciously to its view, believing that both the structure and the meaning of the Qur'an were at stake.

My M.A. thesis, "The Concept of Metaphor as Applied to the Qur'an by the Mu'tazilites," was later published as a book titled *The Trend of Rational Exegesis of the Qur'an: A Study of the Mu'tazilite's Concept of Qur'anic Metaphor*.[4] One of the conclusions I reached during my study was that each side was attempting to shore up its own ideology and impose that meaning onto the Qur'an. In other words, each side attempted to bring the Qur'an in line with its own beliefs. I wondered how the meaning of a text could be so easily manipulated.

When I began reading about hermeneutics (methodological principles of textual interpretation) in the United States (1978–1980), I was already familiar with exegesis, critically examining a text in an attempt to understand the intention of that text. While scouring university libraries in the States for books on the philosophy of hermeneutics and its history, I discovered that the Arabic word ta'wîl closely approximates the English word "hermeneutics." When I returned to Egypt from the United States, I wrote about hermeneutics in Arabic. I believe I was the first scholar to do so.

My basic argument about the Qur'an is that in order to make Islamic thought relevant, the human dimension of the Qur'an needs to be reconsidered. Placing the Qur'an firmly within history does not imply that the origins of the Qur'an are human. I believe the Qur'an to be a divine text revealed from God to the Prophet Muhammad through the mediation of the archangel Gabriel. That revelation took place through the use of language—a language (Arabic) rooted in a historical context. The Qur'an addressed the Arabs living in the seventh century, taking into account the social reality of those particular people living on the Arabian Peninsula at that time. How else could they have understood the revelation?

Without the Word of God being embodied in human language, there is no way for us to understand it. The Qur'an states, "Each apostle We have sent has spoken only in the language of his own people, so that he might make his precepts clear to them" (Sura 14:4). How can we assume, then, that the Qur'an is exclusively and literally the Word of God? God's Word exists in a sphere beyond human knowledge, but we can apply hermeneutical principles to a text that exists in time and place. Historically, most Muslims have insisted that the Qur'an in Arabic is literally and exclusively God's Word. This excludes other Scriptures from presenting the Word of God in a language other than Arabic.

I believe that one of the reasons we currently experience such stagnation in Islamic thought is that we overemphasize the divine dimension of the Qur'an at the expense of acknowledging its human characteristics. I see my scholarship as a continuation of the rational school of thought started by the Mu'tazilites and further developed by Muslim philosophers such as al-Kindî, al-Fârâbî, Ibn Sînâ (Avicenna), and Ibn Rushd (Averroes). My scholarship reflects my roots in classical Islam as well.

When I began to study the Qur'an as interpreted by mystical scholarship, I found myself drawn to the discourse of Ibn 'Arabî, an Andalusian Sufi born in Spain. Ibn 'Arabî is best known for his work *The Meccan Revelation*.[5] He died in Syria in 1279. I decided to focus on Ibn 'Arabî for my doctoral research. I proposed to study the hermeneutics of the Qur'an from a mystical (Sufi) perspective.

Whereas the Mu'tazilites attempted to apply their interpretation of the Qur'an to political and social issues (oftentimes becoming what we call today political activists), I was convinced that Ibn 'Arabî would offer a Qur'anic interpretation void of ideological interest. At the time, I thought Sufis did not concern themselves with the world around them, choosing to concentrate on their own mystical experiences instead. In time, I would learn differently. Just as I had discovered with my study of the Mu'tazilites, I saw all over again with my study on Sufism how all interpretation of text is informed by current sociopolitical and cultural factors. Qur'anic interpretation is no exception.

Ibn 'Arabî wanted to bring modernity (current knowledge) to bear on the Qur'an. He believed that Islamic thought should be flexible enough to absorb all of his society under Islam's umbrella. The "religion of comprehensive love" is how Ibn 'Arabî described his utopian vision in his poetry. He attempted to gather various elements of thought from Christianity, Judaism, Islam, and all other faiths in his society and integrate them into a unified Islamic system. It proved difficult to put Ibn 'Arabî's project into practice. In his attempt to create this utopian society, he did not address social problems in a realistic manner. Even as he was developing his thinking, tensions were mounting within his own society—tensions that could not be diffused through the application of the principles of his "religion of comprehensive love."

Hasan Samak was one of my father's friends who used to hang out in front of our little village grocery store, discussing everything from local gossip to the current political situation. He was a poet. After I had matured somewhat and become a professor at Cairo University, our friendship blossomed. Whenever he was in Cairo, he'd stop in to see me in my office. When I returned to my home village, there he was—a ubiquitous presence. He was a Sufi—a mystic—and I learned a lot about Sufism from him long before doing my formal study of Ibn 'Arabî.

One day he came to see me. I had traveled back to Quhafa for a brief visit, and I was happy to welcome him to my home. I noticed right away, though, that he was trembling from head to foot. "I have to talk with you," he managed to blurt out. I thought for sure disaster had struck him. As soon as he closed the door behind him, he began to cry.

"What's the matter? What happened?" I asked.

"I saw him. I saw him. I saw him. I cannot keep the secret any longer," he lamented.

"What secret? Whom did you see?" I demanded.

Tears rolled down his face. "I saw the Prophet. And I talked to him and I said, 'I love you, Prophet Muhammad.' He said, 'I love you, Hasan.'"

"What is wrong with that?" I wondered aloud.

"Don't you see? Now, I am revealing the secret—the secret of seeing the Prophet in a dream," he said.

I could only look at him blankly. "So what?"

"I will be punished," he insisted. "He will never show himself to me again. But I couldn't keep it inside. I had to talk to someone."

At the time, I didn't fully understand the turmoil Hasan was going through. All I could do was wonder about the nature of the burden he carried. If he believed there would be adverse consequences as a result of his confession, what drove him to do such a thing?

When I read about Ibn 'Arabî—mysticism, the vision, the secret, how to keep the secret, and punishment for revealing the secret to people who are not ready—Hasan's experience began to make some sense. I was in the United States when I began my research about Ibn 'Arabî. While I was reading, Hasan's experience was right there before me, weaving its way in between the words of the text. I think this is what gives my research and writing its flesh and blood. When I write about something, it's not just an intellectual exercise. My reading, my research, and my experience all fuse. This fusion, I believe, is essential to the process of creating knowledge. It's also what's missing from so much work done today in the academy.

I finished work on my doctoral thesis in 1980, the year I returned to Egypt from the States. Within a couple of months, I was awarded my Ph.D. My dissertation on Ibn 'Arabî was published under the title *The Philosophy of Hermeneutics.*[6] It was my second book.

What kept begging to be addressed as a result of my study for both my M.A. and Ph.D. theses, as well as my experiences in life, revolved around several questions. What is Islam? Is it a religion of social justice? Does Islam support capitalism? Does it protect private property? Is Islam a religion of *jihad* against the enemy? Or is the focus on peace? Does the Qur'an support a Mu'tazilite interpretation or that of their opponents, or did the Sufi Ibn 'Arabî best understand what the Qur'an reveals? And just what is the Qur'an? The question must be addressed because the Qur'an is the foundation of Islam. Is the Qur'an clear? Ambiguous? I could find no easy answers.

I had come to the conclusion, based on my M.A. and Ph.D. work, that every interpretation of the Qur'an has never been separate from social and political influence. In other words, it is not possible to speak about the Qur'an as an absolute that transcends space, time, and place. Human beings understand text through some sort of prism that varies depending on experience—both individual and cultural experience.

As a result of further study and research, my third book emerged, which I titled *The Concept of the Text: A Reinvestigation of Classical Qur'anic Disciplines.*[7] Before dealing with questions regarding the interpretation of text, I needed to study and examine rules governing the study of a text and then apply those rules to the Qur'an itself. Without this rigorous application of scholarship, the Qur'an (or any other text) is vulnerable to having the interpreter's ideology made part of that text.

What about the Qur'an's structure? We know that Muhammad received his revelation in installments over a period of twenty-three years. Muhammad could neither read nor write. Scribes wrote as Muhammad recited his revelation. The chronology of the revelation has been rearranged into the order in which we find the Qur'anic text today. This process—canonization—also needs to be taken into account when interpreting the Qur'an.

In addition, we cannot understand the Qur'an properly without studying history in order to learn about the context (geography, politics, society) in which the Qur'an was revealed. People within a particular community raised pertinent questions about a variety of issues—wine, gambling, orphans, menstruation, diet, charity, war. The answers to those questions, found within the Qur'an, became the basis for *shari'a* law, a system of jurisprudence that looks to the legal principles found in Islam's sacred text, and the *hâdith,* sayings of the Prophet, when establishing laws within a particular Islamic community.

I keep returning again and again to the same questions. What is the Qur'an? What does it mean to me, the individual? What does it mean to the *umma*, the community of Muslims? Islamic theology has not developed much beyond the thirteenth century. The basic questions remain frozen. The work that I do—my critical scholarship—has everything to do with making Islam relevant to our lives at the present time.

5 Here I Stand

consider myself to be very, very Egyptian. What I mean by that is that I feel I can communicate at a gut level with Egyptian people. I know how to joke with them. I know how to connect with them no matter what their status within our society. I take them as they are. Perhaps my father's death when I was fourteen years old forced me out into the world at an earlier age than most folks. I didn't have the luxury of lingering in adolescence. I had to learn early on how to survive. I got to know the street and the life of the underprivileged in Egyptian society. I think the ordinary experiences of day-to-day living in my home village of Quhafa set the stage for what later developed into my passion for justice.

Much of my early religious education in the *kuttâb* was rote. Recitation and memorization of the Qur'an took center stage. Correct pronunciation of the Arabic words and clear enunciation of the text were our goals and highly prized by our teachers. Even though I had the entire Qur'an memorized by the time I reached my eighth birthday, I did not comprehend much of what the text said. My father, my mother, the preacher in the mosque, and other folks in the village explained the text's meaning to me. I prayed five times a day and fasted during Ramadân. There were people in my village who did not observe those rituals—rituals so central to Islam. That was OK. These people were not ostracized. I never considered ritual to be the essential part of Islam. Even as a child, I understood that Islam had everything to do with how you lived your life. The emphasis was on orthopraxis (proper behavior), not orthodoxy (proper belief or doctrine). Within my small community, I learned that the spirit of Islam was all about helping the poor and the weak. Today, I stand with the oppressed—whoever they are and wherever they may be.

Between 1992 and 1995—the years I was accused and finally convicted of apostasy—my picture appeared frequently in Egyptian papers and periodicals. Once, a caricature of me in the form of the devil stared me in the eye as I opened my newspaper to catch up on the day's events. The "devil" had just stabbed the Qur'an. Blood gushed copiously from the sacred text. Egyptian people were quite familiar with my situation.

One evening, on our way home from the university, Ebtehal and I stopped at the supermarket to get some provisions for our long week-end. As Ebtehal and I gathered some items together and placed them in our cart, a very old man kept staring at me. He reminded me of my father and my grandfather—all the fathers in Egypt. I knew he recognized me. He walked around me, frowned at me, looked me up and down, and then asked, "Are you . . . ?"

I knew what he was about to ask. Whenever I'd go out in public, people would often ask if I was "that man accused of heresy." I'd always answer, "Yes, yes, I am that man accused of heresy." Often my tone would be one of mock impatience mixed with a healthy dose of boredom.

This elderly man became angry and started to shout at me. Folks gathered all around Ebtehal and me. "Aren't you ashamed of yourself? You should be ashamed. I know that your father is a Muslim. Isn't that right?"

"Yes," I said. "My father's name is Hamed." In the Arab world, if your name is Hamed, there is no doubt about your religious affiliation.

The man kept at me. "How can you call yourself a Muslim? How is it that your father was a Muslim and your mother was a Muslim and now you bring disgrace to the Qur'an, to the Prophet Muhammad, and to Islam? Aren't you ashamed of yourself? You must be crazy." The man repeated these questions several times—only changing the order of his questions and accusations.

"Please, did you finish?" I finally asked him.

"Yes, I have finished," the man replied.

"OK, now please listen to me," I said. "You have been watching me for ten minutes here in this supermarket. You have seen every inch of my body, every inch of my face. Is this true?"

"Yes, it is true," he agreed.

"Tell me," I said. "If you didn't know my reputation, what impression would I give you? Do I look like I'm in need of psychiatric intervention? Or do I appear normal? You actually do not know me personally. What's your verdict?"

"You seem to look like everybody else," he admitted.

"So I'm not out of my mind? I'm not crazy?" I asked.

"No," he said. "You don't seem crazy."

"Tell me," I said, pushing forward with the conversation, "if someone who is not crazy, but normal like you or like your son, and if he worked in the university in a Muslim society like Egypt, and if he wanted to get a promotion in order to raise his salary to meet the ever-rising cost of living, would you think this person normal if he asked for a promotion and then showed himself as an atheist to the university?"

The old man seemed to be listening, so I continued. "I'm not talking about whether or not this man is actually an atheist. We have unbelievers in our society who pass themselves off as believers. But if you were not fasting during Ramadân, would you go out in public and eat? No, of course not. You would eat behind closed doors. So even if I am not a believer, would I flaunt my atheism and then ask the university to promote me? What would you think about someone who would pull a stunt like that?"

"They would be crazy," he said.

"But you just said that I am not crazy," I reminded him. "Do you think I'm crazy?"

"No," he said.

"That's right," I responded. "A sane person like myself would have made a decent presentation to the university—something faithful to Islam. Then, after I had received my promotion, then maybe I would make a show of my atheism because I am just like you. Life is very hard. I need my salary. And this is my wife. [I introduced Ebtehal to the man.] You know the prices here."

The man, who just a few minutes ago had been ready to attack me, started to calm down and asked me, "What is the problem, then? Those people who have accused you—they are not stupid, they are good, holy men."

"Yes," I agreed. "They are good, holy men. "Do you want to know what the problem is?"

"Tell me," he insisted.

"I criticized those holy men who supported the Islamic investment companies. These are the same men who robbed the Egyptian people," I said.

"God curse all of those people," the old man shouted. Every Egyptian was familiar with the scandal surrounding the Islamic investment companies. As he told me his story, I learned that the old man's son had worked in Kuwait for ten years. He had put all of the money he earned overseas into one of these investment companies and lost it all.

"So this is the reason for all this commotion around you?" he asked.

"This is exactly the reason," I answered. "You know the name of this man—he was a religious counselor to these companies. That's why I criticized him. I'm just an Egyptian like you. Because I had no money to invest, I didn't get bilked out of my savings, but I was defending you, your son, and your grandson. Those people have been able to steal money from the people in the name of religion."

The man broke down. "Oh, my son, I didn't know. I am so sorry. I didn't know." And he came toward me and kissed me and hugged me, and I held him close to me right there in the middle of the busy supermarket.

I felt relief and contentment on the forty-kilometer drive home. I said to Ebtehal, "What I really need to do is meet every Egyptian citizen and explain myself. How can I do that?" With TV, of course, I could communicate well with folks. However, it would have to be live TV. Piecing together fragments of conversation just would not work.

This is what I mean when I say I'm very, very Egyptian. I'm able to communicate with people from different educational backgrounds as well as with people who have no education at all. Egyptian people have always expressed themselves in a wide variety of ways. Our recent history in particular reflects this variety.

While I was growing up, Egypt had what came to be known as the Free Officers Revolution (1952). A select number of Egypt's military officers went up against the royal regime, wresting power from the monarchy. This became a turning point for Egypt. People were tired of the corruption that had seeped into every part of the society, much of this corruption stemming from the royal family, the British occupation (since 1882), and some minor parties all vying for power. The Egyptian people were suffering. So the Free Officers got themselves together, got rid of the king, declared Egypt a republic, and started

instituting reforms. People welcomed this turn of events. Egypt was finally being governed by Egyptians. During this upheaval, everybody
had an opinion about what direction the country should take. Different ideologies—ways of thinking—developed. All of them tried to in-
ject Islam with their particular perspective. In other words, in order to
be heard, your opinion had to square with Islamic thought.

From the mid-1950s through the 1960s, Arab nationalism took
hold of the country's imagination. Scores of books were published
about Islam and Arab nationalism. These authors interpreted Islam
according to their own ideas about the shape and direction an Islamic
state should take—loyalty and devotion to Egypt. During this time, the
state's ideology began to incorporate socialism into its politics and
policies. It's quite easy to make the claim that Islam teaches socialism.

I was in my late teens and early twenties during this time. I agreed
with this socialist interpretation of Islam—it made a lot of sense to me.
The Islam that I learned growing up in Quhafa practiced social justice
and believed in equality among people—even equality between
women and men. During the 1960s in Egypt, women gained considerable ground as socialism crept into Egypt's consciousness. Most no-
table were the expansion of women's education and women's suffrage.
Frankly, I loved this interpretation of religion.

During the 1950s and 1960s, any opposition to the regime in
power was quickly squelched—Communists as well as Islamists.
Gamal Abdel Nasser (1918–1970) became the leader of a new Egypt
in 1954. He was a member of the Free Officers who overthrew the
royal regime. (Anwar al-Sadat, Nasser's successor, was a member of
the Free Officers as well.) Nasser established a new social structure
in the country—a structure that included free education for everybody. Tâhâ Husayn had the same idea during the earlier part of the
century. He believed education should be available to all—just like
air and water. Without this sweeping social change instituted by
Nasser, I would never have dared to dream of becoming a university student. The cost would have been prohibitive. Eventually,
though, I became quite critical of Nasser's regime. There was one
political voice—the voice of the state under a military regime—a system that did not take kindly to criticism.

As an Egyptian citizen, I was appalled that those who criticized
the government were subject to persecution. At the time, I had friends
who were Communists, some who were Socialists, and some who even
belonged to the Islamic Society of Muslim Brotherhood. During the

1950s, I remember Quhafa, my home village, hosting a branch of this Society of Muslim Brotherhood. They made an effort to educate people about the Society's philosophy and activities. Above all, they wanted an Islamic Egypt, an Egypt governed by Islamic principles alone. Even though I was quite young at the time, I listened to what the Brotherhood had to say. Like all reformers at this time, they put their particular spin on Islam, based on their own ideology.

The Muslim Brotherhood rested on the following points:

1. Since God revealed Himself in the Qur'an and in the Prophetic Tradition (*sunna*), all aspects of living ought to be subsumed under the Qur'an and the *sunna*. Both the Qur'an and the *sunna* were seen as universally valid. ("The Qur'an is our Constitution and the Prophet is our leader" became the Society's motto.)
2. Muslims should return to an early expression of Islam understood as being untainted by the influence of Greek theology and philosophy. A believer could know God only through descriptions of God in the Qur'an and the words of His prophet, Muhammad.
3. Since the structure of Egypt's society—greetings, the use of foreign languages, working hours, the calendar, recreation—had been infected by the West, an overhauling through the use of *shari'a* (body of legislation based on the Qur'an and the *sunna*) was in order.
4. These steps would ultimately lead to a restoration of the caliphate (the caliphate, a system of government historically used by Muslims, was abolished in 1924) by bringing all Muslims together in a single state.

Shortly after the Free Officers assumed power, they abolished all political parties (1953). They exempted the Muslim Brotherhood because they considered it a religious organization, not a political party. There were reasons for this exemption. Some of the members of the Free Officers had belonged to the Muslim Brotherhood before the revolution. The Brotherhood appealed to people from all walks of life and all sectors of Egyptian society.

The Muslim Brotherhood asked Nasser's government to appoint five men from within their ranks to official government positions. They wanted enough clout and power to chart Egypt's future, and they wanted to start with getting rid of the monarchy and all its trappings once and for all. The new government accepted only one minister from within the ranks of the Brotherhood. A power struggle followed as Nasser's regime clashed with the Brotherhood. Nasser felt threatened by its push toward the establishment of an Islamic state, and he reacted by dissolving the group in 1954.

On October 26, 1954, Mahmûd Abd al-Latif, a member of the Muslim Brotherhood, shot Nasser during a political rally. Nasser survived this attempt on his life and subsequently came down hard on the Brotherhood. Thousands were arrested. Many served long prison terms. Some were executed. The Brotherhood appeared to have been crushed. What looked like defeat, though, was merely illusion.

During all this upheaval, I couldn't help but think that Egypt certainly needed a good political overhaul, but I believed (and still do) that force and coercion were improper methods to bring about lasting reform. A society needs to be open enough so people feel free to discuss and exchange ideas in the public sphere. Discussion—hammering out those ideas—brings resolution. Sometimes it takes a while, but without the freedom to discuss and debate—when people feel as though they have no voice—a society can easily turn violent. Nasser's regime squelched this freedom of expression.

Hasan al-Banna (1906–1949), a schoolteacher, founded the Muslim Brotherhood in 1928. His ideas were influenced by the journalist Rashîd Rida (1865–1935), a moderate who believed Egypt could be both modern and Islamic. The Indian influence on the Muslim Brotherhood became apparent when Abul al-Mawdudi (1903–1979), a journalist, politician, and founder of Jamaat-I Islami in Pakistan, came on the scene. Al-Mawdudi was convinced that the encroachment of the West would eventually destroy Islam. He felt Muslims needed to band together in order to fight this encroachment. Al-Mawdudi's ideology paved the way for and influenced Sayyid Qutb (1906–1966), an active reformer in the Muslim Brotherhood since 1953. Qutb had spent two years (1948–1950) at Colorado State College of Education in Greeley. He had been a literary critic in Cairo and was one of the first people to recognize Naguib Mahfouz, the Egyptian author who won the Nobel Prize for Literature in 1988. (Islamists stabbed Mahfouz in the neck in 1994, leaving him barely able to write.) Egyptian nationalism had captured Qutb's imagination during the early 1950s. While studying in the States, he grew disillusioned with the West because of what he perceived to be a lack of spiritual values evidenced in the loose way Americans lived their everyday lives.

Sayyid Qutb was among those who spent years in prison for his membership and activity within the Brotherhood. After seeing members of the Brotherhood tortured and murdered in prison, Qutb reacted by coming up with even more of a fundamentalist interpretation of Islam than al-Mawdudi's. Qutb proclaimed that even though Nasser claimed to be Muslim, his behavior "proved" he was not. Nasser's government, he thought, would neutralize Islam. Therefore, it was every Muslim's duty to do what they could to remove him from power. These were unusually difficult times that called for dramatic action.

Qutb wrote:

> The Muslim community has long ago vanished from existence. . . . It is crushed under the weight of those false laws and customs which are not even remotely related to Islamic teachings. . . . We need to initiate the movement of Islamic revival in some Muslim country . . . in order to fashion an example that will eventually lead Islam to its destiny of world dominion. There should be a vanguard which sets out with this determination and then keeps walking on the path.[1]

In 1961, an underground movement of the dissolved and illegal Brotherhood was uncovered. Qutb was among those arrested and persecuted. Five years later, he was sentenced to death and executed. Before he was hanged on August 29, 1966, he said, "Thank God, I performed jihad for fifteen years until I earned this martyrdom."[2]

The Brotherhood—those left after the purge—went on about their business in secret. Nasser had pushed them underground. Nasser's regime, aware of the Brotherhood's clandestine meetings and activities, kept on hounding them, arresting them when feasible, jailing them when possible. What the government could not do was stamp out its ideas. Until the 1960s, I sympathized with the Muslim Brotherhood. I liked their interpretation of Islam. Social justice was at the heart of their message. I applauded that message.

The Brotherhood tried to establish a more just society by penetrating social institutions such as schools and hospitals. They even branched out into commercial establishments. Many Egyptian people supported their cause. The Brotherhood filled a need. Even the more radical Islamic groups that arose in the 1980s and 1990s continued to provide services to people who had no other means of obtaining such things as education and health care.

The 1960s, though, saw the Muslim Brotherhood veer in a fundamentalist direction. More than anything else, the Brotherhood feared that Egypt's move toward modernization meant that religion would be eradicated from Egyptian society. It felt squeezed out, unable to participate in Egypt's development. The members felt that their identity as Egyptian Muslims was at stake.

During the 1960s, I remained convinced that a proper understanding of Islam had everything to do with social justice, with equality, and with tolerance. I was distressed with the way Egyptian politics excluded any kind of opposition such as the Muslim Brotherhood. Those in power persecuted people without reason—just arrested them and slammed them in prison. Those imprisoned had no legal recourse. It was inhumane and unjust.

Even though many countries in the West thought of Nasser as a secularist, Egyptians understood him differently. A conversation I had with a medical doctor while studying in the United States (1978–1980) was quite telling. When the doctor realized I was Egyptian, he began speaking of Sadat as a national hero and a great statesman. I didn't agree with him. My demeanor must have reflected that disagreement. "Oh, you are a Nasserist?" he asked. When I answered affirmatively, he immediately concluded, "Then you are a Communist."

"Absolutely not," I shot back. "Nasser was not a Communist." This brief conversation showed me that sometimes the image a leader has within his own country is vastly different from his image outside his own country. To this day I feel that without the social reforms brought about by Nasser's regime—even with the absence of political freedom—many of the positive changes in Egypt could not have taken place. I respected Nasser, yet at the same time, I became critical of him.

I graduated from technical school in 1960 and began working in the town of al-Mahallala Kubra at the police headquarters, maintaining electronic communication equipment. I did this kind of work for the next twelve years. In 1961, I joined a small literary group composed of poets and short story writers from the area. These people had been excluded from the local youth organization because they thought too deeply—too critically. Interestingly enough, all of these folks went on to become highly respected authors. During this time, I remember being quite critical of Egypt from an Islamic point of view. The secret police became suspicious of our group and began following several of us. One of our members was arrested and spent fifteen years in jail. I went down to the police headquarters after this harassment and arrest—uninvited. It was not a particularly prudent thing to do. "Why are you following me?" I asked. The officer merely said that it was their duty "to investigate." I became increasingly offended with this militarization of society.

During this time, intellectuals began producing novels and poems criticizing the Egyptian political system—not explicitly, of course,
but through the use of symbols. In a society where freedom of speech
cannot be taken for granted, the intellectual crowd needed to be cir-
cumspect as they expressed their opposition to the political system
in power.

Working at the police headquarters allowed me to observe, and
sometimes even to get involved with, a whole array of social problems—especially problems that plagued the underprivileged, the poor,
and those on the margins of society. I remember a particular incident
where a woman came to the police station, complaining that her husband had hit her. She was bleeding—it was difficult to tell from where.
The staff at the police station ignored her while she waited and waited.
What else could she do? The policy, of course, when somebody comes
in bleeding is to take the individual directly to a hospital. For some
reason, the police ignored her. In Egypt, we don't think of police as
public servants. In an authoritarian society where public officials are
given power just because they occupy a certain position, abuse of that
power happens frequently. An authoritarian system assumes that those
in power "know." Because they "know," you, the one without power,
have no business questioning them. Forget about demanding that
something be done. We Egyptians generally have unpleasant experiences with the police.

I stuck my nose into this situation. Because I was so offended by
the inaction of the department, I questioned, not very meekly, the
police officer in charge. The officer lit into me. "Why are you angry?"
he demanded. "Do you know this woman?"

"No. Would that make any difference?" I asked. "She should be
taken to a hospital and you should bring her husband in for questioning. Isn't this the procedure?" I knew that if I aggravated the police too
much, I would put myself in the path of their wrath and ultimately
would not accomplish what I wanted to by interfering in the first place—
getting help for the woman. I ended up taking the woman to the hospital, staying with her until she was treated and released. I went back
to the police headquarters, handed them the hospital report, and went
on with my duties. Two days later, the police brought her husband in,
but I did not get involved with the situation.

A little later on that same day, the woman came to my office. She
had brought me a hot meal—rice and chicken. I was afraid that the
police officers would think that her familiarity with me indicated that

somehow I really did know the woman and had been unwilling to admit that when I got involved with this situation.

"Look," I said, "this is very nice, but I cannot accept this. I am at work. I cannot eat on the job."

"Please take it home," she suggested. "Consider it as a gift from your sister." I did as she suggested. I was living alone at the time.

The woman had come in to withdraw her complaint against her husband. She explained to me that what she wanted was for the police to admonish her husband in some way, not to be physically abusive with him. "After all, he is my husband and the father of my children."

"Do you love him?" I asked.

She didn't seem to understand the question. "He is my children's father," she said again.

"Does your husband hit you often?" I asked.

"No," she said. "He was very angry about some problems." The man was a street peddler, selling fruit. Because we were in the middle of summer, Cairo was hot. A lot of the fruit had spoiled that fateful day, and in anger he had lashed out at his wife.

"Would it help if I visited you?" I asked the woman. "After all, you brought me some food, which means you invited me to your house."

"That would be wonderful," she said.

"I will come only with your husband's permission, though. But bringing me food indicates that we are friends." I didn't want her husband to feel threatened by my presence.

I visited them. They had three children. They were extremely poor. The man was quite a decent fellow. She had told him about my interfering with her case at the police station and that I had taken her to the hospital. She wasn't at all shy. She had also told him that he, her husband, should have been the one to take her to the hospital.

This incident showed me that sometimes the poverty that people endure affects them to such an extent that it taxes their unstated love and respect for each other in ways that the wealthy cannot even imagine. I saw a host of problems like this one—many of them appeared to me to stem from an unbalanced power structure.

The woman's husband asked me, "Why aren't you married? You have a good job and are steadily employed."

I told him I had a family to care for. This incident happened when I was living alone—before the family joined me in Cairo from al-Mahallala Kubra and just before I began teaching at Cairo University. "I cannot get married because I cannot afford to." When my family eventually did settle in Cairo, our two families developed a comfortable friendship.

The Free Officers Revolution was a huge turning point for Egypt. Another of Egypt's turning points happened in 1967. In fact, the whole Arab world changed as a result of the Arab armies' humiliating defeat by Israel in what became known as the Six-Day War. We Egyptians thought we had created a strong society, one that included a strong military. We thought we should have been able to easily push Israel into the Mediterranean Sea. At that time, Arabs supported *jihad* against the enemy—Zionism—as a good and proper thing to do.

Zionism is all about the creation of a homeland—a specific piece of real estate—for the Jewish people. The Jews have been scattered and persecuted ever since the Romans squelched the Jewish revolt in Jerusalem, an event that led to the destruction of their Temple in 70 C.E. Centuries later (1897), in Basel, Switzerland, Theodor Herzl organized the First Zionist Congress. But it was the Balfour Declaration of 1917 that gave Zionism its real impetus. The Balfour Declaration established the legitimacy of a home for Jewish people in Palestine. Ever since then, Jewish settlements have mushroomed in Palestine, encroaching on and taking over Palestinian land, displacing families, wreaking havoc, and causing economic hardship.

The defeat in 1967 did not come as a total surprise to me, nor was it a surprise to most intellectuals. But being defeated in a matter of hours was shocking. I was not married at this time, but had many friends who were. I heard story after story from my friends about how they were unable to engage in regular sexual intercourse with their wives—it was as though they had been castrated. The whole country was abuzz with this kind of testimony. Men felt their manhood had been severely compromised. The defeat was understood in religious terms. God was punishing us—Muslims—because we had abandoned Islam. Apparently, God was rewarding the Jews. Judaism had triumphed over secularism. How could Muslims bring about a solution to this humiliation? Return to Islam. Establish a strong Islamic state to compete with a Jewish state.

My brother Muhammad took part in this Six-Day War, which broke out on June 5, 1967. We had received a letter from Muhammad the day before, June 4. Toward the end of June, we began to see soldiers trickling back from Sinai, where the fighting had taken place.

There was no organization, no leadership—nothing but chaos in the train and bus stations as the remnants of an army began arriving home. We looked for, but did not find, Muhammad. My mother was beside herself, wailing for her son. "I just want to know his whereabouts."

We were prepared to accept his death. We just wanted to find his body. So I went to Cairo, going from office to office, looking for any scrap of information that might lead me to Muhammad. Nothing. I then went to every hospital in Cairo, checking lists of the dead and injured, lists that were updated every hour or so. People from all over Egypt had come to the hospitals in Cairo—all searching for their sons, brothers, and fathers. Some of these folks were illiterate. Often I would read aloud the names of the dead and wounded from these lists. It was a terrible experience watching family members realize that their fathers, brothers, and sons were wounded or—worse yet—dead. I spent a month in Cairo searching for my brother.

Finally, I came across the name of Muhammad Abu Zaid in one of the hospitals. I felt nothing but relief. I had found him. According to the list, he was in a coma. I didn't care. He was alive. I took what was left of my money and bought some fruit, candy, and nuts. I arrived at his bedside with my offering. Much to my surprise, this was not my brother. It was another man with the same name. I left everything there. With no money in my pocket, I was forced to walk an hour and a half to the home of one of my friends from Quhafa who had moved to Cairo. I then had to wait ten hours for my friend to arrive home from work. I must have been a sight. "What is wrong?" he asked me immediately.

After some food and rest, I returned home. My efforts to locate Muhammad were fruitless. About a month later, we received a letter telling us the location of his army unit. Sayyid (Badriyya's husband) and I, laden with food my mother had prepared, raced to the military camp. Thousands of people were sitting on the sand outside the gate— all waiting for sons, fathers, and brothers to be notified that their relatives had come to see them. Sayyid and I kept straining our necks, looking for Muhammad to come through the gate. Finally, a young man approached us. We had not recognized him. "Oh, my God, is it really you, Muhammad?" I asked. To this day, Muhammad does not speak of this experience. I've stopped asking him about it.

In Cairo, just after the Six-Day War, there were reports that the Virgin Mary had suddenly appeared on top of one of the churches—a Coptic church. Millions of people gathered around the church, hoping to get a glimpse of the Virgin. People at this time felt a need for support from sacred figures like Mary. (Mary is a sacred figure to both Muslims and Copts.) At the same time, *sheikhs* (spiritual leaders in the Muslim community) began reporting that the Prophet was appearing to them in dreams, telling them, "Of course you must suffer this defeat, you have to learn. If you return to the Prophet's teachings, you will be restored and triumph over your enemies."

By this time, I had long since applied my critical thinking skills to evaluate and make sense of what was going on around me. Not only had I graduated from technical school, I was learning a lot from the day-to-day experiences of my job. I also continued to read on my own, a habit begun in childhood. When I first began to read seriously, literature (poetry and novels) intrigued me most. Literature became a stepping-stone to academic texts. Philosophy fascinated me, particularly the idea of God. I managed to get hold of books that had been translated into Arabic from English and French. Through these translations, I started to read about Islam from an array of viewpoints. Even though I situated myself comfortably within a socialist ideology (and Egypt at this time had definite socialist leanings), there was a lack of freedom within the society that grated on me. The military, trying to create this just and equitable society they talked about, tightly controlled the people they were working to free. It struck me as odd, ironic, and ultimately unjust.

The Six-Day War (1967) and the war in 1973 (my brother Muhammad took part in this war as well) marked the end of nationalism and socialism in Egypt. Islam was no longer understood in terms of social justice, but in terms of power. People gradually began to turn to a radicalized understanding of Islam. The state should be established, using Islam itself.

After Nasser's death in 1970, Anwar al-Sadat came to power. He desperately fought to keep nationalism and socialism at bay—especially as manifested within the student body of the university. Sadat put his own twist on Islam. He talked about Egypt as a state of religion and science. It was the first time anybody tried to cover so many bases—Egypt as a state of religion, of faith, of science and faith, and knowledge and faith. He also put on quite a show as he tried to get the message across to the people that he was, at heart, a devout Muslim. Every Friday, he would wear the *jalabbiyya* (long white robe) on his way to the mosque, and as he worshiped, television cameras captured his image and broadcast it all over Egypt. He had the very recognizable black forehead—a sign that he had prostrated himself often in prayer. He was eager to be seen fingering *sibha* (prayer beads) in public. He adopted the title of The Faithful President—this phrase has a connotation of "inspired" in a religious sense. He also initiated the televised call to prayer five times daily.

All over Egypt, prices of basic needs were skyrocketing. The bread strike (January 19–20, 1977) instigated violence in the big cities, especially Cairo and Alexandria. The army finally took over in order to restore a modicum of peace. On another front, Sadat released members of the Muslim Brotherhood who still lingered in jail, and for the first time, the Brotherhood was recognized—though not officially—as a political party. It became active in the universities.

In November 1977, Sadat decided—on his own—to visit Jerusalem. The decision seemed to come out of the blue. The message he was trying to convey was "Look, I am willing even to go to the devil to bring about peace between Israel and Palestine." Many Egyptians, including myself, thought his visit quite inappropriate. We resented what appeared to us to be maverick behavior. It was around this time that Sadat became involved in the process of establishing peace with Israel at Camp David in the United States. He again made a major decision (going to Camp David) without consulting the Egyptian people or other Arab leaders. As a result, he received quite a bit of opposition.

In spite of all of this, Sadat did begin to allow some political opposition. He quickly grew irritated with this opposition, though, which prompted him in September 1980 to issue a slew of decrees that led to the arrest of more than five thousand people from different political affiliations, including Islamists. He then fired faculty from Cairo University who disagreed with his policies—at least sixty-five professors. I was one of those professors. Sadat accused us of stirring up conflict between the Copts and Muslims. In October 1981 the radical underground Islamic organization al-Jihad assassinated Sadat. Egypt was shocked.

During the 1970s, while an assistant lecturer at Cairo University, I would often bring current political issues before the students, hoping to open a space for discussion. I tied Sadat's political discourse to religious discourse, showing how intertwined the two really are. On the surface, Sadat's speeches were political, but if we looked at them on a deeper level, they were religious.

By peppering his speeches with an inordinate number of Islamic symbols, Sadat tried to make certain ideologies (the transformation of a state-controlled economy to a free-market economy, for example) palatable to the Egyptian people. Even as living conditions continued to deteriorate, Sadat kept assuring the people that by enacting certain policies, Islam would be protecting private property. All that had been accomplished since the Free Officers Revolution for the benefit of the poor—land reform, for example—went up in smoke. The land reform law, passed in 1954, limited the size of a piece of property that any one person could own to one hundred acres. Anything over one hundred acres was taken by the government and distributed to farmers. Sadat's government made an about-face and decided that the land reform law went against *shari'a*, the body of law derived from the Qur'an and the *sunna*.

When Sadat came to power, he attempted to placate the Muslim Brotherhood by changing the Egyptian Constitution from "*shari'a* is one of the sources of legislation" to read "*shari'a* is the principle source of legislation." This makes a big difference. So the government took the land from families who had worked that land for over twenty-five years and returned it to the original landowners. A reshuffling. The inheritance tax law also went against *shari'a*, according to Sadat's government. Taxes ought not to be taken from people who have inherited property. This goes against God's will. All the laws intended to create economic justice were considered to be against *shari'a*.

Sadat also spoke to the people with the authority of an *imam* (religious leader), quoting long passages from the Qur'an before addressing Egyptians as though they were his subjects. He'd say, "When I was assigned to rule you," and then continue with his prepared speech. Nasser had always addressed Egyptians as "Brothers and Sisters" or "Ladies and Gentlemen," and sometimes just "Citizens." Sadat exuded a pomposity that I found difficult to swallow.

In spite of Sadat's outward display of religiosity, Egypt's wealth remained in the hands of an elite minority. Most Egyptians were dirt poor. It was hard to believe that a president who sanctioned such economic disparity would really be interested in what I always considered to be the heart of Islam—social justice.

Egypt in the 1970s produced a type of businessman who seemed to get rich overnight. These businessmen created no productive projects in Egypt, nor did they employ people. They were commissioners, exporting things. They were not engaged in a productive economic system. The middle class started to lose ground. As a university professor, I belonged to this middle class, but I found it harder and harder to make ends meet. With the salary I earned at the university, I was not able to rent my own apartment. Even though I was thirty-plus years old, I was forced to continue to live with my family in a very small apartment. The gap between rich and poor widened. Young people could see no comfortable future for themselves. I remember being quite vocal at this time, questioning how in the world anybody could use Islam to justify a political system that produced such economic suffering. Sadat, using all the religious symbolism he could muster (TV, prayer beads, blackened forehead, The Faithful President), attempted to bend Islam to serve his own purposes. It galled me.

I come from a poor family. I belong to the poor. I defend the rights of the poor. This is where I stand. For years, I believed that Islam could be interpreted only as a religion of social justice. Of course, I have to apply the same critique to my thinking as I do to all other thinking. But how is it that the meaning of Islam could be manipulated so easily? Islam's meaning kept changing and transforming, depending on what ideology one brought to the religion. Just what is the relationship between ideology and interpretation of text? That became a burning question for me.

Today, I still identify with the oppressed, although my vision has expanded to include not just the weak or the poor in the Muslim world, but the oppressed throughout the entire world. And this is where I find myself—defending the rights of the poor no matter who they are or where they might be.

I don't restrict my efforts on behalf of the poor and oppressed to the religious realm. How can I hold to certain beliefs (justice, compassion, freedom), beliefs taken from the Qur'an, and not have those beliefs spill over into my thinking in the political arena? So, given the question of what many people, especially in the West, refer to as suicide bombing, where do I stand? I stand with the oppressed—people who are fighting for the freedom of their land.

I was invited to a Palestinian camp when I visited Damascus in April 2002. During this visit, many people asked me, "What do you think of the Islam of martyrdom? Where do you stand?" Of course, I stand with the Palestinians. I am all for fighting against the Israeli Occupation. When people have no weapons with which to fight, they make themselves into weapons. This is legitimate. To give this whole thing the label of a religious war, well, that's worrisome.

I am well aware of the Arab publicity regarding martyrdom bombing. You know the scene. A father and mother rejoice—praise God—when they realize their child has just been blown to bits. Unfortunately, people believe the publicity—the marketing of these kinds of images has been effective. What much of the world fails to understand is that people in Arab societies are not allowed to express their true feelings. They express what they are expected to express. Do you really believe that a mother and father are happy because their son or daughter died? If so, you are swallowing the propaganda. And that's exactly what I told the Palestinians who asked me what I thought of the Islam of martyrdom.

Do we really believe that these parents at the end of the day, when they close the door behind them to go into their home, are rejoicing over the death of their child? We need to learn to express our true feelings. Are we really happy that our children have to be bombs? We don't have to celebrate death. I understand that when people feel there is no other way to defend themselves, martyrdom bombing seems the only way to go. However, we have to think about innocent people, and frankly, I don't buy the idea that all Israelis support their own military society. We really should explain to the world that we are sorry for what we are doing, but we feel we have no other option. This is not a religious war. Labeling it as such (and it has been called a religious war since 1948) is counterproductive to finding a solution to the fighting. Don't believe this line. If we are indeed fighting a religious war, then we have already lost. Our religion is based on Judaism. You cannot destroy Judaism without destroying Islam. We are not against the Jewish people. We are against the Israeli Occupation—perhaps even against the concept of an Israeli state for the Jewish people.

I was trying my best not to offend the people, but I wanted to expand their vision of the world and, at the same time, be sincere about my feelings. I talked about the French resistance against the Nazis during World War II. When a soldier went up against the Nazis, he carried no name and no rank. We are stupid. When we go up against our oppressors, we publicize the name of the soldier and the names of his or her family. What kind of war is this? This is a show. We are making a show of the blood of our children—something we ought not to be very happy about. If death is an option, it should come as a last resort and we should feel very sorry that we could find no other way to resolve our problems.

When I look at Jewish history, there is no way not to stand against the oppression that the Jews have been subject to over the years—including the Holocaust. To downplay the Holocaust is a gross mistake. It doesn't matter how many Jewish people were killed. It's not a matter of numbers. It's a matter of persecuting people just because they are different in some way. Israel, though, has at this point become an oppressor.

Along that same line, nothing justifies the cowardly, terrible attack against the American people on September 11, 2001. Nothing! This was criminal behavior, and criminals must be confronted with their crime.

I am against any kind of oppression. Sometimes it is difficult to differentiate between an oppressor and one who is oppressed. I see it in terms of the powerful and the weak. Power can be wielded in the political sphere, within the military, and certainly within the religious cadre. People can use physical power to exploit as well. Sometimes the powerless become powerful and then become oppressors themselves. The issue has nothing to do with specific religious or social affiliation. These boundaries are fluid, changing easily.

Nowadays, I am a defender of the rights of Copts in my country. Also, I work for the rights of women. I've written a book on that subject, titled *Circles of Fear: Analysis of the Discourse about Women*.[3] Sometimes, within an Egyptian context, I'll defend the right of Islamists to speak out in a free political market. How could I not?

So, even though I had some initial misgivings, it pleased me no end to accept the Freedom of Worship Medal in conjunction with four other recipients at the Franklin D. Roosevelt Four Freedoms Awards ceremony in June 2002. The Four Freedoms Medal was given to Nelson Mandela; the Freedom of Speech Award went to Radio Free Europe/Radio Liberty; the Freedom from Want Medal was awarded to Dr. Gro Harlem Brundtland; and the Freedom from Fear Medal was presented to Ernesto Zedillo Ponce de Leon.

I was in Paris when I received the letter nominating me for the Freedom of Worship Medal. I wondered why the Franklin and Eleanor Roosevelt Institute, an American institution, would select me to be the recipient of this award. Why me? Why this year? Blame it all on my critical mind. When Ebtehal and I discussed my misgivings, she thought that the reputation of an institute such as the one carrying Roosevelt's name went beyond America.

I agreed. But I feared the reaction in Egypt as well as the rest of the Muslim world. I just knew people would say, "OK. You now have the official blessing of America. We thought you were their puppet all along, and it looks as though our suspicions were not unfounded." Fellow Muslims have often accused me—especially since 1992—of being heavily influenced by the West.

I discussed my dilemma with friends, of course. One friend— someone I thought for sure would tell me to steer clear of accepting such an award—told me he'd come from Cairo to be with me during the presentation. I ended up taking the advice of my friends, but I remember telling Ebtehal, "I will go to the ceremony where the queen of the Netherlands and American people will be present. I will insist on wearing the Palestinian scarf on my shoulders because I want to send a message to the American people and to the world."

A few days before the ceremony, Ambassador William J. Vanden Heuvel, the co-chairman of the Franklin and Eleanor Roosevelt Institute, came to the Netherlands. We had dinner together. He said, "I've read about you. I'm fascinated with your ideas."

"Thank you," I said. "I do have a question for you, and I need an honest answer. Were you specifically looking for a Muslim to award this prize to this year?"

"Honestly," he said, "yes." His candor took me aback. I'm not accustomed to such honesty from officials. He continued, "We needed to give a message to the Muslim world and to the American people that we are not against Muslims. To tell you the truth, we had no idea about you."

"How is it, then, that you found out about me?" I asked. I knew that the prize is given during odd years in America and in the Netherlands during even years. The Roosevelts, of course, come from a Dutch background.

Ambassador Vanden Heuvel said that they had held a meeting and decided that if they could find a Muslim scholar or individual who believed in the basic principles Roosevelt stood for, they'd like very much to award the prize to that individual. "We left that matter in the hands of the people of Zeeland in the Netherlands, and to our surprise the editor of the newspaper of Zeeland pointed us in your direction."

The editor was at Leiden University in 1995 on a six-month scholarship. He knew me only by name, and forwarded my name to a representative from the Institute with this caveat, "I don't know anything about Abu Zaid's work." During the time this particular editor was studying at Leiden, most people knew about the problems I had faced in my country—problems that eventually forced me into exile. The editor also passed on the name of Professor William Stokhof, executive director of Leiden University's International Institute for Asian Studies, the man behind bringing me to Leiden University in 1995. Ambassador Vanden Heuvel contacted Professor Stokhof, who then nominated me for the award.

"We believe the professor's nomination was remarkable—quite excellent," the ambassador assured me. In light of this conversation, it became an even more pressing issue for me to wear the Palestinian scarf draped over my shoulders as a symbol of solidarity with the Palestinians who suffer daily. The Americans have something to say, and I have something to say as well.

A Dutch reporter at the ceremony asked me, "Don't you think that the Institute is exposing itself to a lot of criticism, giving you this medal because you are a Muslim?"

"You may be right," I said, "but I'm always exposed to a lot of criticism. If the Institute is sacrificing something, please be aware that I am making a sacrifice as well in accepting it."

"This is very arrogant," he shot back at me.

"No, your question is arrogant," I insisted. "If this Institute is making a sacrifice, I, too, am making a sacrifice," I repeated.

In the end, the ceremony went off well. The American ambassador attended the event. I was especially moved by the speech of Anna Eleanor Roosevelt, a direct descendant of Franklin and Eleanor.[4] Both Ebtehal and I wore the black and white Palestinian scarf around our shoulders, symbolically representing our brothers and sisters whose voices are not being heard.

6 My American Adventure

I greatly benefited from an exchange program in place between Cairo University and the University of Pennsylvania in Philadelphia. I was awarded a scholarship that enabled me to live and study in the United States for two years, 1978 through 1980. I was working toward my Ph.D. at the time. Officially, I was to study folklore and learn about the methodology of fieldwork. And I did—on my own terms.

I traveled all over the United States, visiting several campuses, including UCLA, Berkeley, and Princeton. I also visited libraries throughout the country and toured interesting places in the West—Nevada, California, and Oregon. I was young. I purchased round-trip tickets on buses, planes, and trains. I spent a good deal of my money on transportation. It was worth it. I wanted to learn as much as possible. What better way than to visit a wide variety of places?

One day, just after I had returned to Philadelphia from a trip around the country, Tom Neff caught up with me. Tom was the director of the Institute of Middle Eastern Studies, and I was responsible to him. He looked somewhat frazzled. He grabbed me by the arm and asked, "Where have you been for the past two months?"

"I made a trip across the United States," I answered.

"Did you visit universities?" he asked.

"Of course. I visited libraries as well." I told him about the stack of photocopied books I had managed to gather together.

"OK," he said. "I can pay you back for this trip. Bring me your ticket stubs. What you've been doing is all part of your scholastic effort—I don't consider it a waste of time at all."

I was stunned, but deliriously happy. I had eleven dollars and some change left over from my travels.

When I first arrived in the States, I began my exploration with Philadelphia itself. I found that Philadelphia is divided—not just into North Philly and South Philly, but underground and aboveground. Buses, generally speaking, were for white folks. Subways, on the other hand, were the domain of black people. Sometimes, I'd go to clubs that black people frequented. I always had a good time listening to the music and letting myself get caught up in the atmosphere.

I had a terrifying experience, though, one night after leaving one of these clubs to head home. It was quite late, and I noticed several black teenagers just hanging about in the subway station. They encircled me. I thought for sure my number was up. I played it as cool as I could. One of them asked me, "Where are you from?"

"Africa," I answered. They seemed interested, so I asked them, "Are you familiar with Africa? I am from a place in Africa called Egypt." I had been in the States long enough by this time to know that most black Americans knew their ancestors came from Africa, but they didn't know much else about that continent. "I am teaching and studying," I continued.

"Oh, he's a teacher. You hear that? He teaches." They were mocking me. "What do you teach?" one of the more outspoken boys demanded.

"I teach Arabic," I answered.

He then asked, "Why don't you invite us to your place to have a drink?"

"Yes, why not?" I answered. "It's very late. If you would like to come, we can have something to drink together. However, I must get to bed soon because I have to teach a class in the morning."

They seemed surprised at my response. Frankly, I could not believe I was asking these young men to come home with me to have a drink, but I was afraid to tell them no. We took the subway. For the entire trip, my thoughts centered on the six of them getting inside my apartment and killing me. When we finally did arrive at my apartment, one of them asked, "What do you have to drink? I'd like a beer."

"Well," I said, "I don't have any beer, because I don't drink alcohol. But you can have tea, coffee, orange juice, or milk."

"Why don't you drink alcohol?" They seemed to all ask me at once before one of them got specific. "Are you a Jehovah's Witness?"

"No, I am Muslim. Drinking alcohol is against my religious tradition," I replied. They looked at me somewhat suspiciously, but didn't press me any further. So I served these six teenagers drinks from among the choices I had given them. While they were in my apartment, they were quite polite. They asked serious questions about my teaching, and after a few minutes, each one of them thanked me, saying, "We really enjoyed your company." And they left in peace. I like to think that my respectful attitude toward them had averted a violent attack. Most of all, I felt lucky that I had not been slaughtered in cold blood.

While I was traveling around the United States (I believe I was in Portland, Oregon), I stumbled across what looked like one of the black clubs that I hung out at occasionally in Philadelphia. I was hungry, and ducked inside to get a bite to eat. It took a minute or two to take in the whole scene, but after looking around a bit, I thought I had dropped into a gay bar.

I sat down at a table. A woman (this seemed odd) approached me. "Do you mind if I sit with you?" she asked. I motioned for her to sit down, and we began to talk. After exchanging a few pleasantries, we spoke on more personal terms. I got the impression that she was interested in what Americans call having some fun. She wanted a sexual encounter. "Where are you staying?" she asked me.

"I'm staying at a hotel down the street," I replied. I think she just assumed I would be interested in having a sexual escapade with her.

She continued speaking with that assumption in mind. "I have to tell you something before we go on." And she told me she was a man, waiting for a sex-change operation. Her or his emotions, she or he assured me, were that of a woman. If I were willing, she or he could really satisfy me.

I was taken somewhat aback, but did not want to be rude. I had never before been approached by a man (under the guise of a woman) for sex. I must have appeared a little disoriented to him. "Do you despise me now?" he asked.

"No, of course not," I answered. I could honestly say that I had no contempt for him. I could only imagine how difficult he must have found his current situation.

"We can continue to talk?" he asked.

"Why not?" I replied.

"Would you like me to show you around the city?" he asked. "You've just arrived and you are leaving tomorrow. I have a car. We could spend the day together." We did just that. I had a wonderful time.

My culture does not easily tolerate what Islam defines to be aberrant sexual behavior. Homosexuality and transvestism fall under that category. People call it all kinds of things—sin, crime, going against nature, and going against God's will. Must I, though, as a Muslim stand behind my culture, judging and condemning people who color outside orthodox lines? It's easy to get on the bandwagon and take cheap shots at people who are different. Through my experience in this transvestite bar, I discovered that I am open to understanding behavior that perhaps theoretically I cannot accept.

I developed friendships with homosexual people while living in the States—some of them I remember as extremely creative people, working as artists and musicians. I liked many of them and even grew to admire some of them. I never was able to write about this experience in Egypt, though. Even my intellectual friends would not have understood. They would have thought it all so weird. I could only imagine what the reaction in the press might have been.

Much later (May 1996), after I had begun my life in exile in the Netherlands, I received a phone call from Dr. Rudolph Steinberger, a psychologist, asking to meet with me. Turns out that his specialty was dealing with homosexuality in the Muslim world. He told me that many homosexuals come to the Netherlands from Afghanistan, Pakistan, Iran, and other Middle Eastern Muslim countries when they realize they are homosexual. It's difficult for them to live in societies where homosexuality is looked upon as criminal behavior.

There is no specific verse in the Qur'an condemning homosexuality; however, the story of Sodom and Gomorrah (God destroys these cities with fire) implies condemnation of men having sex with one another. I wasn't sure how I could help Dr. Steinberger and told him as much. He assured me that if I gave him a little time, he was sure our discussion would impact his work positively.

He came to my office. We talked for over three hours, hitting on a whole array of subjects. What is the relationship between Islamic culture and Arabic culture? What about pre-Islamic culture? What does manhood mean in Arabic culture? What about friendship? How do women and men relate to one another in Muslim societies? The man could really dig.

Dr. Steinberger was catalytic in my enlightenment. I learned from him that homosexuality is not a disease. This was new information to me. Biologically speaking, he said, homosexuals are different—genetically. We discussed the history of homosexuality. "Something has gone askew in a society," the doctor said, "when that society doesn't recognize and accept differences between and among its individual members." I became more aware of homosexuality as a natural phenomenon. I have made friends with people within the homosexual community in the Netherlands. They feel free to discuss with me some of the difficulties they experience with their partners. I listen. People are people. They experience the same kind of dynamics within their relationships as everybody else does.

Will Islam ever accept homosexuality as anything other than aberrant? Not until we have a real revolution—a change in the way we think about the Qur'an in conjunction with our lives.

Jurists, scholars of law, throughout Islamic history have culled legal principles from the Qur'an based on induction and deduction of certain texts. These scholars incorporated another source—the Prophetic tradition, or *sunna*. This became the second source of legislation. The Qur'an and the *sunna* were not sufficient to deal with the increasing political, social, economic, and criminal problems, so the jurists adopted a third principle based on already agreed-upon, practiced legal rules called consensus (*ijmâ*) of the earliest Muslim generation—the companions of the Prophet. A fourth principle, rational inquiry (*ijtihâd*), needed to be established in order to solve the problems not solved by using the three other sources. This principle of *ijtihâd*, though, was restricted to the use of analogy. A solution to a certain problem could be reached only by comparing its position to a similar problem previously solved by any of the other three sources. These four sources make up what Muslims call *shari'a* law.

Shari'a law is human law. There is nothing divine about it. When we look at certain legal stipulations spoken about in the Qur'an, such as the penalties for fornication, robbery, murder, or causing social disorder, we need to ask certain questions. Are the stipulated penalties initiated by Islam? Can we consider them to be Islamic? Definitely not. The penalties meted out for such offenses were used in pre-Islamic times—some of them come from Roman law and some from Jewish tradition. Others go further back. In modern times—times in which all kinds of human rights legislation is initiated—many people balk at the thought of amputating parts of the human body or taking the life of an individual as divinely inspired and, therefore, obligatory as punishment for crime.

Other aspects of shari'a, such as those dealing with religious minorities, women's rights, and other human rights (such as those of homosexuals) need to be reconsidered as well. The job of the jurists has always been to look for principles of law within shari'a and then apply those principles in different social contexts. The Qur'an is not a law book. There are legal principles found within the Qur'an. These principles leave a wide space for human interpretation and reinterpretation. To claim that the body of shari'a literature is binding for all Muslim communities, regardless of time and place, is to ascribe divinity to human thought as it has developed throughout history.

When jurists look for legal principles, they work under the umbrella of five agreed-upon Qur'anic objectives. Any law drawn up by jurists must be in agreement with those objectives. If there is any contradiction between a law and the principles set out by the objectives, the law cannot be considered Qur'anic. Those objectives are protection of life, protection of progeny, protection of sanity, protection of property, and protection of religion or faith. They have a universal scope and have become part of what is known as classical Islam.

Classical Islam reached its final expression in the thirteenth century. All the books today on shari'a law repeat the understanding our ancestors had reached by the thirteenth century. There has been no development in shari'a law since that time. The conclusions our ancestors came to were on the cutting edge of their time. Today we have more knowledge to work with, yet Islamic thought in all its aspects remains static, having come to a screeching halt centuries ago.

It was also through discussion with Dr. Steinberger that I realized something about my culture that heretofore I had not been able to see. Our society, at least publicly, is based on friendship between men. Men feel ownership toward their male friends in a way that men and women often feel toward each other when they are in a committed relationship. It is not unusual to hear a man say to his friend, "You are my friend. Why did you do this [whatever] to me? How could you make such a decision without consulting me?" I discovered—and it was quite a revelation to me at the time—that in a society where there is little opportunity for the sexes to mix freely, men easily form strong bonds with other men. An unhealthy possessiveness toward one another can and does emerge. Wherever this kind of possessiveness (parent/child, husband/wife) takes root, trouble follows close behind. A person needs to be free to make his or her own choices according to his or her conscience, not be constrained by another's.

When I married Ebtehal in 1992, my friends were surprised. Ebtehal is outspoken, an intellectual, and a professor at Cairo University. In Egyptian society, her outspoken behavior and intellectual bent label her as unfeminine. I like to think that human beings, both female and male, possess traits that culture labels masculine or feminine. Forcing women into specific roles defined by a society as feminine and men into specific roles defined as masculine is oppressive—mainly to women. Women, generally speaking, are more constrained. Ebtehal's father was unusual in that he went against conventional family wisdom and allowed his only daughter (Ebtehal has a brother) to travel alone to France, study, and come home again.

At any rate, my male friends had no inkling whatsoever that I was about to marry Ebtehal. When the nuptials were over and they realized that I had not discussed the matter with them, they were angry, saying that I had betrayed them by not consulting with them. Now, I am thoroughly Egyptian. Egyptian ways of being and doing ooze from my pores. But it seemed inappropriate to me that those friends expressed such anger. Getting married was a decision Ebtehal and I made together. But my friends had expected me to consult with them.

Privacy is something I learned to appreciate while living in the States. When I returned to Egypt after my two-year sojourn in America, one of my professors, who is like my godfather, greeted me with a barrage of questions—some of them innocuous and general (What did you study? Where did you visit?), others more intrusive and offensive (How much money did you save?). I answered as best I could before he started to report on what every one of my friends had done while I studied in the States. I stopped him.

"Please don't," I said. "No doubt if one of our friends told you something, he told you in confidence. If he would like to tell me, then he will. There is this thing called privacy. What I tell you about myself, maybe I would not tell others. We have to respect that."

The professor laughed—either out of embarrassment or out of surprise. Perhaps a mixture of the two. "So this is what you have learned in the States?" he asked.

"Yes, one of the things I learned. And what a relief it is not to have everybody's nose in everybody else's business and to respect the secrets people give to you."

Perhaps my father's death when I was fourteen gave me space to move about—a space that would not have been there had he lived. I discovered I did not need to get permission or approval from folks as I went about my business. Since I could not depend on the authority of a father as I approached manhood, and because mothers do not carry that same authority in Egyptian society, I learned early in life that there were consequences I had to live with as a result of making certain choices. I made some inappropriate choices. I learned by making mistakes. But having that freedom to make my own decisions—well, I wouldn't want it any other way.

So I chided my friends a bit, asking them, "When you decided to marry, did you consider my opinion? Not that I believe you should have, but if you don't like my wife, this is your problem. I'm not asking you to love my wife. What is your complaint with me?" Most of them did not understand. How could they? The Egyptian way of doing things was the only way they knew.

My experience in America broadened my worldview. I would often get together with other students and chat with them over coffee. I still count many of these people as my friends. By living in a culture different from my own, I learned not to judge another culture by my own society's standards. I became less ethnocentric. I became eager to learn what makes American people tick. What kind of thinking fuels their perspective on things?

When I first moved to Philadelphia, I rented an apartment from an elderly woman. As she handed me the key to my new quarters, she asked me, "Where are you from, son?" In the late 1970s, people took one look at me and knew I wasn't American-born and -bred. I'm short and round, and have a dark complexion.

"I am from Egypt," I said.

"Egypt? Where is Egypt?" she asked.

"Egypt is in Africa," I answered. She stared at me with a blank expression, so I continued. "You know, the Pyramids, the Sphinx. Egyptian civilization has been around for at least seven thousand years."

"No, that's impossible," she was quick to reply.

"How so?" I asked. "We are talking about history."

"Well, according to the Bible, life began only about five thousand years ago," she said.

I didn't discuss the issue further with her. It did not seem to me that anything fruitful would have emerged had we continued our conversation—so sure was she about her biblical facts. But as I began piecing American culture together, I realized that there are a significant number of folks in the States who rely on the Bible as a primary source of historical fact. (Many Muslims rely on the Qur'an in the same way.)

I had another conversation with an elderly woman in an American supermarket. She was wheeling a cat around in her shopping cart. As the cat was about to jump out, I caught it and placed it back in the cart. She thanked me and then asked me where I was from. I told her I was from Egypt.

The woman frowned. No doubt, in her mind, Arabs were a monolithic lot. She asked, "Why don't you accept the Jews to live with you?" I assumed she was referring to Palestine and Israel.

"I believe it is the Jews in Israel who cannot accept the Palestinians living with them," I said.

The woman continued to frown. "This is the Promised Land that Isaac inherited from his father, Abraham."

I calmly responded, "This is true. We are talking about the Promised Land, but Abraham had two sons—Isaac and Ishmael. Does it seem right to you that Abraham would single out just one son, Isaac, for an inheritance?"

She surprised me by saying, "Yes, yes, of course, Abraham had two sons."

"You are right," I replied. "I think that's one of the reasons why the Jewish people need to accept the Palestinians—the descendants of Ishmael—to live with them."

Engaging folks in conversations such as this helped me to understand the inherent assumptions people have—assumptions that play out in concrete ways through the behavior of individuals in any given society. When enough individual people behave alike, the society takes on a distinctive shape or flavor.

Dating American women was a daunting experience for me. In Egypt, there was never any question as to who pays the bill for dinner or even just coffee. The man does, of course. Sometimes, in my haste to pay the bill, some American women accused me of patronizing them. If I were to hold a door open for a college coed, I'd run the risk of being accused of patronizing her. I learned to adjust. Finding humor in my "mistakes" went miles in easing these social situations.

Once I was telling my friends about the great time my date and I had together. I mentioned that I wanted "to satisfy" her. They laughed, telling me that it would be more appropriate for me to say that I wanted "to please" her. "Satisfy" carries a sexual connotation. I learned a lot about American culture by looking at how Americans use language. I would not have learned nearly as much had I stuck to the language of academic discourse prevalent in the university. That's why I went outside the university as much as possible and mixed with people from all walks of life.

While living in Philadelphia, I felt right at home with Tom Neff, the director of the Institute of Middle Eastern Studies, and his wife, Jane. The couple had lived in Egypt for seven years while Tom worked at the American University in Cairo. The first time I had dinner at their house, Jane gave me pointers on how best to maneuver mealtime with American families. "Look, Nasr," she said, "I am going to act with you as I would with an Egyptian family. I am just going to put food on your plate. If you say, 'Thank you, that's enough,' I won't stop piling the food on your plate." She told me that I'd probably be invited to eat with American families. "If you say, 'Thank you,' people will think you don't want any more food. They will take you at your word and not offer you any more food."

Jane also told me that if some item (Coke, mustard, tea) was not on the table, it was not impolite to ask for it. This is very impolite in Egyptian society. I appreciated her telling me these things. Nonetheless, I still found it difficult to put the information she passed on to me into practice.

One day, Jane called me on the phone. "Let's have lunch together," she suggested. I made some small talk, asking her how Tom was doing even though I saw Tom every day at the university. "You know we are separated," she offered.

"No, I didn't know. Tom did not tell me." Their separation surprised me. They had been married a long time and had grown children. She then told me she wanted to meet with me. We were acting like Egyptians. In Egypt, if there is a dispute between a husband and a wife, a third party can feel quite free to step in and try to bring the couple back together. But I knew how Americans felt about marriage—it is a private matter. I still offered to help. "If there's anything I can do," I said, my voice trailing off.

"Do what your heart tells you to do," Jane responded. I figured she was asking me to do something.

The next day I met Tom in the office. "I had lunch with Jane yesterday and she told me that you are separated."

Tom was kind, but he cut me off nonetheless. "Nasr, I'm sorry, but this is not your business. In addition, we don't want to add to your troubles and burden you with our problems." (My sister Badriyya had recently died.)

I may have called Jane once after my conversation with Tom, but for all intents and purposes, that conversation with Tom ended further contact with her. Through this experience, I understood a little more about the way Americans go about marriage and divorce. Generally speaking, in Egypt, it's unusual to even think about separation and divorce after twenty years of marriage—especially if there are grown children. I made no judgment about Tom and Jane. As an outsider, I felt I could not possibly know all the ins and outs of the situation. Egyptian Arabs in a similar predicament would wonder, "How can I start my life over again at this point?" I had no way of knowing it then, but a dozen or so years down the road, I would face a situation similar to the one Tom and Jane faced during this time.

Among the things I took advantage of while studying at the University of Pennsylvania was the huge offering of courses—courses that pointed the way to other disciplines—especially sociology and anthropology and the study of culture in general. My academic experience in the States turned out to be quite fruitful. I did a lot of reading on my own, especially in the fields of philosophy and hermeneutics. Hermeneutics, the science of interpreting texts, opened up a brand-new world for me.

The science of hermeneutics was first applied to biblical texts. Literature, anthropology, and even psychology have appropriated hermeneutical principles as a tool in their research. Human sciences rely on textual interpretation (texts include speech, dreams, and individual cultures), not on the controlled laboratory experiment, as a way of coming to knowledge.

The Qur'an, the sacred text of Islam, is God's speech. God took the initiative and communicated with human beings through the Prophet Muhammad at a particular time (seventh century) and in a particular place (Arabian Peninsula). Muslims are in agreement with each other about this. The word Qur'an itself means "to recite."

When analyzing the first vision of Muhammad—the first session of revelation— what we notice is that Muhammad reported information to us. We were not there. Nobody was there. After his vision, Muhammad told his companions that he had met an angel who had spoken to him. What we have is Muhammad's word that this angel who spoke to him revealed to him the Word of God.

Did God really speak through an angel to Muhammad? If so, we have no idea what kind of language the angel used. There is no way we can know such a thing. Muslims have speculated ever since the seventh century about this first session of revelation. Speculation inevitably leads to the making of hypotheses. But all we know for sure is that Muhammad told his companions that an angel revealed to him the Word of God. Muhammad then repeated the message. So what do we have? The word of Muhammad reporting what he asserts is the Word of God. This is the Qur'an.

Muslims believe that Muhammad received the Word of God. There is no dispute among Muslims about this. We believe Muhammad. We believe he is telling us the truth. But, at the end of the day, it is Muhammad, the human being, reporting to us the Word of God. There is no way to test or prove that the Qur'an is the Word of God. Based on the information we have, we cannot establish absolute facts. We have room to maneuver, though, when we think of the Word of God as reported to Muhammad as a means to understand the Word of God. So just what is the Word of God?

There are passages in the Qur'an that tell us that God's Word cannot be contained. I cited one of these passages earlier. God's Word goes beyond anything we can take in through the use of our senses and then record. If you were to take the Qur'an—the text we have today—you could easily write it all down in a couple of hours, using one pen and a container of ink.

A distinction must be made between the absolute Word of God and the Qur'an. The Word of God in the Qur'an can best be described as a manifestation of the Word of God. Therefore, there are other manifestations of the Word of God. God does not speak only Arabic. God speaks no specific language as we understand language. So if God has no specific language, this opens up a space for other Scriptures to be recognized as manifestations of God's Word as well. All these manifestations of the Word of God come to us by way of human beings. Human beings such as Moses, Jesus, the apostles, and Muhammad report the Word of God through language. We've come, then, to an important point. What do we mean when we talk about language?

Language does not emerge from a vacuum. Language has a cultural, social, and political context. Human beings populate these contexts. Human beings, living throughout the world in specific places at specific times, leave their mark on language. So if we look to understand the Word of God as manifested in a specific text (Qur'an, Hebrew Bible, or the New Testament), it is imperative that we understand the history of the text.

Some people resist looking at God's Word as a document expressed in human language, thinking that understanding sacred text in such a way goes against belief or faith. What kind of language did God use to communicate with humanity? When you speak to a young child, what does that language look and sound like? Would you speak to a youngster with the same language you would use with a mature adult? Would you use academic language to get your point across? Not if you want the child to understand. You use a language the child can access. You adapt your language to the child's language. If you don't, there is no communication.

So when we talk about God communicating with humanity, what we have in the Qur'an is human language. The Word of God needed to adapt itself—become human—because God wanted to communicate to human beings. If God spoke God-language, human beings would understand nothing. It's like a professor talking about Aristotelian philosophy to his two-year-old. The child has no context in which to receive Aristotelian philosophy. Christians believe that God revealed himself in the actual humanity (flesh and blood) of Jesus. Therefore, Jesus is both human and divine. Muslims believe that God revealed himself in the Qur'an. Therefore, the Qur'an is both human and divine.

How are we to understand this dual nature of the Qur'an? How do the human aspect and the divine aspect fit together? Was the human aspect made divine, or was the divine aspect made human? When we read the Qur'an, we certainly find the imprint of history. It is obvious in so many passages. We follow Muhammad to specific geographic places as he travels about with his family. He interacts with the community. He advises the community about specific things. Muhammad is firmly situated within a historical context. At the same time, the Qur'an goes beyond historicity. There are passages that speak about the cosmos, creation, God, attributes of God, the mission of prophets, heaven, earth, mountains, animals, beauty of the universe, and morality. A careful investigation into the Qur'an reveals both a divine aspect and a historical, human aspect.

The divine text became a human text at the moment it was revealed to Muhammad. How else could human beings understand it? Once it is in human form, a text becomes governed by the principles of mutability or change. The text becomes a book like any other. Religious texts are essentially linguistic texts. They belong to a specific culture and are produced within that historical setting. The Qur'an is a historical discourse—it has no fixed, intrinsic meaning.

What is a text? What is the structure of a text? How do we go about interpreting a text? Is there such a thing as an objective interpretation?

Does meaning reside within a text, waiting to be discovered? Just what is the relationship between a text and the reader? Perhaps the reader belongs to the same culture as the author, perhaps not. Within any culture there resides a host of factors that affect our understanding of the language used in a text. Is the reader a contemporary of the author? If not, then the relationship is not direct—the text has been interpreted throughout a period of time, and that interpretation easily worms its way into the original text. A reader cannot avoid this accumulated interpretation around the text.

We live in a world of interpretation. When you look at your watch, for example, and say, "It is noon," you are expressing a natural phenomenon. But you are actually looking at a piece of machinery and declaring that it is noontime. You have learned how to interpret a particular configuration on your watch with a natural event.

Spoken language is aural. Written language is visual. At the end of the day, both spoken and written language refer to concepts, and these concepts have a relationship to this thing we call reality. What is the relationship between concept and reality and the relationship between concept and language? This takes us into wider fields such as linguistics (the study of human speech) and semiotics (the study of how signs and symbols function in language).

One of the things I discovered while doing research in the States was that there is no such thing as a pure interpretation of a text. Any given text carries a point of view. At the same time, readers/interpreters of text carry their own ideologies that affect their understanding of that text.

Islamic theology early on divided itself along two main interpretive lines, literal interpretation and metaphoric understanding of the Qur'an. Each assumes a different idea about the nature of the text and how that text relates to God, humanity, language, and culture.

A metaphoric view of the Qur'an considers language to be a human invention. Language does not directly reflect reality. What language does reflect is the way human beings conceive, conceptualize, and symbolize reality. The Mu'tazilites understood this because they conceived of the Qur'an as a created action, not the eternal, verbal utterance of God. This idea of a created Qur'an implies that the bond between the signifier (language) and the signified (reality) exists only by human convention—there is nothing divine in this relationship. In addition, being a cultural and historical product, the Qur'an cannot be understood properly without studying the specific historical context where the text came about. All Muslims agree that the Qur'an is God's speech. Disagreement over whether the Qur'an is eternal and uncreated or temporal and created led to dispute and persecution. This great persecution or inquisition lasted from 833 until 848. Ahmad ibn Hanbal (780–855) objected to the temporality and creation of the Qur'an. His view emerged victorious.

A literal understanding of the Qur'an holds language to be a divine gift, not a human invention. God's speech is not something created, but one of God's eternal attributes. When the Qur'an refers to something nonexistent in the real world, the assumption is that this something exists in the unseen realm. Literalists believe that before being revealed to the Prophet Muhammad, the Qur'an existed in heaven, where it is recorded on the well-preserved Holy Tablet in magnificent Arabic letters, each of which is as great as Mount Qâf. When you see the Arabic letter representing Qâf, you note a small closed circle resting on the right top of a larger half circle. From this visual image, it is easy to see Mount Qâf encompassing the whole Earth.

Classical Islamic thought believes the Qur'an existed before it was revealed. I argue that the Qur'an is a cultural product that takes its shape from a particular time in history. The historicity of the Qur'an in no way implies that the text is human. Because the text is grounded in history, I can interpret and understand that text. We should not be afraid to apply all the tools at our disposal in order to get at the meaning of the text. God's actual words, though, exist in a sphere beyond human knowledge—a metaphysical space that we can know nothing about except that which the text itself mentions.

The message of Islam could not have had any effect if the people who first received the revelation could not understand that message. Because the community could—and in fact did—understand its message, the Qur'an produced a new culture. Simply stated, the Qur'an first emerged as a text within a specific sociocultural time, place, and space with a specific language (Arabic). From this time, place, and space, a new and different kind of culture emerged.

We must keep in mind that the Qur'an comes to us via a historical and ever-changing human community. Because interpretation of text often intertwines with the actual text, it's important to understand how the original Muslim community interpreted the Qur'an. However, we ought not to accept their conclusions as final or absolute. Neither should we think of the interpretations that succeeding generations arrived at as being etched in stone. After the text is decoded in the light of history, culture, and language, it must then be recoded into the current cultural and linguistic context. The Qur'an's message has to be continuously discovered and rediscovered.

The notion that religious texts are historically determined and culturally constructed is not only rejected but also condemned in most of the Islamic world as atheism. The idea of the Qur'an as the eternal and exact utterance of God has become the accepted doctrine in classical theological thought. Denying the textuality of the Qur'an leads to a wooden or literal interpretation of the text—an interpretation that freezes the meaning of the message. There is never a space to reinterpret the Qur'an based on changing circumstances. No difference exists between the letter and the spirit of divine revelation. When the meaning of the text becomes frozen, an authority of some sort (the state, theologians, or politicians) easily emerges, claiming to be the rightful guardian of Islam. These guardians all too often have imposed their own agenda onto the Qur'an, manipulating the sacred text to suit their own purposes.

Metaphorically understanding God's Word leaves room for reinterpretation of *shari'a* or religious law because that understanding stems from the spirit of the text, not the letter. What logically follows, then, is that a society, through its public authorities, becomes free to interpret and apply *shari'a* to its present circumstances.

When I study the Qur'an and other religious texts, I attempt to create an objective and scientific framework to analyze and interpret those texts. This framework has two parts. One aspect of my work tries to recover the original meaning of the text by placing it within a sociohistorical context. The other aspect of my work attempts to make crystal clear the contemporary sociocultural framework and political goals that motivate and steer Qur'anic interpretation. All interpretation has an ideological content—interpretation that rarely squares with historical meaning.

Current religious discourse obliterates the historical dimension of the Qur'an by assuming that we can apply solutions that worked well in the past to problems we face in the present. I easily grow weary when I hear the Qur'an quoted as a way of offering solutions to all the current social, economic, political, and cultural problems in the Muslim world. Most times, those quoting verses from the Qur'an assume the meaning of the quoted verses to be self-evident. It's not that simple.

Much Qur'anic imagery speaks of God as a king with a throne and an army of angels. Some verses speak of a pen and the Preserved

Tablet. This imagery, if taken literally, leads to an understanding of the universe that sustains a social order of royalty and tyranny. The early Muslim community may have understood only the literal level of meaning. It is more likely that the text reflects the early community's "lived reality." This would be natural. What is not natural is that in spite of culture's forward thrust, much modern Islamic discourse clings to an interpretation of text attributed to the earliest community. This interpretation takes on a wooden, lifeless quality irrelevant to our modern-day sensibilities and needs.

A metaphoric reading of the Qur'an is alluded to within its own text. Several verses in the Qur'an admonish believers, by way of almsgiving, to lend only to God. This loan will be returned to them multiplied several times. The Jews living in Medina at the time of the Prophet asked a logical question: "How is it that Muhammad's God prohibits usury, yet promises to give profits on loans?" In order to make sense, a literal understanding of the text—one that prohibits usury—cannot logically be sustained.

I owe much of my understanding of hermeneutics to opportunities offered me during my brief sojourn in the United States. The science of hermeneutics widened my vision—a vision I hope many more Muslims will glimpse as well.

7 Going Japanese

When I received an invitation to go to Japan as a visiting professor in the Department of Arabic at Osaka University for Foreign Languages, I jumped at the opportunity. I didn't think I'd ever be in a position to afford a ticket to such an exotic place, so this seemed to me to be the best shot I'd ever get to see the Far East. I was in Japan for a little over four years—March 1985 through July 1989. The Japanese higher educational system has a policy requiring that their foreign language departments be staffed with at least one native-speaking professor for each language they offer. I filled a particular niche. Colleagues of mine from Cairo University filled the position before me as well as after me.

My teaching responsibilities at Osaka did not tax me as they did in Cairo. In Osaka, a full class meant twenty-seven or thirty students, not the one hundred or so I had been used to in Egypt. In addition, the courses I taught were elementary—two classes in Arabic, one class in literature, and one class in Islamic thought. I also supervised one student working on his M.A. I didn't need a whole lot of time to prepare for class. I discovered that I liked this slower pace. It allowed me to travel around the country a bit. As in the States, I developed my own fieldwork and was also able to concentrate on my own writing.

Japanese students impressed me. They were hardworking and extremely conscientious. Whatever work I assigned, they completed. Without complaint! Sometimes I would give them a two-hundred-verse, classic poem to read in English. In spite of English not being their native language, they always came to class ready—even eager—to learn and contribute.

In the first-year Arabic language class, the students knew nothing at first. I had had some experience in Egypt teaching Arabic to students from other countries: Germany, England, France, and even Mexico. I applied some of the teaching techniques that I had learned in Egypt to my Japanese students and found they worked well in Japan. I used gestures and body language to begin building some vocabulary before stringing that vocabulary into sentences such as "I am a teacher"; "My name is Nasr"; "I am from Egypt"; "How are you?" After the first month, they were able to say a few simple phrases, an ability that gave them a sense of accomplishment. That ability encouraged them to forge ahead into more difficult things.

It didn't take long for me to form a bond with my Japanese students, something highly unusual within Japanese educational tradition. The Japanese keep a respectful distance between professors and students. It's not a harsh distance, but it definitely is there. The student is the student. The professor is the professor.

My experience with professors in the States couldn't have been more different. There, I could (and was expected to) address my professor by his first name, although I never found it within me to do so. I always rose to my feet when a professor spoke to me, and I never would initiate conversation with him from a sitting position. In addition, I always prefaced his name with the title Professor.

On one occasion, one of my professors chided me. "Why do you continue to address me in such a formal manner?" he asked. I was the only student who did.

I told him that I understood American tradition. I respected it. I even loved it. "But I am unable to address you by your first name."

In Japan, the pendulum swung completely in the other direction. I tried to bridge some of this distance between professor and student when I taught at Osaka University. I invited students to my home and introduced them to Egyptian food. I took them to the mosque in Kyoto to watch the Ramadân festivities. I made arrangements with the *imam* (leader of the Muslim community) to bring my students to one of the big feasts at the mosque. The *imam* was eager to have them come. He thought this was a great way to bring people to Islam. This, of course, was never my objective. Islam is part of Arab culture. You cannot know about Arab culture without knowing something about Islam. It only made sense to have my students experience Arab culture in order to learn about it. Just being outside of the classroom and taking the train together to the mosque created an atmosphere of expectancy and possibility.

The Japanese are quite capable of displaying a wide range of emotions. Many people stereotypically think of Japanese people as stoic. This is a mask. I learned how important the mask is to the Japanese by attending the Kabuki Theater. The mask keeps emotion from the actor's face. It's the voice that becomes the vehicle through which emotion is expressed. Sometimes I stood seven hours in the Kabuki. I understood nothing. I realized later on that the Japanese people themselves don't understand the language used in the Kabuki. The language of the Kabuki is an archaic one. But, as in all cultures, the Japanese use semiotics, the language of signs.

While living in Japan, I began to see differently—my perspective changed. I read voraciously about Japanese culture and history. I also traipsed about, visiting temples, but not as a tourist. I looked for (and found) people within the temples who could speak English. I brought them my questions and used a tape recorder to hold on to their answers. I lived at one of the temples for three weeks. They provided me with a room—even welcomed me as a participant in their rituals. They had no objection to my having an Egyptian student with me, working as a translator. I ate their food, mostly vegetarian fare. The day before my three-week stay ended, the temple priest came to me and said, "You have been quite a presence here among us. I would like to invite you to have a good dinner. You must miss eating meat. There is a steak house not too far from here. I would like you to be my guest." While we ate, I don't remember meat ever having tasted so good.

When we speak of Japanese religion, we usually think of Shintoism and Buddhism coming together. However, we cannot ignore Christianity in this mix. There has been a viable Christian presence in Japan since the seventeenth century. (Christian missionaries traveled to China and India as well.) I experienced Shintoism as a result of my temple stay. I had read some about Shintoism, the traditional Japanese religion. But by living in an actual temple, the experience became etched in my consciousness in a way that no amount of reading could have given me.

I have a Japanese friend who graduated from Cairo University. He and I took several undergraduate classes together; however, he had some difficulties with his studies, so we did not graduate together. After

I graduated and had become an assistant lecturer, I helped him move along with his studies. His name is Muhsin Ogasawara.

Muhsin loved Egyptian food, especially *molokhiyya*. This dish is like a soup, but it's substantial enough to be a meal in itself. The *molokhiyya* plant has traditionally been grown as a companion crop with cotton. The soup is prepared by simmering the *molokhiyya* leaf in chicken broth before adding vegetables. When cooked, the soup has a dark green color and a gelatinous consistency. Served piping hot with rice or bread, it is delicious. This is the quintessential Egyptian dish. So I'd invite Muhsin to come home with me especially when my mother planned on making *molokhiyya*. She loved the fact that Muhsin could speak Arabic, but what really moved her was that this boy had been away from his mother for seven years. She extended her care toward him by giving him a great big dose of mother love—something she was sure he was missing terribly.

Japanese are a very polite people. If you were to say to Muhsin, as my mother often did, "You should eat," Muhsin would eat even if he felt he were about to explode.

As Muhsin grew more comfortable with us, he'd say, "My mother, you will kill me. You love me, but you will kill me." It made me happy to see my mother laugh. She didn't laugh often, so when she did, it delighted me. So Muhsin became part of our family for a while.

When I went to Japan, one of the first things I did was look up Mr. Ogasawara, my friend. He wasn't difficult to find. He was a professor at one of the universities in Tokyo. As I roamed about the university one day, I asked several people, "Where might I find Muhsin?" Nobody knew to whom I was referring. However, when I said Ogasawara, they knew immediately. We had a delightful visit—even spoke in Arabic, using language and phrases that took us both back to the time he had spent studying in Egypt and had, for all too brief a time, become part of our family.

The next day, Muhsin came to Osaka to invite me to visit his village. He had told his family that I was his *sensei* (teacher). When I arrived at his home, Muhsin ceremoniously presented me to each member of his family. I don't remember ever feeling so welcomed anywhere—not even in Egypt. I spent a week in his village near Tokyo, the *sensei* of the *sensei* (teacher of the teacher). It was the week before the Japanese New Year. There were celebrations and festivities galore. This experience opened up a window for me to peek a bit into traditional family life in Japan. Most meaningful, though, was the respect and love I experienced from this humble professor in his home village—a man who had once upon a time brought laughter into my mother's life.

When I was in Osaka, I used to walk from my house to the university. It took me about an hour, but I figured the exercise could only be good for me. Sometimes, women would be in front of their houses, cleaning the sidewalk. One of them stopped me one day, and with gestures and simple words we managed to communicate. She knew about Egypt when I told her that was my home. She couldn't figure out what Arabic was when I told her I taught Arabic. I spoke to her in Arabic and she then seemed to grasp that I taught language. She considered my teaching Arabic to "our boys" to be a huge favor. It was as if I were on a great mission to Japan. I don't remember getting a reception such as this in any other place I've taught.

While living in Japan, I often rode the train to get around. On crowded trains, I noticed that men did not offer their seats to women. Quite the opposite, in fact. If a husband and wife traveled together on a crowded train, the man would be seated. The woman stood. On one particular occasion, an elderly woman got on the train and it was an automatic reflex for me—I gave her my seat. She was quite moved, kept talking to me in Japanese, but all I understood was "Thank you." When she got off the train, she handed me her card. This is a common practice. I reciprocated by giving her one of my cards. A month later, I got a phone call from her son. His English was difficult to decipher, but I did understand that he was the son of the lady to whom I had given my seat on the train. He invited me to have dinner with him. I accepted. English was our common language, but conversation was quite limited. I remember gesturing a lot during the meal.

Besides enjoying my students and attempting to experience as much of Japan as I could absorb, I translated Inazo Nitobe's book *Bushido: The Way of the Samurai*.[1] Inazo Nitobe (1863–1933) wrote in English, and this particular book deals with traditional Japanese culture. Along with translating the text into Arabic, I did a sort of comparative analysis as well. In my own field, after receiving my Ph.D., I wrote my first book, *The Concept of the Text: A Study of the Sciences of the Qur'an*.[2] I also wrote *Critique of Islamic Discourse*[3] while in Japan. I had plenty of time to concentrate on my academic work while learning about the country.

My studies in the States focused on hermeneutics—how to go about interpreting a text. In Japan, I realized that the Japanese religious experience does not center on a text, but on personal experience. Religion expresses itself through individual interpretation of a person's experience. There is no dogma.

Many folks become confused when they ask a Japanese person, "What is your religion?" Japanese people will hesitate, think for a while, and say, "I don't have a religion." Often the conclusion people draw is that the Japanese have no belief system. This, of course, is not true. They have no specific dogma. They believe certain things, but their practical lives are not dependent on an authoritative text.

The Japanese do not struggle between tradition and modernity in the same way as people who claim a religion with a revealed text. No perceptible tension exists between tradition and modernity in Japan. At home, tradition reigns. I could hardly find a chair to sit on when I visited a Japanese family. In the university setting, I could hardly find an indication that I was in Japan. Technology and all the up-to-date amenities surrounded me.

As I focused on my writing in Japan, I saw quite clearly that many of the difficulties we face in Islam regarding the meaning of our sacred text become irrelevant in religious traditions that have no authoritative text. If God spoke, verbally spoke, literally spoke, then every letter of the text has divine significance. Literalism insists on a fixed understanding of text. Fundamentalists—people who insist on a literal interpretation of text—etch their particular understanding in stone. Of course, having no authoritative text does not render a religion immune to fundamentalism. Fundamentalism knows no ideological boundaries. The possibility of fundamentalism exists within any religious, political, or social ideology.

As attractive as the concept of a pure text may be to some folks, there really is no such thing. A text comes into being through a process. We can talk about religion, though, within the context of a fixed text—where meaning becomes frozen. Without understanding how a text comes into being, fundamentalism can easily take root. Communism, a political system of thought, can carry fundamentalist fervor. Communism centers itself on Marxist text. Communism is a text-centered ideology. People have differed on just how to interpret what Marx said. What did Marx really mean? The moment you make a dogma of any text, you are in danger, even if the text is a literary text such as a poem. The authority of the text is not something inherent to the text. The authority of any text comes when people give it authority. It's as simple as that.

I was born into an Arab-Islamic culture. I identify myself as Muslim. Like all of us, I am a product of my culture, having been shaped by that culture's historical and sociopolitical forces. The Qur'an, a text, is at the very center of every Muslim's identity. In 1996, long after I had left Japan for Egypt and then left Egypt for the Netherlands, Professor Dieter Senghaas from the Institute for Intercultural and International Studies, University of Bremen, and I engaged in a dialogue titled "The Islamic World and the Modern Age." This dialogue was later published in a pamphlet that marked the tenth anniversary of the Development and Peace Foundation.[4] During the course of our conversation, Professor Senghaas asked me, "Why are you yourself so fixated on the Text?"

The Qur'an is the very heart of Islam. Consequently, the crucial question for Muslims revolves around the nature of this text. Does the text have an inherent authority? What is the relationship between the authority of the text, the authority of the interpreter, and the social authority at large? Those who insist on a literal interpretation of the Qur'an (as fundamentalists do) subscribe, whether they are aware of it or not, to a set of hermeneutical principles. They believe that meaning resides in the text itself. The text speaks by itself.

When a religion is centered on a sacred text, religious intellectual activity becomes all about hermeneutics—interpretation. This is mainly true of the three major monotheistic faiths—Judaism, Christianity, and Islam. Asian religions have texts, but those texts do not have an inherent authority. Asian religions center on personal experience. Buddha, for example, was neither a god nor a prophet. He was a case. Everybody has a chance to be a Buddha. Shintoism, the religion most associated with Japan, does not even have a foundational text.

But how does a particular interpretation of a sacred text (and all understanding is derived from interpretation) become the only valid interpretation? Every text has its context. Social and political forces influenced the chronology of the Qur'an as well as its content. The text, when it was revealed to Muhammad, responded to current problems experienced within the community and answered specific questions regarding those problems.

Let's take the example of usury. Why does the Qur'an condemn usury? Meccan society, like any society, had people who preyed upon the poor and powerless. Prophets, such as Muhammad, invariably champion the cause of the widowed, the orphaned—those who have no voice within their society. The wealthy elite exploited those who were in financial need through the practice of usury. The Qur'anic injunction against usury serves a specific purpose: to protect Mecca's poorer citizens from the wealthy elite taking advantage of them. The broader question is one of justice.

In order to make sense of religion, especially those religions with an authoritative, sacred text, you have to start by addressing the nature of this text. I am trying to tell my Muslim colleagues all over the Islamic world that the text is a message. It has no authority in itself. We human beings give this text its authority. The theologian's job is to apply hermeneutical principles to the text in order to discover meaning from the text. Do those principles point to a literal interpretation? A metaphoric interpretation? Perhaps some combination? Through application of tools (linguistics, lexicology, semiotics) to the text, the text yields meaning. This is the kind of work I do. This became the content of my fourth book, *Critique of Islamic Discourse.*

I intentionally used the words *Islamic Discourse* in the title, not *Islamic Thought.* Discourse refers to any kind of speech or writing—it even includes social behavior. When you speak of thought, you necessarily deal with intention. It is possible for a discourse (and discourse can be political, religious, or social) to convey ideas that have nothing to do with the intentions of the author. In spite of people's good intentions, their discourse can wreak havoc. Speech, writing, and social behavior carry meaning with them.

As I began to write *Critique of Islamic Discourse,* I wanted to determine just what assumptions were inherent in religious discourse. What's the starting point? What do folks take for granted at the outset? I discovered that political and religious discourses were similar. Both base themselves firmly upon two untested presuppositions.

The first presupposition of religious discourse is this: Divine authority is absolute. A dualism follows. God possesses knowledge and wisdom. Humanity is ignorant. God is powerful. Human beings are weak. So, whatever God commands, you take literally. The text speaks by itself. What do you, an ignorant and weak human being, know anyway? Furthermore, human beings are conceived as machines, created by an engineer—God. Since God created human beings, God knows them inside and out. Scripture is seen as an instruction manual on how to care for the machine. Human beings have the responsibility to apply those instructions to their lives. Should they mess up, the machine gets destroyed.

To fundamentalist Islamic thinkers—and there are plenty of them who produce this kind of discourse in Egypt—this is exactly the image they have. They don't think of human beings as social beings active in conversation with God. Human beings are mere creatures. God and creation exist in separate vacuums. Bringing the social sciences to bear on their understanding of the Qur'an—well, this is all nonsense to them.

The political discourse in the Muslim world is not quite as rigid as the religious discourse, but it follows a similar pattern. Those who hold political power do not consult the people when they make decisions that affect those people they govern. People will often ask, "Why didn't you consult with us?"

Those in power respond, "Our decision was based on certain facts you do not know." Those in power possess knowledge. Others do not.

There's a message that comes across clearly. "We are privy to information you are not entitled to. Since you are ignorant, you don't have the right to protest. We know. We base our decision on knowledge that you have no access to."

It's outrageous. This is exclusion. In the religious expression, this exclusion plays itself out through the assertion that an unbridgeable gulf exists between God and human beings. In the political expression, we see knowledge and power, grasped tightly by the elite, coming up against those the elite label as ignorant. Ordinary people internalize this understanding. It's not unusual to hear ordinary people saying, "The government knows. We don't."

This power disparity also appears in different social arenas. The teacher, for example. The teacher knows. Students are ignorant. What about the father? The father knows. Children have only to obey. When it comes to women, the power structure remains in place. The wife's duty is to obey her husband—a woman must even obey her younger brothers. They are men, and because they are men, the assumption is that their life experience has given them knowledge. Women, for the most part, are not given the same opportunities to experience life, so they remain ignorant.

This kind of thinking infiltrates all institutions—social, religious, and political. When the preacher in the mosque tires of people asking him questions, he will often say, "Don't ask. Asking too much is a sign of disbelief." By using God as a shield, religious discourse manipulates people. In the political realm, using knowledge as a shield controls and dominates people in much the same way. In each case, people are intentionally kept in the dark, unable to get hold of power for themselves.

Using a critical approach to challenge this kind of structural power shakes up the status quo. Saying that knowledge and education should be freely available to everybody, and that women should get out and have their own life experience, threatens to turn society upside down. Not everybody wants society turned topsy-turvy—especially those who stand to lose, the ones who wield power. Other folks—those who have internalized their society's assumptions: "The government knows. We don't"—may initially lose the illusory sense of personal well-being that comes with uncritically accepting their society's givens. Arab culture is one of obedience. From infancy, children are taught that obedience is virtuous. It's difficult and often dangerous to go against the tide. The rewards—freedom and autonomy—are well worth the effort, though. Our dignity, our worth, our very survival are at stake.

Saying that human beings operate under a degree of autonomy scandalizes those who hold religious power. God, however, created humanity after creating the universe. Human beings were created within a context. Within this context, human beings developed a society. To say that the world keeps spinning as a result of God's power does not mean that God interferes in all the details of the world. If God ordains everything that happens, why do many theologians believe and preach that God punishes people for going against God's will? If God ordains all that happens, then it follows that a person's disobedience is ordained as well. On the other hand, if God does interfere, what happens to personal responsibility?

Challenging the religious and political discourse in Muslim society is not just about flexing intellectual muscle. It's shaking the foundation of an authoritative society in order to establish another kind of society where every individual has the right to know and the right to choose.

When I am critical of conventional religious discourse—a discourse that claims to speak on God's behalf—my goal is to show how that discourse uses religion as a political tool. Political rulers, patterning themselves after this first presupposition—divine authority is absolute—use religion as a way to boost their agenda and fortify their power. Both religious and political discourses in Egypt believe in the right to rule, and both use Truth to justify their ambitions.

The second presupposition inherent in religious discourse is this: The unfolding of history has no effect on how we interpret our sacred text and apply it to our present-day lives. In other words, this second assumption attempts to solve current political, social, and ethical problems by resurrecting solutions that the Muslim community of a bygone era used. These solutions were effective at one time; hence, they'll be effective now. That's the spin.

Our current problems stem, so we're told, from our having strayed so far from Islam. The solution? Return to Islam. Within the phrase "Return to Islam" there is the sense that Islam as practiced by the earliest community enjoyed a purity which subsequent generations lost. As a result of this—dare I call it thinking?—the saying "Islam is the solution" has taken hold in Muslim society. (Not any different from bumper stickers I've seen in the States that say, "Jesus is the answer.") Just exactly what is the question? Those who glibly spout such a simplistic formula as a cure-all for our present-day problems offer no plan, nor do they speak about what kind of solution they envision Islam would bring to the social, political, and economic problems that plague us. They fill the gap between the past and the present by simply stating that since Islam solved the problems of the seventh century, it can just as easily solve our problems today.

What kind of Islam are we talking about? When we speak of Islamic civilization today, we must understand that we are talking about something different from Islamic civilizations of the eighth and ninth centuries. During this time, Muslims rubbed shoulders with a variety of other cultures—Indian, Egyptian, and Greek. Muslims incorporated knowledge obtained from neighboring cultures and integrated that knowledge into the structure of Islam, producing new knowledge that reconfigured Muslim theology, philosophy, language, and even jurisprudence. Islam has evolved over time and throughout history. Thinking that Islam, as it was understood in the seventh century, is identical to Islam of the eighth, ninth, tenth, eleventh, and subsequent centuries reflects an understanding of human history as a static phenomenon.

Many Muslim theologians either do not recognize or refuse to admit that history's influence on religion has been incorporated into the religion itself. They fail to distinguish between Islam as a divine message and the human, historical way Islam played itself out during the thirteen or fourteen centuries since the Qur'an was revealed to Muhammad.

Many folks have a dichotomous way of viewing Islam. There is a pure expression of Islam and a contaminated, corrupted Islam. Abul Ala Mawdudi (1903–1979), the founder of Jamaat-I Islami in Pakistan, said that the real Islam existed during the lives of the Prophet and the four guided caliphs. Because of subsequent foreign influence, Islam has become corrupt—al-Mawdudi even went so far as to say that Islam's history is totally corrupt because that foreign influence has infected all of society's institutions. Coming to this conclusion can be done only by ignoring the fact that Islam is a historical phenomenon, a dynamic phenomenon that gets its shape from coming up against specific social and political forces. Islam is not static. Islam, like all other religions, has evolved over time.

How does Islam become meaningful to those within the *umma*, the community of believers? When Muslims, in collaboration with the foundational texts, produce appropriate solutions to current problems—solutions that meet the present needs of individuals and community alike. This production of meaning is never-ending. Life is in a constant state of flux. New problems arise—problems that call for creative solutions, not solutions taken from the past and superimposed on problems of the present. Survival of any religion depends on the ability of the community of believers to produce updated religious discourse, reinterpreting texts according to present needs. Without this ongoing process, religion dies.

All of this thinking made its way into my writing while I lived in Japan. As I've noted, my teaching schedule was not all that taxing. I had time to develop my thinking along certain lines and to focus on my writing. My original intention was to stay in Japan for two years, but I found myself content and satisfied. I extended my stay for another two years. It would be great to be able to return there some day. While in the States, not a day went by that I did not long for Egypt. While living in Japan, I found myself longing to stay.

I learned more about Christianity while living in the States, as you might imagine. I visited a variety of churches there—black churches, born-again churches, Pentecostal Holiness. It seemed to me that whenever I went to visit a church in the States, people considered me fair game for conversion. I would politely tell them, "Thank you for your interest, but I'm a Muslim and very happy about that. I'm just here to understand." They would tell me that Jesus loved me and died for my sins. I made friends with some of these folks, but they never seemed to tire of trying to convert me.

I watched baptismal ceremonies with a certain degree of awe as preachers submerged people for a second or two in small pools of water—pools built right into the sanctuary of their churches. I spent days around the Christmas season with American families who hosted students from the university. Usually it was the elderly women in these families, determined to mold my behavior into their understanding of how a good Christian should behave, who admonished me about my smoking. I've since given up the habit. Nevertheless, these elderly women told me that smoking was sinful. I had to ask, of course, if they could show me one single verse in the Bible that would back them up. They tried, but the texts they pulled up never satisfied me. But here we were again with the text. What does the text say? In Japan, finding meaning from a sacred text was never an issue.

Traveling abroad was something I eagerly did in order to experience and understand other cultures. What part does religion play in shaping these cultures? How do cultures shape religion? As a student and scholar of Islamic Studies, I felt the need to know about the practice of other religions. I knew about Islam. I was born a Muslim, meaning my perspective on the world was shaped through the prism of the Qur'an. I wanted to expand my understanding—not depend solely on information from books, but to gather information from the experiences of people living their religion. I learned this well while in Japan.

I learned this in the States as well, but the experience wasn't as dramatic as it was in Japan. In addition, I didn't sense there was as wide a cultural gap between Egypt and America as there was between Egypt and Japan. In Egypt, we have all the American movies, all the European styles, but we don't have much Japanese influence. I soaked up as much Japanese culture as I could, and even learned to eat Japanese food.

To an Egyptian, Japanese food initially appears gross. Egyptians are used to meat such as shish kebab, a dish that is inherently greasy. Japanese food is not at all greasy. It doesn't smell the way I was used to having food smell. Japanese people like the delicate scent of their food. In due time, I got over this initial repugnance toward their cuisine. I saw Japanese people enjoying, even relishing, their meals. I said to myself, "These people are not stupid. There must be something to what they're enjoying." Gradually, I learned to appreciate the aesthetic dimension of Japanese food. I even began to imitate my hosts' way of eating, paying close attention to the table setting. It's colorful. In addition, the distribution of colors within the food shows an artistic flair. Over time, I learned to savor food with my eyes, not just my tongue.

It's a mark of honor and respect when you, the guest, are offered raw fish in Japan. It's equivalent to an Egyptian or a Saudi slaughtering a lamb for guests. People are bringing you the best they have. Raw fish needs to be fresh. Sitting in the refrigerator for more than an hour makes raw fish unacceptable to present to a guest. And when the host serves up this fish, the meal itself is like a ceremony. There's music involved. Colors must be compatible. There's a protocol that everybody follows. It's the way Japanese people eat. And when they drink a little too much, they start to sing. Then they cry. I enjoyed it all—especially their tears.

Over the years I taught in Japan, my students and I bonded. Even though in their day-to-day living, they were not demonstrative of their feelings toward me, I was always keenly aware of their affection. When I arrived at the airport on my way home to Egypt after my four years in Osaka, I found out just how strong this bond of affection was. Common courtesy dictates that university officials receive you when you arrive in their country and accompany you when you leave. You are their guest. They even carry your luggage. What came as a surprise to me was that all of the students in the department—one hundred of them over the four years I taught there—were waiting at the airport for me, ready to give me a royal send-off. They stood in two lines in front of the gate area where I presented my passport to Japanese officials. The whole airport began to get a little jittery. What was happening here?

Much to my delight, the students had made a gigantic paper heart. Each of the students had signed it and had written one sentence in Arabic. I still have that heart, although it is in Egypt. They also sang a song—a Japanese farewell song—while I was going into the gate area. I had to stop. Everything seemed to stop at the airport. It was as though I were leaving my own country. I had given a lot to these Japanese students, but in the process they had given me so much more. Later, I ran in to some of these students in Germany and other parts of the world. They'd come up to me and say, "You don't remember me, but I was your student when you taught in Japan." My heart would feel as though it were about to burst.

I did find some similarities between Japan and my own traditional culture. In the Egypt of my childhood, we used to sit on the floor. We did not use chairs, just cushions. We also used the kind of toilet that was just a hole in the ground—the same kind used in Japan. A friend of mine came to visit me while I taught in Osaka. He was unable to sit on the floor or use the toilet. He asked me, "How do you manage?"

"It's just like my childhood," I answered. Even though I am quite heavy and sitting on the ground, tucking my legs underneath me, is quite a feat, it was familiar to me. It's the same posture we Muslims assume when we pray. In many ways, I was much happier learning in Japan than I was in the States. Not a day went by in the States when I wasn't homesick. Homesickness was not even a small part of my experience in Japan.

Nevertheless, visiting both the States and Japan enriched me in ways that would not have been possible had I not ventured outside the borders of my own country. My perspective widened as a result, giving me valuable insights that have found their way into my writing.

8 Ebtehal

When Ebtehal and I fell in love and married, it was as though the ship I had been sailing in all of my life had finally found a place to dock. Ever since my father's death in 1957, I had felt like an orphan—alone and bereft. Circumstances forced me to think continuously about my family's welfare, something that took most of my time and energy. I spent little time focusing on my own needs. And then one night in 1992, with Ebtehal by my side, I finally released all the grief I had stored up—grief I had kept bottled up since the day of my father's funeral when my relatives and friends were so concerned about my stiff upper lip. As Ebtehal's love encompassed me, I wept. I had been unable to shed those tears for twenty-five years.

When I married Ebtehal, it was my second marriage. My first marriage happened in 1981, shortly after I returned to Egypt from my two years of study in the United States. I was thirty-eight years old. I should have been married much earlier, according to traditional Egyptian standards. My mother, along with other members of my family, exerted considerable pressure on me to tie the knot, and I eventually gave in.

A tragedy hit our family while I was in the States. Badriyya, my elder sister, died. She was not quite forty years old. It tore my mother to pieces. She became depressed. She wept openly. The first thing she asked me when I returned to Egypt from the United States after our two-year separation was, "When are you going to marry? Your brothers and sisters have all married and settled down. What about you now?"

I had finished the job of raising my siblings. My mother thought I should settle down and establish my own home. She had a young woman in mind. She saw no reason not to go ahead with a wedding.

I had no interest in getting married immediately after returning to Egypt. I tried to buy some time. I told my mother, "People don't get married in a month's time, even two months' time. It's not that simple."

When I lived in Philadelphia, I had fallen in love with Janet, an American girl who was extremely proud of her Greek heritage. She worked as a secretary at the University of Pennsylvania, where I was studying. We enjoyed one another's company, sometimes talking and discussing things into the wee hours of the morning. Our relationship never became physical. We never even kissed. I did propose marriage, though. She turned me down.

"Even though I love you," she explained, "this will not work." She knew I wasn't all that comfortable living in the States. And I knew I still had a lot of things to learn and many more things to see. All that potential learning and adventure would have probably taken a backseat had we married. She showed a remarkable maturity when she said, "If we allow this relationship to develop, both of us will suffer. I don't think I would be able to live in Egypt and I don't believe you would agree to live with me in the States. Besides, I know you have a job to do back in Egypt."

We remained friends. When I left the States to return to Egypt, I told her I would write. I did. She said she would send me postcards occasionally. She did. I saved them all. She stopped sending the post-cards when I married in 1981.

Falling in love with Janet broadened my understanding of court-ship and marriage. I experienced firsthand how these rituals vary from culture to culture. Now that my family began pushing me toward mar-riage, I couldn't help but contrast my courtship with Janet in the States with courtship and marriage in Egypt. In Egypt, to marry someone you are not in love with is no catastrophe. It is enough for each family to know the other and to have approved the union. After that, commu-nity support generally provides sufficient glue to keep a marriage intact.

I discovered that in the States, dating is a means of getting to know a woman. Initially, you have little information about her and even less about her family. Courtship becomes a give-and-take, a dance between two people. I found that I liked this process of discovering the charac-ter and personality of a woman before deciding about marriage.

As my mother kept the pressure on me to marry, I thought about how much I would have preferred to go about courtship and marriage the way I discovered it could be done in the States. When my wedding seemed like a done deal, I told myself that traditional marriage isn't always such a bad thing. I could adjust. I had known Ahlâm, the woman who was soon to become my wife, for some time. She worked at Cairo University with my sister Karima. Karima and I met with Ahlâm and her family, and everybody agreed that our getting married would be an excellent way to go.

I wanted to be honest with Ahlâm about my feelings. One day when we were alone, I spoke quite frankly with her. "Look," I said, "we are going to get married. I'm not sure it will work. I suppose love can develop between us, but if at any time, you feel that this marriage is not working, please tell me, and I promise to do the same with you."

She seemed puzzled when I told her that I could not commit to her forever. "We cannot speak about an everlasting future," I said repeatedly. She was twenty-eight years old, a traditional young woman with little life experience. She wanted to get married. "Nice" would be the best way to describe her.

I talked about love, about commitment, about human nature, and about change. I wanted her to know where I was coming from. She simply stated, "I don't understand what you are saying."

I replied, "To put it simply, I have every intention to love you."

"But I already love you," she declared.

"Yes, thank you very much," I answered. "But how do you love me? What do you know about me?"

Looking back on the whole scene, I believe the idea of getting married made her happy. I don't think the identity of the groom would have mattered much to her. She was eager to assume the role of wife.

I kept telling her, "Love is not something that is guaranteed forever. There is no such thing. Love is like a dream. It could die." I continued to assure her that I would do my best to make this marriage work.

We went to Japan in 1985 after I accepted a position as visiting professor in the Department of Arabic in Osaka University for Foreign Languages. We lived together in Japan for four years. Problems developed between us. In Egypt, problems could be diffused more easily. I had my friends. She had her family. But even so, when we lived in Egypt, she resented the time I spent with my students. "Your students are more important to you than I am," she'd complain. In addition, we never had children. As far as I know, she could have borne children, but when we consulted a fertility specialist in Egypt after we had married a while, we discovered my low sperm count was the reason we remained childless.

I remember the doctor asking me, "Where do you work?"

"I am a professor at Cairo University just like you," I told him.

The doctor was clear and to the point when he spoke to us. If we were determined to try to become parents, the way forward would not be smooth. He said, "This is a long, dark, and very expensive road. The medicine costs a lot, and in the end, there are no guarantees." University professors in Egypt do not earn a lot of money.

I remember my mother asking me, "When are we going to have the prince?"

Many people in Egypt, even educated people, assume that the woman bears total responsibility for a couple's childlessness. I didn't want anybody—especially my family—to blame Ahlâm for our failure to produce offspring. I was blunt with my mother. "You are not going to see a prince from our union because medically I am unable to have children." And I left it at that.

To tell you the truth, I have never been ashamed, nor have I been sorry, that I could not sire children. By the time I married in 1981, I felt that I had already raised my children—my younger siblings. They eventually grew up. I felt as though I'd been a father for years, and frankly, I was tired of assuming a parental role. I really didn't want to go that route again. I explained all this to Ahlâm. Perhaps a dog or some other kind of pet would help fill what she perceived as a void. I offered to release her from the marriage. Perhaps with another partner she would conceive a child. In the end, though, the idea of being divorced was just too much for her. We stayed married—at least for a while.

While we were living in Japan, it became clearer than ever that we lived in two distinct worlds. That bothered me. As I was writing my book, *The Concept of the Text: A Study of the Sciences of the Qur'an*,[1] I asked Ahlâm to type the manuscript. (Computers had not yet become commonplace.) She did. She typed the manuscript, but she did not read it. Because she did not engage the text as she typed, she made many careless mistakes along the way. I had hoped that through her typing the material I had researched and was currently shaping into a book, a door would open and we'd find some mutual ground for discussion. It didn't work as I had hoped. We did visit several museums and historical sites together. She appeared to enjoy herself on these outings, but nothing she saw in these places ever interested her enough to delve more deeply into the subject. She preferred to spend her days shopping.

We were together alone. Life became increasingly tense and difficult. I did not want to live like this. However, I continued to plod along—adjusting myself the best I knew how to our mutual disappointment. When we returned to Egypt in 1989, the problems we experienced in Japan continue to flare. The glue that had sealed our traditional marriage was losing its adhesive quality. The edges were fraying, and our life together was coming undone.

Once back in Egypt, I threw myself into my duties at Cairo University. I supervised a large number of students. Ahlâm became jealous of the time I spent with them as they worked towards their M.A. and Ph.D. degrees. She accused me of behaving in inappropriate ways toward certain students. She named several. All of them were women. They were beautiful as well.

"Look," I explained, "these students are like my daughters." Some of them were brilliant. We enjoyed hearty discussions. These students were extremely polite and respectful to Ahlâm. After all, it wouldn't do to be disrespectful to the wife of your professor.

Ahlâm and I began to drift even further apart. She traveled with her family to the beach. She expected me to accompany her. "No, I cannot spend so much time away from the university," I said, "I have my students and my research."

"No, no, you should act like a proper husband and come with me to the beach," she said. Inevitably, an argument would erupt.

Finally I told her, "Look, I am wearing myself out trying to explain to you my role with my students. It's not what you think. I have been a father all my life. These students are like my daughters, nothing else."

Ahlâm just didn't get it. Her family tried to help smooth things out. "How come after ten years of marriage you cannot settle down with him?" they'd ask.

We separated, but continued to live in the same apartment. Cairo has a severe housing shortage. Living together, but apart, seemed the practical thing to do. For some reason, neither of us could or would initiate divorce proceedings.

In the Arab world, it is very easy to live separately, but together—all the while giving the appearance to your family, your friends, and your colleagues of a happily married couple. But this kind of life got old very quickly. It was within this context that Ebtehal and I came together. The year was 1991, two years after we returned to Egypt from Japan.

Ebtehal and I had met before 1991 on several occasions. She was an assistant lecturer in the French Department of Cairo University. She had gone to France. I went to Japan. We were colleagues. Cairo University, in 1991, agreed to host a big conference on Tâhâ Husayn, the illustrious Egyptian pioneer of modern Arab thought. Ebtehal was a member of the organizing committee of the conference. I was a participant.

Most male university professors in Egypt treat women, especially women on organizing committees, as their servants. With supercilious condescension, they'd repeatedly ask Ebtehal questions such as "Where is the bathroom?" or "Do you have an extra pen?"

Ebtehal could hold her own ground quite well. "Don't ask me!" she'd come right back at them.

At this point in my career, I had been to hundreds of academic conferences. I knew to keep papers, pen, and certain books on hand. I had no need to bug Ebtehal or anybody else for supplies. When I got to know her better, she told me that because I did not hound her for directions and supplies, she sat up and took notice of me.

About this time, my name was becoming well known in Egypt. The first edition of my book *The Concept of the Text: A Study of the Sciences of the Qur'an*, was published in Cairo in 1990. Books I'd written about the Mu'tazilites and Ibn 'Arabi had been published in Beirut, but it was my book on the Qur'an, published in Cairo, that enjoyed a good reception—at least initially. Every couple of weeks or so, I had an interview with a newspaper or magazine reporter. So, during the conference on Tâhâ Husayn, Ebtehal had expected me, a professor in the university and an up-and-coming author, to be just as demanding as most of the professors. She attended my lecture at the conference. Afterward, she asked for a copy of my lecture. I gave it to her. And that was the end of it—at least that's what I thought at the time.

At the conclusion of the conference, we held a ceremony honoring the legacy of Tâhâ Husayn. In order to make the event a truly festive occasion, the organizing committee had planned a dinner party, a cruise along the Nile. It was all quite pleasant. Ebtehal and I bantered back and forth as we stood on the deck, looking at the stars. Her wit meshed quite nicely with my own.

Shortly after the conference, Ebtehal phoned. "I have read a newspaper article about you. The reporter interviewing you said, 'a great thinker, but still young.' Yes, I will agree you are a great thinker, but young? Hardly. That's an exaggeration. Great thinker? But of course. Young? No way!"

I liked her style. We became good friends. After she had finished reading the copy of my lecture, she visited me at my office. She had written a few comments in the margins of the paper, comments that acted as springboards for further discussion. We began to see one another more frequently while going about our teaching responsibilities at Cairo University. My domestic problems did not let up.

I lacked courage. I admit it. Ahlâm and I had been married ten years. We were living in the same apartment (I have never owned a house), but we were not together. We were separated. In Egypt, nobody notices if a husband and wife separate unless they make it a point to tell folks.

Because I had recently returned to Egypt from Japan, I had some money saved up. I bought a new apartment—a bigger apartment—and Ahlâm and I moved in together. She thought that as long as I was buying and furnishing a new apartment, our life was safe from disruption. Since we had shared four years together in Japan, I felt that she was entitled to part of whatever money I had made while living abroad. When she realized that what I really wanted was out of the marriage, she was astonished. "Why?" she asked. "We have a new apartment."

I finally found the courage to say, "We have a problem, and this problem is not going to resolve itself. You have your world. I have my world. There is no common meeting ground. I'm sorry. This is the way it is."

The decision to divorce is a serious undertaking in Egypt—not just for the couple, but for their families as well. In our particular case, our problem was never made public. I never spoke about Ahlâm with my family, nor did I speak about her with my colleagues. It is unfortunate but quite common in Egypt for men to speak openly about the "stupidity" of their wives. I never did. It's not my way. Nobody knew about our problems except her family. As far as my colleagues knew, I was the happiest husband in the world.

I desperately wanted to speak to Ebtehal about my feelings for her. Immediately, I censored that thought. "No, no, don't do this to her," I said to myself. "She is young. She is like your daughter. No, no, don't do it." But, as we rubbed elbows during the following semester, we found ourselves growing closer and closer, day after day, week after week.

At times, Ebtehal would ask me, "Why do you seem unhappy? We know you don't have problems, but in spite of that, you look unhappy. What is wrong?"

"It has nothing to do with my life now," I lied. "It has to do with some unhappy events in my childhood. The problems always seem to be there, close to the surface."

Occasionally, Ebtehal would visit us in our apartment. Ahlâm knew her. When Ebtehal's father died, Ahlâm and I paid our respects to the family. Ebtehal became a family friend, the kind of person that Ahlâm welcomed into our circle of friends. Since she did not consider Ebtehal to be a beautiful woman in the popular sense, she expressed no jealousy toward her, as she had done with some of my students. Ahlâm was not able to see in Ebtehal what I clearly saw—the beauty and strength of her character.

Ebtehal's friendship nurtured me, taking me into all sorts of interesting places. Here was a woman I could talk with about ideas, about concepts—about life. I didn't want to damage this friendship by saying something out of turn. I didn't dare show my cards. I determined to be satisfied with enjoying our friendship and to forget about anything more than that. But it didn't work out that way.

One day Ebtehal and I were waiting for some friends just outside the gate of Cairo University. They were late. We were on our way to a function of some sort. It was autumn, a lovely time to be in Cairo. We were bantering back and forth as we usually did when I said, "It's very strange, Ebtehal. You have many friends, but you are not married or even engaged. Is that right?"

"Yes, that's right," she said.

"Very strange," I offered, "that you have not yet married."

"Do you have someone in mind?" she asked. "Are you now a matchmaker?"

"Probably," I said.

"OK," she replied. "Put your cards on the table."

So I did. "What about somebody like me?"

"Somebody like you, or you?" she asked.

"Me," I meekly responded.

"OK. I agree," she said.

"I'm not joking," I told her.

"Who said you are joking?" she asked.

"Do you mean that? If you don't mean that, take it back." I could hardly believe she was serious.

"Yes, I mean it," she said.

"But you know that I am already married," I reminded her.

"I know. I also know that you are unhappy and I know that you are separated."

"How do you know that?" I asked.

"Look, we have been friends for a year now, and I think I can read you. I know that you are unhappy. I visited you at home. I've met your wife. She's a nice lady, but I know that you are unhappy." Ebtehal had read me right.

That was it—it took just a few moments. The year was 1992. It all came out on that bright autumn day in front of the university gate. "There must have been an underground current flowing between us for some time," I said. Did I really think this was news to Ebtehal?

"Yes, yes. I wondered why it took you so long to tell me," she mused.

"Maybe it's because I think I don't deserve you."

In spite of the fact that we were (and continue to be) intellectually well matched, I felt as though I didn't deserve her. She is fifteen years younger than I am—the same age as Ayat, my youngest sister. I raised my sister. She is like a daughter to me.

I suddenly felt old. It wasn't so much a matter of chronology. I felt as though I had accumulated enough experience in my forty-nine years to fill several lifetimes. But here I was, just having confessed to being head over heels in love with a woman who was not my wife. It was the push I needed to initiate divorce proceedings. Even so, initiating such action was hard.

I approached Ahlâm, explaining that the time had come for us to divorce. "I promised I would tell you if and when I thought our marriage was not working out. Now is the time. I have fallen in love."

She asked immediately, "Who is it?" She rattled off a bunch of names. Ebtehal's name was not on the list.

Even though I wanted to keep the divorce low key, Ahlâm didn't. Her family understood my position. I bent over backward trying to be fair and just with the settlement. I legally transferred the new apartment and all the furniture we had purchased together into her name. She didn't ask for it; I gave it to her. And even though we split all the money I had right down the middle, Ahlâm grew angry and embittered.

Her sister told her, "Look, at least the man is honest. He didn't go sneaking around behind your back like so many husbands do. Divorcing you is a sign of respect. You have been his partner for a number of years and he has given you a generous settlement." This whole divorce thing was difficult for all of us.

I don't know if Ahlâm ever remarried. I lost touch with her. My divorce and remarriage happened in 1992. Ebtehal and I started our life from scratch. My trouble with Cairo University began in 1992 as well. I don't know how Ahlâm would have reacted to the scenario that resulted in my eventual exile. Would she have understood what was at stake? Ebtehal supported me through the trial, the animosity from fellow Egyptians, the charge of apostasy, the call for my death, and all the rest of the gory affair. But to say she supported me would be telling only part of the story. The case became our case, not just my case. We are partners. We weather things together.

The court's verdict that annulled our marriage wounded Ebtehal in a way that could not touch me. Since she was unable to attend the Fourth World Conference on Women held in Beijing, China, in September 1995, she sent a timely and poignant message to the group. She spoke about rape. She had been raped, she noted. Not physically, but nonetheless, it was a real and painful experience. "In order to punish my husband," her statement read, "Islamists attempted to deprive him of me—something they considered to be an object of pleasure." I was (and still am) angry about the court's meddling in our marriage. Ebtehal was deeply wounded.

Ebtehal has found ways to be productive while living with me in exile. She has published a number of papers in French and Spanish periodicals while living in the Netherlands. She works at home, developing her ideas. She has also participated in many conferences in France and Spain—even in Egypt.

While living in exile, Ebtehal applied for a full professorship at Cairo University. Under Egyptian law, it is possible to do this while on unpaid sabbatical. Professors in Egypt, upon reaching sixty years of age, are officially pensioned. However, they can continue at the university as professors emeriti. Professors who reach sixty years of age cannot teach undergraduate courses. Between sixty and seventy years of age, professors are limited to teaching M.A. and Ph.D. courses along with supervising M.A. and Ph.D. students.

The French Department granted Ebtehal the title of full professor. One of the remarkable things about her department is that all of the faculty members are women. Her department has supported her, keeping her well informed about developments there ever since we moved to the Netherlands. Her junior status made no difference to them—they included her in departmental discussions, keeping her abreast of new policies. She never lost her sense of affiliation with her colleagues in the French Department. This, of course, is completely opposite to my own experience with my department.

Recently, the chairperson of the French Department asked Ebtehal to return to Cairo University to teach for one semester each year. "You are now a full professor in your field, and as you know, according to law, the older professors cannot teach undergraduate classes, so please come."

Ebtehal hesitated. Ever since our exile, we have often talked together about how Ebtehal could best continue her own career. I never thought that giving up her teaching would be the best course for her to take. Just because I am no longer welcome to teach at Cairo University does not mean that Ebtehal should suffer the same fate. Initially—just after coming to the Netherlands—we were fearful that due to the dramatic circumstances surrounding our decision to leave Egypt, if Ebtehal had stayed on at Cairo University, an inaccurate message would have been sent to those people in Egypt eager to silence and censor me. If she had continued to teach in Egypt, we would have lived in separate countries. People would think we had separated, and neither one of us wanted to give that impression.

Ebtehal felt torn. On the one hand, she finds the classroom experience challenging and meaningful. It was difficult for her to suddenly be wrenched away from her students in 1995 after being immersed in the academic culture of the university for so many years. On the other hand, she did not want to leave me. Nonetheless, she agreed to teach French Civilization one semester each year. As much as I wanted us to be together, I never wanted Ebtehal to sacrifice her career because of me.

I enjoy the vibrant atmosphere of Leiden University. I have students and colleagues who keep me on my toes, engaged in academic pursuits. Ebtehal does not have those same benefits in the Netherlands. I thought the time was right for her to return to her teaching. I'm glad she accepted the offer to return to Egypt. She went back into the classroom in September 2002. We were apart for five months. I missed her. The timing was good, though. I had an invitation to go to Berlin's Institute of Advanced Studies on a fellowship, and I worked with other scholars at the Institute on Islamic and Jewish hermeneutics. I told Ebtehal, "I'm going to Berlin for six months and you'll be in Egypt almost as long. We are not really separated—just traveling along different paths for part of our journey together."

Even after spending over a decade together, we are still the best of friends. In fact, friendship is the most important aspect of our relationship. We want to keep it that way. We are both Egyptian, but our backgrounds are vastly different. Ebtehal comes from an upper-middle-class background. Her father was a diplomat. Her mother was a teacher and eventually became head of a school. Ebtehal was raised in what I call a regulated atmosphere—an atmosphere where daily life molded itself around Emily Post–type etiquette. There were right ways to eat, proper ways to dress, correct ways to sit and stand. I found it all very funny.

I, on the other hand, come from a poor family. Since my father died when I was only fourteen years old, I lacked a certain structure and direction that Egyptian fathers provide for their children. Experience became my father—the one thing I could count on to give me direction. Having the freedom to make mistakes is of course essential to the process that allows human beings to learn, develop, and (hopefully) eventually to thrive.

So, initially, Ebtehal struck me as rigid. I struck her as undisciplined. Gradually, we learned to adjust to one another's differences. She accepted a lot of my disorganized lifestyle. I accepted her need to go about things decently and in order. I tend to push rules to the breaking point. I believe rules eventually need to be broken. This paves the way for the establishment of new rules. Since life is in a continual state of flux, rules we create need to reflect that inevitable change. There is nothing worse than living in a frozen state of shoulds and oughts.

In spite of Ebtehal's need to follow certain social conventions, in other areas of living she is not conventional at all. Our marriage, for example. Her family was not eager to see us married for many reasons: the class difference; my previous marriage; my being fifteen years older than Ebtehal. And I can't rule out the element of surprise. Our decision to marry seemed to come out of the blue. Her family saw me as a happily married man. I never talked about my private life in public. Even after my divorce, my standard response when people asked what happened was, "There was no particular problem. It just didn't work." Always guarding against the proclivity of Egyptian society to blame the woman for a failed marriage, I would inevitably add, "It's not Ahlâm's fault. I have the utmost respect for her."

Ebtehal's family was extremely reluctant to bless our marriage. Ebtehal, though, did not agree with the stand they took. She has a fiercely independent spirit, one of things I most admire about her.

There were several paths that we could have chosen to take when all my difficulties started with Cairo University. For example, when the university refused my application for promotion to full professor, we could have just kept silent. After a period of time, I could have applied again. This is the normal procedure. This, of course, was not my choice. I felt I needed to speak out against what I perceived to be a gross injustice. Nonetheless, Ebtehal was my partner. It would not be fair to her to make this decision on my own. We discussed the situation at length. She was as determined as I to speak out. She said, "No, it's not just your promotion. It's the integrity of the academic institution that is at stake—an institution to which we both belong. If we keep silent, it would mean that everyone who comes after you will be punished." Any discouragement that I experienced due to her family's reluctance to accept our marriage evaporated when Ebtehal spoke so clearly from her heart.

These days, my mother-in-law and I are good friends. When she visits us, she tells her daughter, "I came here to visit Nasr, not you." Of course, she's speaking tongue-in-cheek, but it shows the complete turnabout she and the rest of her family have had with respect to our marriage. It never was any secret that my mother-in-law was dead set against our marriage. I understood. Never did I force my way into the family, but I did go to meet with one of Ebtehal's uncles before we officially tied the knot. After all, I was the groom. In traditional Egyptian society, the groom's responsibility is to go to the bride's family and ask permission to marry their daughter. Since Ebtehal's father had died, her uncle assumed a parental role. Ebtehal's mother was noticeably absent from this encounter.

Nevertheless, I presented myself to the family. It was all superficially polite. We had coffee. Her uncle said, "Welcome." A deadly silence followed. I figured I had nothing to lose so I jumped right in with both feet.

"OK. Let me quickly get to the point," I said. "You are angry. I understand. I have nieces. If one of them came to me wanting to marry a man I didn't like and said, 'I have decided to marry such-and-such a man,' I would be angry, too. There is a big difference, though, between your reaction to me and my response in a similar situation. I would be angry, but I would support my niece."

I felt I was on a roll, so I continued, "I'm not asking the family to love me. I don't need your love. I'm asking you to love your daughter.

That's all. Hate me as much as you want. It makes no difference to me."

Ebtehal's uncle quickly broke into my soliloquy. "No, no, no, we don't hate you. Please don't misunderstand."

"I'm using hyperbole here to drive home a point," I assured him. "I would just like you to support your daughter. We are not talking about a minor or even a student. We are talking about Dr. Ebtehal. It seems to me that you still think of Ebtehal as a girl. She is a professor at Cairo University. She has earned an M.A. and a Ph.D. degree, and you are not giving her free rein to decide whom she will marry?!"

Ebtehal's uncle shifted uncomfortably in his chair, but I was not finished. "Suppose this marriage fails? So what? The world does not guarantee us success. I believe Ebtehal has every right to take on this responsibility herself. Please convey to her mother and other members of her family that I love your daughter. I'm not asking for your consent, nor am I asking for your blessing. I'm not really interested in knowing just what it is that you object to. All I ask is that you stand behind Ebtehal."

In Ebtehal's family, tradition dictates that a huge celebration take place whenever people marry—perhaps with up to five hundred guests. Because her family does things by the book, Ebtehal's mother began making plans for a gala affair. Ebtehal and I wanted just a small ceremony with minimal frills. Ebtehal told her mother, "OK, go ahead and make reservations at the biggest hotel in Cairo, prepare to pay the costs, invite the people you'd like to have present, plan a big party. Unfortunately, Nasr and I will not be there. We are busy. He and I have made other arrangements." Her mother got the point.

We married in an understated fashion. After the ceremony, which took place in the mosque, the family would not even talk to me. In spite of that, I never wanted Ebtehal to sever ties with her family. Neither did she, even though they would not give me the time of day. She'd phone her mother when we happened to stop in Cairo to see our mutual friends and she'd take the time to visit her family, but always without me. I'm strong enough to take all of this nonsense. That's exactly what their shunning me amounted to—nonsense. I felt that eventually the rift would somehow mend, although at the time, I wasn't sure just how this would come about.

One evening Ebtehal's mother called to tell her daughter about the death of one of her aunts, her mother's sister. "Don't come," her mother advised. "We live so far from you." The car we drove at the time was unreliable, and we never knew when the thing would just stop dead in its tracks as we sped along the highway. There was a stretch of desert between our home and Ebtehal's family. Her mother was firm. "Don't come now. It will be dark soon. You can come tomorrow."

Ebtehal's face was ashen as she hung up the phone. "What happened?" I asked.

"My aunt died. My mother told me not to come tonight, so I will be going over there in the morning."

"Your mother gave you good advice," I offered. "It would not be safe for you to drive to Cairo alone at this hour." I dressed quickly and told Ebtehal, "I am going out."

"Where are you going?" She had a puzzled look on her face.

"I am going to Cairo," I replied.

"Why? And are you going to take the bus?" she asked. Bus transportation in Egypt is notoriously inefficient.

"I'll find some mode of transportation," I assured her.

"Where are you going?" she asked again.

"I believe I am going to your uncle's house to offer my condolences. Your uncle is your aunt's brother. Is that correct?"

"Yes," she said.

"Well, I know the man, so it is my duty to go to him at this time," I said.

"If you are going, I will go as well," she said.

"But your mother told you not to go alone," I reminded her.

"If you are with me, then I will not be alone. We will go together." She was getting excited.

I had never really been involved with the family since our marriage, so I'm sure Ebtehal's mother thought I would not darken the door of the house—even to offer condolences after the death of a family member. On such occasions, the women and men sit in separate places. Even so, Ebtehal's mother had an inkling that her daughter had not come alone when we arrived at her house. "Is Nasr with you?" she asked Ebtehal.

"Yes," Ebtehal answered, and told her the sequence of events that led to our coming together.

As is the custom, I sat with the men and expressed my condolences to her uncle. He then asked me, "Would you like to offer condolences to Ebtehal's mother?"

"Of course," I replied, "if she would like that." So I went to the women's room and expressed my sorrow regarding her loss. We spent some time together. Before long, it was time for Ebtehal and me to be on our way home.

This event was catalytic in mending the familial rift. After we had said our good-byes, Ebtehal's mother walked with us to the car, lingering along the way. It was as if she did not want the visit to end. The incident underscored to me the importance of supporting people during life-altering events. It would have been a shame not to take advantage of the opportunity to mend the broken fences that a time such as this offered.

9 My Teaching Journey

"Teaching is not a one-way trip," I tell my students after they've settled into the classroom on the first day of class. "In here you will need a round-trip ticket."

Teaching involves so much more than doling out information. Teaching and learning go hand in hand. Neither one happens in a vacuum. The teaching process requires that students be engaged. To me, the classroom is like a laboratory. The atmosphere must be open and free as students bring their questions and their arguments to bear on whatever material we cover. As we experiment and wrestle with that material together, they help me develop my ideas and refine my thoughts.

When I first started teaching at Cairo University, my students thought me strange. I didn't just lecture—the teaching method most professors use exclusively. I incorporated dialogue and discussion in my classroom. I wanted to know what my students were thinking. I wanted to hear what they had to say. In Egypt's authoritarian atmosphere—an atmosphere that spills over into the universities—my teaching methods seemed odd to them. Gradually, as they became more comfortable participating in the process, they opened up. Little tender shoots tentatively poked their heads through the stuff of our discussion, and before I knew it, love bloomed. I believe love is essential to education. If you do not love your students, you cannot be a good teacher. If your students do not love you, they experience difficulty learning. Although I have no biological children, I feel as though I have thousands of children all over the world—students I have taught over the past thirty years.

My adviser for my master's and Ph.D. theses, Abd al-Azîz al-Ahwânî, was my role model. He never gave me answers. He taught me by raising questions. And he never seemed to run out of questions. As I read and studied while working on the thesis for my M.A., I'd come up with ideas that addressed some of the questions he had posed. I incorporated that speculation into the draft of my thesis. We kept discussing and I kept working.

One day we were reviewing the work I had done so far when he said, "Go ahead, print this up, and bring me a copy in a couple of days."

Even though I was uncomfortable with his request—I didn't feel the thesis was at all finished—I did as he asked. He read my work. He approved it. But those hard questions he raised, the ones that I did not address in my thesis, rattled around in my head. I was not satisfied with my approved thesis. I felt the work needed more development, based on those difficult questions that my adviser had posed. I kept working. Every couple of months he would ask me, "Where are you? Where is your finished thesis?"

"I'm still working on it," I'd answer.

"But I've already approved it," he'd reply.

"But I have not," I reminded him. "Some of your questions challenge the basic argument. I have to be sure." It took me an extra year to get to the point where I felt the thesis passed muster.

Those days when I used to hang out in front of my father's grocery store, reading to my father's illiterate friends, vividly showed me that through the process of teaching, I learned. Back then, I was very proud of the fact that these men, my father's friends, needed me because they could not read for themselves. And yes, they did need me to get the text off the page for them, but they opened up the text to me, giving me insight and understanding. I never knew at what point they might interrupt my reading and get into a heavy discussion among themselves, grabbing and shaping into ideas those words which had suddenly taken on life for them as they leaped from the page. My students are not illiterate. Nevertheless, whenever material comes alive and malleable in the classroom through discussion with my students, I'm reminded all over again that the teaching process requires a round-trip ticket.

Much of my teaching at Cairo University focused on uncovering the ideological basis behind religious and political discourse. What's the agenda behind the rhetoric? Who stands to benefit? I developed this subject in my book *Critique of Islamic Discourse*.[1] This book became the catalyst that brought the charge of apostasy against me in 1992. In it, I criticized established Islamic institutions; therefore, I was considered dangerous by established religious, economic, and political institutions.

Bottom line, my conviction of apostasy had nothing to do with my views about the Qur'an. Challenging the monopoly of power and knowledge is what shakes up the political establishment. And my writing did just that—it touched the sacred cow of established power. I want religion to be freed from the monopoly of those in power. All of my books, including *Critique of Islamic Discourse*, emerged as a result of class discussions with my students. In a real sense, the classroom is a laboratory where ideas are born, nurtured, developed, and tested. It's a microcosm of contemporary society.

University education in Egypt is free thanks to the efforts of Tâhâ Husayn. I understand from my nieces and nephews, though, that there is very little teaching in the university these days. Instead, professors shout at students gathered in large lecture halls, telling them they will fail for sure. Those students who can afford to do so hire tutors to teach them privately. It's unfortunate. Nevertheless, I never took for granted the fact that the Egyptian people paid for my education. I consider it a gift. Teaching, to me, provides a way to give back to the Egyptian people what has been freely given to me. Paying back a debt, though, is just part of it.

Being pronounced a heretic by the courts barred me from doing what I loved doing most—teaching at Cairo University. When I could no longer teach there, something essential to who I am was wrenched away from me. Teaching Egyptian students infused me with life and energy. Showing them how to think critically and rationally was at the heart of my work. Without critical and rational thought, developing a better society—a society based on principles of freedom and justice—goes up in smoke.

Teaching is not something I do in order to persuade students to see things from my point of view. Dogma and propaganda have no place in the academy. If I were to use the classroom to dogmatize and propagandize, I would be cutting off the path that leads to the future—a future I would like to see come about as a result of the free flow and discussion of ideas in the public sphere. I feel I'm part of a chain of intellectual development. Knowledge will develop after me—work that will be done by my students. The fact that I am no longer a part of this process in Egypt is the cause of so much of my pain. Egypt is my mother. I love her. I care about her welfare.

I remember one of my students in particular. Ahmed was a fundamentalist, accused of being a member of the *jihad* group who assassinated President Anwar Sadat in 1981. He went to prison for a time. But even though Ahmed had graduated with high marks from the university, the university did not appoint him as an assistant lecturer, something customarily done for the top students. He took his case to court. And he won! (This happened in one of the universities in Mansûra, not Cairo University. Mansûra is a city located in the Nile Delta.)

When I returned to Egypt from Japan in 1989, several professors were readying to take leave, just as I had done in 1985. Returning professors like me had to oversee those M.A. and Ph.D. candidates who needed a supervisor. As a result, I had the job of supervising students who under normal circumstances would have belonged to other professors. One of these students, Ahmed, was working at Mansûra University, but due to a staffing shortage at Mansûra, he was forced to finish his M.A. and Ph.D. work at Cairo University. My department assigned Ahmed to me.

I knew nothing about him at first. I knew only his topic of interest—the linguistic theory of Ahmad ibn Taymiyyah (1263–1328), a great scholar from Damascus. Ibn Taymiyyah belonged to the Hanbali School, one of the most orthodox schools of Islamic thought. He believed everything in the Qur'an and *sunna* (sayings and actions of the Prophet) could be clearly understood by applying a literal understanding to the text. Understanding the Qur'an metaphorically or applying rational thought in order to derive meaning from the text went against his belief system. He also rejected the concept of a created Qur'an.

Ibn Taymiyyah lived during the Mongol invasions, a time of great social upheaval in the Muslim world. Many Mongols converted to Islam but kept their own code of living—a code not in keeping with accepted Islamic practice. Ibn Taymiyyah, as many Islamic leaders have done, fused religion with politics as a way of wielding power during a time of great change in society. There were those who opposed him, of course. According to legend, Ibn Taymiyyah is reputed to have said,

"If they imprison me, I am in solitary [like a pious mystic]. If they kill me, I am a martyr. If they force me into exile, I wander in the land of God." He inspired much of modern Islamic fundamentalism. The topic of Ahmed's thesis interested me.

Cairo University had sent letters to graduate students affected by professors going abroad or taking sabbaticals. "Because the professor supervising your work is not available at this time, you have been assigned a new supervisor." My name was on Ahmed's letter. He made an appointment to come and see me one morning. I was sitting in my office when the secretary of the department came in and said, "Ahmed is waiting for you. He seems terrified. He's even whispering verses of the Qur'an to himself. I have never seen him like this."

"Who is Ahmed?" I asked.

"He is the student who was assigned to you after his supervisor took leave," she answered.

"Why is he so afraid?" I asked.

"I'm not sure, but he has a very long beard. He is an Islamist," she replied.

Then I understood. He was an Islamist and he was going to be under my supervision. At that time, there was no case against me, but I had a reputation regarding my ideas on Qur'anic interpretation.

"Should I show him into your office?" she asked.

"No," I answered. "I will go out to meet him."

I left my office, walked over to the reception area, and said, "Hello, Ahmed." Based on the secretary's description, I knew I had identified him correctly. "Would you like to walk around the campus? I want to stretch my legs."

He agreed, and as we were walking, I said, "Look, Ahmed, you have been transferred to me to be your supervisor, no doubt against your will. Take your time. Think about it, tell me which supervisor you would like to work with, and then let me make a suggestion to the department."

He immediately protested my suggestion, but I interrupted him. "No, no, don't say anything now. Take your time," I said. "We don't have to rush. You are just at the beginning of your work. You have every right to be comfortable with your supervisor. This right may not be recognized in our system, but it is your right nevertheless. Let me see what I can do as far as getting you a different supervisor. Which professor would you like to work with?" I gave him my home phone number. "Just call me and let me know. I assure you I will go about your transfer in a proper manner."

He became more and more agitated as he vehemently protested my suggestion.

"Are you sick?" I asked.

"No, no, I am tired. I think I'll go home to Mansûra now, get some rest, and think about it." Mansûra is about a two-hour bus ride from Cairo.

One week elapsed before he called me. "Have you come to a decision?" I asked.

"No, I would like to come and meet with you again," he said.

He came, and I took him on another walk around the campus. I didn't want him to be sitting in my office. I felt it would be less formal and a lot less threatening to Ahmed if we went somewhere other than my office. I didn't have a private office, but shared space with many other people. I was hoping, too, to make Ahmed feel a little special. As we walked, he said, "Professor Abu Zaid, I would like to work with you."

I was somewhat surprised. "OK, if that is what you would like. But, I must be up-front with you. Please understand that it's not my job to convert you or sway you from your own convictions. My job is to make a scholar out of you."

I explained to Ahmed that I took no issue with whatever religious or political convictions he held. He had every right to come to his own conclusions. But under my supervision, I would expect him to do research. I explained that a researcher does not choose standpoints to begin with. Only a missionary does that. A researcher begins by asking questions based on his or her scientific research. Researchers are human beings. All human beings perceive knowledge through a particular lens. As the researcher looks through that lens, gaps become evident, and this is where a focus of study can emerge.

Scientific research means having an effective method of squeezing information from references and sources, categorizing and arranging it according to its importance, analyzing it in its historical and social contexts in order to discover meaning. Any conclusions the researcher comes to are by no means final. Methods of research and tools of analysis and criticism constantly change and rapidly evolve. Stagnation in a society happens when knowledge freezes. That's why it's so important to train new generations of researchers where knowledge can always be reforming and evolving.

"I will not accept a thesis in which you make Ibn Taymiyyah a hero or an inspired genius," I continued. "I know he's a source of inspiration for people who think as you do. I believe Ibn Taymiyyah is a great thinker, but he is not the best thinker in the world. If you'd like to be a scholar, then great, I'll agree to be your supervisor, but if you'd like to be a preacher, find somebody else."

"I would like to be scholar," Ahmed assured me.

We worked hard. Just as I had been taught to do by Abd al-Azîz al-Ahwânî, the professor who supervised my theses, I brought tons of questions to our meetings and plopped those questions down in front of Ahmed. I never answered those questions. Ahmed would read, think about what he read, discuss it with me, and come to some tentative conclusions about Ibn Taymiyyah. Over time, Ahmed's zeal for this scholar ebbed. He realized that the man had no brilliant, innovative, or original ideas. Ibn Taymiyyah brought nothing new to the study of Islam. He knew Islam well, but like most traditionalists, there was nothing creative about his work.

Ahmed finished his thesis. I was quite pleased with it. What made me even happier was that much of Ahmed's biased thinking melted away as a result of applying critical and rational thinking to his study. The next step involved choosing a committee to discuss the thesis. (In Egypt, we have adopted the French system to evaluate M.A. and Ph.D. candidates.) I rounded up a professor who specialized in linguistics and theology.

Graduation Day came. The ceremony is public. The university prepares a large hall to accommodate the huge crowd that comes to the event. During Ahmed's graduation ceremony, the hall bulged with fundamentalists. The men sported long beards. The women completely covered themselves—even hid their faces behind veils. Some of my colleagues, noting the makeup of the audience, made jokes about the scene, even asking me, "Did you bring us here to be assassinated or what? What's this all about?"

I reminded my colleagues that they had read Ahmed's thesis. "You know he is a scholar. It shouldn't matter what he looks like." But, frankly, as I looked out over the audience, I thought the scene strange. All those beards and all those veils!

The only woman in the audience who did not cover was Ebtehal. Ahmed's wife sat behind Ebtehal. She cradled her newborn baby in her arms. During the program, Ebtehal realized that Ahmed's wife wanted to feed her baby. No way could she take her breast out and feed the baby in public. So Ebtehal asked her, "Would you like to find a room in the department where you can feed your baby?"

As Ebtehal escorted her to a suitable room, she asked Ebtehal, "You are Professor Abu Zaid's wife, right?"

"How did you know?" Ebtehal asked. Of course, Ebtehal was the only woman at the graduation ceremony who was not covered. It could not have been difficult to guess. "Yes, I am."

Ahmed's wife began talking nonstop, telling Ebtehal how much Ahmed talked about me to his family and how truly happy Ahmed had been working with me. "Ahmed's parents would like very much to meet your husband," she added.

Meanwhile, in the ceremonial hall, some of my colleagues were making fun of Ibn Taymiyyah right there in front of the whole audience, asking Ahmed questions such as, "Do you think that Ibn Taymiyyah was really all that good in Arabic? Look at his writing style. It's awful. What do you have to say about this style? Certainly looks like somebody who has not mastered the Arabic language." And they'd laugh out loud. Ahmed stumbled about, attempting to give a coherent answer. I wish he had said that what we have in the text is not the actual writing of Ibn Taymiyyah. Ibn Taymiyyah lectured while other people took down his words. How can we judge the man's Arabic based on the documents we have, since all we have is his recorded speech? In spite of this, Ahmed was given a grade of Excellent. I was very proud of him.

I met Ahmed's father after the ceremony. He was elderly—seemed quite pleasant. "Ahmed is your son," he said.

"No," I replied. "Ahmed is your son. He is my student. You are his father."

The elderly man disagreed. "No, he really feels as though he is your son. I am grateful to you and Mrs. Ebtehal for taking such good care of him. Thank you."

"We were happy to do so," I said sincerely. "But tell me, what do you think about all that has been said here today?"

I was referring specifically to my final comment during the ceremony where I commended Ahmed's work, reiterating for the sake of those in the audience that scholarship is not about agreement or disagreement with any particular point of view—exactly what I had told Ahmed at the outset of our work together. "Ahmed," I continued, "is a serious scholar, researched his material meticulously, and reached certain conclusions I don't think he really wanted to reach."

By the time Ahmed earned his M.A. degree, the case against me had become public.

"Well, Professor Abu Zaid," Ahmed's father said, "a lot of people don't understand where you are coming from. They think you are against Islam. After today, I can see that is not the case. You are not against Islam at all."

After Ahmed had been awarded his M.A. degree, he had to make a proposal for his Ph.D. He wanted to continue studying the work of Ibn Taymiyyah and do some work with the Wahhabis. Muhammad ibn 'Abd al-Wahhab (1703–1792), the founder of Wahhabi ideology, established with the collaboration of Muhammad ibn Sa'ud, the prince of Dar'iyya, a theocratic state in central Arabia. Wahhabism became Saudi Arabia's official state ideology. It's the most conservative of all the schools of thought within Islam.

I wasn't thrilled with his direction. "Well," I said, "there has been a lot of research done about Wahhabism. If you were to visit Saudi Arabia, you would see thousands of theses about the Wahhabis. Wahhabism is a good topic, but I think it's more appropriate for an M.A. thesis." I suggested some topics for him to consider and then said, "I do have a topic in mind that might work well for you, but I'm not sure you would agree."

"Which topic?" he eagerly asked.

"Hermeneutics of the Shi'i," I replied. He was visibly shocked. He began to tremble. I thought he might even start to whisper verses of the Qur'an to himself, as he had done just before meeting me for the first time. After he gathered himself together a bit, I said, "OK, you are not my student. Go search for another professor to supervise your Ph.D. thesis." I was serious. "If you react to a topic—just a topic—by falling apart at the seams, you are thinking about Shi'i in terms of deviation. You do not demonstrate that you are able to think about Islamic tradition in its totality regardless of your own personal convictions. No, I will not supervise your Ph.D. thesis on Wahhabism."

Both Shi'i and Sunni, the two major branches of Islam, anchor themselves firmly in the Qur'an. Nevertheless, each branch, because of specific historical events surrounding succession of leadership after Muhammad's death, interprets the sacred text differently. I thought Ahmed would benefit tremendously from looking at how the Shi'i community does its hermeneutics or interpretation of the Qur'an. Shi'i compose only about twenty percent of all Muslims. Iran is predominantly a Shi'i state. There are some Shi'i communities in India and Pakistan as well.

Muslims have always struggled with the question of who should rule the *umma* (community of believers). Muhammad's charisma enabled him to unify the people in the Arabian Peninsula, but after he died, a crisis developed. Muhammad's close companions succeeded in putting Abû Bakr (c. 570–634) up as the first *khalîfa* (caliph, a successor or deputy) from 632 until his death in 634. The term *khalîfa* has a strong religious connotation. The Qur'an refers to King David as someone whom God made a *khalîfa* (or vicegerent) on Earth (Sura 38:26).

We cannot pinpoint a specific date for the emergence of the Shi'i as a separate group. Shi'i ideology developed over time. The political conflict between the two houses of the Prophet's tribe, the Quraysh, is convoluted and difficult to follow. Without getting too mired within the story, we can begin with the third caliph, 'Uthmân ibn 'Affân, who held the office from 644 to 655. 'Uthmân made the first canonical edition of the Qur'an—he belonged to the cousins' branch of the Prophet's tree. 'Uthmân's nepotism eventually got him killed, and then 'Alî ibn Abû Tâlib (the Prophet's cousin and son-in-law) became the fourth caliph (656–661). Conflict emerged between the supporters of 'Uthmân and the supporters of 'Alî. 'Uthmân's followers accused 'Alî of being involved in 'Uthmân's assassination. But at this point, there was no Sunni and Shi'i division.

Mu'âwiya ibn Abû Sufyân (from 'Uthmân's family) fought 'Alî's claim to rule the Muslim community, resulting in the creation of three distinct camps: the Shi'i, literally "the supporter of someone"—in this case 'Alî; the Mu'âwiya camp (Mu'âwiya ruled from 661 until 680, establishing the Umayyad Dynasty, headquartered in Damascus); and the Khawârij, literally "the outsider." The Khawârij excluded themselves from both of the other factions.

Not all Muslims accepted Mu'âwiya's leadership. To many Muslims it felt as though the caliphate had been hijacked and transformed into a monarchy. The Abbasids, headquartered in Baghdad, later succeeded the Umayyads, taking on the monarchical trappings just as their predecessors had done.

When 'Alî became caliph in 656, he moved his headquarters to Kufa, Iraq. He and his followers continued to fight for their right to assume power within the Muslim community. 'Alî eventually became recognized as the first *imam* (leader) of what came to be known as the Shi'i branch of Islam.

'Alî had two sons. Al-Hasan, the elder son, succeeded 'Alî, but Mu'âwiya, the first Umayyad caliph, prevented him from assuming power. In his attempt to keep things on an even keel and avoid bloodshed, al-Hasan gave up his right to the caliphate. Al-Hasan's younger brother, al-Husayn, was next in line to lead the community. Al-Husayn and some of his followers traveled to Iraq, a strategy intended to confirm al-Husayn as the new leader of the Muslim world. While en route, they were ambushed by an Umayyad force that annihilated them. Al-Husayn became a martyr. You can see his shrine in Karbala. The Shi'i community commemorates his death by torturing themselves and chanting, "We left him alone, we did not support him and we are now paying the price." The real tragedy here is the fact that the Prophet's grandson had been killed by fellow Muslims. Perhaps this can be called the beginning of the Shi'i movement. From a political standpoint, we begin to see the emergence of two distinct factions, supporters of 'Alî (Shi'i) and supporters of Mu'âwiya (Sunni).

The Shi'i community gradually developed a specific ideology. According to Sunni understanding, the Prophet did not leave any indication as to who should succeed him. The caliph should be from the tribe of Quraysh, but not from a specific house. According to Shi'i understanding, the Prophet nominated 'Alî as his successor. 'Alî was initially deprived of his right to succeed the Prophet by the usurpation of Abû Bakr, Umar ibn al-Khattâb (the second caliph), and then 'Uthmân. This is a major ideological difference between Sunni and Shi'i.

Another major difference deals with a theological understanding. According to the Shi'i, the Prophet had two kinds of knowledge: the knowledge that he delivered to the people in seventh-century Arabia, and a deep reservoir of knowledge that he could not convey because the people were unable to receive it. This deep level of knowledge has been inherited by the imams. 'Alî was the first one to inherit this gift, followed by his son, and from then on, all the imams who have belonged to the house of 'Alî have inherited this deep knowledge. That's why in Shi'i theology the imam has authority. This authority comes from an inner knowledge inherited from the spirit of the Prophet. According to Sunni understanding, there is no inherited knowledge. Knowledge is acquired, and the community of believers plays an important role in selecting those who rule.

The Shi'i believe in what is known as the disappearing imam. Whether this is the seventh imam or the twelfth varies among the Shi'i. The Shi'i have what we can call a messianic vision, but of course, they do not use this terminology. When the *imam* returns, the world—currently bogged down with injustice—will suddenly be made right. Justice will seep into every corner of the world. In the meantime, the Shi'i community needs to do nothing but wait for the *imam*'s appearance. Activity on the part of human beings to bring about complete justice would be ineffective anyway. Best to keep hands off. Given this theology, the Khomeini revolution in Iran becomes understandable. Khomeini gave authority to jurists (those who determine laws based on the Qur'an and the *sunna*) to act as *wilayati faqîh* (vice *imam*).

Between the tenth and fourteenth centuries, Egypt was a Shi'i state. I find it quite funny when I hear that a secret Shi'i organization has been uncovered or discovered in Egypt. I like to say that the Egyptians are Sunni by ideology and Shi'i by emotion. That's why we have so many shrines for both males and females of the 'Alî family. In Egyptian society, on a popular level there is no distinction between Sunni and Shi'i—the distinction exists on an ideological plane. We all love the Prophet's house. The Shi'i have a unique theory of hermeneutics because of their view of the *imam*'s function—an infallible guide and intermediary between God and the believers.

A few weeks after I spoke rather brusquely with Ahmed, he came to me with a Ph.D. proposal that was quite good: the hermeneutics of the Zahirites. When interpreting the Qur'an, the Zahirites relied exclusively on a literal understanding of the text. They believed the text sufficed to explain itself. I think, though, that by saying, "I don't need knowledge except for the sayings of the Prophet and I don't need rational thinking," the job of interpreting text becomes much more complicated than it is for those who use a variety of methods and theories to understand the text. If the Qur'an says everything, a scholar must find everything within the text, without help from other sources. The text becomes its own source. My assumption was that the Zahirites used a complex linguistic method to interpret the Qur'an. The moment you begin with an autonomous text, you need a sophisticated linguistic methodology in order to derive meaning from that text.

Ultimately, I don't know what happened with Ahmed's academic career. I left Egypt shortly after our brief discussion about his proposed Ph.D. dissertation topic. I like to think that he made a thorough investigation. Certainly the examples he presented to me initially reflected the complexity of the Zahirites' linguistic method. Ahmed's job was to research and study in order to determine the coherence of the particular linguistic method they used.

Working with a student who shared my vision and ideas would have been a breeze. Rarely do those kinds of winds blow in an academic setting. I'm not convinced that working with such a compatible student would necessarily be a good thing. I see the challenge of education like this: How do I convey to my students that academic scholarship is not about agreement or disagreement? It has everything to do with research and the creation of knowledge. I firmly believe that this is the heart of education. Education involves being a troublemaker—perhaps "gadfly" expresses the idea better—as I challenge my students, pushing them to think hard and deep. Education does not mean applying a more sophisticated language to old ideas, a common practice in the Arab world.

I don't believe in secluding myself in an ivory tower—something many professors do. There they sit, pristine and pretty, never thinking or caring about what effect their ideas might have on people's lives. They are convinced that the world of ideas can easily be separated from the world of experience. This is nonsense.

When God decided to reveal Himself to human beings, God humanized Himself, breaking through a barrier in order to have contact with ordinary people living on the Arabian Peninsula during the seventh century. The Qur'an, God's spoken Word, gives us instruction on how to go about this business of living. Following God's example, Muslims have traditionally broken through societal barriers and impediments in their quest to establish a just and equitable society here on Earth.

One of my students said, "Professor Abu Zaid, you stay in this polemic mode of discussion by always talking about the text—about how the Qur'an is our reference, our only reference."

"You are right," I said. "We cannot disclaim our sacred text, the Qur'an. It's our paradigm. What's important to keep in mind is that the Qur'an is just that—our paradigm. We have no business claiming it to be absolute truth."

I appreciated this student's critical observation. I hope succeeding generations of scholars will be able to create their own paradigms. Are we ever able, though, to get out from under any kind of model in order to get our ideas across? I'm not sure.

I suffered when the Egyptian court handed down its verdict declaring me an apostate. I'm still experiencing fallout from that verdict. I live in exile. I've missed my family back in Egypt. The heaviest loss, though—the loss that causes me untold agony—is that I no longer can teach Egyptian students. At this point, no compensation would be possible. Even if there would be the unexpected department apology filtered down from the top authority of Egypt, it wouldn't be enough. I've lost years.

Sometimes Ebtehal, trying to ease my feelings of loss, will say, "You are not being fair to yourself. I visit Egypt. You don't. It's evident to me that you have students whom you have never even seen. They know you from your books." Several people have told her as much.

I'm happy that students have access to my ideas through my writing. But the admiration of students is not the same thing as working to develop a school that opens the way to the future through the creation of knowledge. I'm not the first one by any means to have suffered such a loss. I'm thinking especially of Professor al-Khûlî, but there have been others who have gone before me—others whom the system has tried to silence. I'm concerned about the future of Islamic Studies. At the present time in Egypt, there is no research in Islamic Studies being done. It's all about preaching.

How to ask a question, how to question something before accepting an answer, how to look at the answer in a critical way—all of these things need to be part of the modus operandi of a scholar. Scholarship is not something we find much of in Arab countries these days—especially in Egypt, where the situation has gone from bad to worse. Nowadays in Egypt, there is no discussion about the Qur'an except within the established or orthodox framework of al-Azhar. Al-Azhar as an institution was founded in the tenth century by the Fatimides, a Shi'i dynasty which reigned in North Africa and then in Egypt from 909 until 1171. It has evolved into the most important Islamic university in the Sunni world. There are no symposia unless al-Azhar sponsors, supervises, and controls the gathering. Outside the orthodox box, there is no thinking officially allowed.

Education in Egypt remains stagnant. If new thought peeks out through the academic soil, the old guard plucks it from that ground before it has any chance to take root. Education in the university consists of lecturing students about what has been already said. Sometimes the language is a bit different, perhaps a couple of new vocabulary words are thrown in here and there in an attempt to spice things up, but fundamentalist and traditionalist thinking don't become useful in contemporary society by merely varnishing the vocabulary of emerging disciplines on them. This is a huge problem throughout the Arab and Muslim world.

How do we integrate the modern world with our spiritual values? Reformers and political leaders have struggled with this question for years. Muhammad 'Abduh (1849–1905) attempted to bring new insights into the meaning of Islam while integrating modernity (democracy, scientific agricultural practices, women's suffrage and education) into Egyptian society. How can some kind of fusion take place without compromising our identity as Muslims? That's the question.

Muslims came to view the West—first Europe and then America—like this: We need modern science and technology to live in an ever-changing world. Science is a pure kind of knowledge, devoid of any spiritual or ethical values. Importing technology is all well and good, but when it comes to those values that define our humanity, we cannot accept what we see offered from the West. The Qur'an and the *sunna,* our sacred text and traditions, are more than sufficient to show us how to live good and decent lives.

Muslims made a clear distinction between the products and technology that emerged from the West's application of scientific thinking and the scientific thinking itself. It was like saying, "I can borrow your technology, I can borrow your science, but I'm not interested in the thinking behind that science and technology, and I'm certainly not interested in the way you live your life—your lifestyle." But it wasn't quite that simple.

Europe was a puzzle to Muslims. Most of the time, Muslims came into contact with the West by way of foreign occupation. By the end of the nineteenth century, the British had successfully colonized much of India. The French, under Napoleon Bonaparte, occupied Egypt in 1798. France then went into Algeria in 1830 and occupied Tunisia in 1881, and Britain marched into Egypt in 1882. There were many other excursions as the West's program of colonization unfolded throughout the Muslim world.

Some Egyptian reformers and political leaders thought it feasible to become part of Europe. Others balked at such an idea. All this upheaval in a traditional society took its toll. Imagine what it must have been like to see a group of French soldiers—all dressed strangely, odd-looking as well, publicly keeping company with women. Egyptians (and other colonized people) were impressed with much of what the West could offer: libraries, printing presses, and machines that worked with precision. Europe was advanced and strong. But the ever-present downside was that Europe consisted of the occupiers—the enemy to fight against. But how do we go about fighting something that we benefit from? Can we not be devout Muslims and still enjoy the fruits of scientific technology? 'Abduh tried to come to terms with this paradox.

Then came a tremendous change. Turkey (Ottoman Empire) had been the headquarters of the Islamic world, the cradle of the caliphate, ever since the fourteenth century. The caliphate is a system of government—office and institution—that governs all Muslims. The caliph was first and foremost a political and military leader. However, to be considered a legitimate ruler, the caliph was responsible to safeguard *shari'a* and those trained to interpret *shari'a* law. Turkey, under the leadership of Mustafa Kemal Ataturk (1881–1938), adopted a secular state based on a nationalistic ideology. Turkey abolished the caliphate in 1924, sending shock waves throughout the Muslim world. Even though the caliphate no longer functioned as it had in Islam's earlier history, the institution was still a symbol of unity in the Muslim world. Its abolition created an emotional reaction among Muslims.

Muhammad 'Abduh had desperately tried to balance tradition with modernity. Muslims, though, after losing that symbolic seat of power—the caliphate—felt stripped of their identity. Many blamed the West for this loss. Without the caliphate, it felt like they were returning to the age of *jâhiliyyah*, commonly understood as the Age of Ignorance, although Age of Ignorance does not cover the term adequately. *Jâhiliyyah* refers to the pre-Islamic era—a time when the tribal code of behavior took precedence over acting according to one's own conscience and applying rational thinking to a situation.

Hasan al-Banna (1906–1949) also attempted to bring a solution to this tension between tradition and modernity. As noted earlier, he founded the Islamic Society of Muslim Brotherhood in 1928. This organization appealed to ordinary citizens. By 1948, the membership was in the millions. Al-Banna saw the value of Western science and technology. He was well aware that Egypt's institutions were in dire need of reform. He believed that spiritual renewal, based on Islamic heritage, was an essential part of the whole equation of reform. With this in mind, al-Banna instituted many social reforms—built schools, factories, and hospitals, and even founded a modern scout movement. Most significant, though, was that the Brotherhood looked for ways to reestablish the caliphate.

There were political leaders who believed that the Muslim world had no chance to catch up with modernity as long as Muslims held on to Islam. Since Islam seemed to be such an impediment to the modernization process, just get rid of it. 'Abduh responded by saying, "Yes, Muslims are backward, but we are not backward because we are Muslims; we are backward because we don't understand Islam. If we look at our heritage, we could recapture what Muslims did during the seventh, eighth, and ninth centuries, when Muslims ruled the world." The problem, as 'Abduh saw it, was one of understanding Islam properly.

Later on, as the modern world kept encroaching on Muslims, traditionalism took hold. A shift in thinking came about. Yes, we are backward, but not because we are Muslims; it is because we are not Muslims anymore. This makes a difference. The solution, then, is to return to the real Islam. How can we get back to this real Islam?

Many factors played a part in shaping the path Muslims took in their attempt to regain their identity as Muslims. A big factor was the discovery of huge reservoirs of oil in Saudi Arabia, bringing wealth and prosperity not just to Saudi Arabia but to the hordes of people (professors, intellectuals, teachers, and others) who flocked to the Arabian Peninsula in search of a better way of life. I believe one of the reasons for Egypt's stagnation has much to do with the exodus of thousands of Egyptians who went to the Persian Gulf region to work in order to afford an apartment, a house, even a car once they returned home. While they labored in the Gulf area, they became acquainted with Bedouin Islam, an Islam that teaches you not to think. No need to think. Why? Because underneath Islam—our heritage—we have reservoirs of knowledge.

Oil-producing countries throughout the Arab world have become extraordinarily rich. How? Not through work, but by digging. Digging brings wealth. If you are not able to dig, hire somebody to do it for you. And wealth comes—it's as easy as that. Money pours in as long as oil spouts out. Why work? In much of the Muslim world, thinking is too much like labor, and folks just don't make the connection between work and prosperity. Just dig into the past. Uncover those solutions that lay buried. The *sheikh* or some other authority will interpret the find. No need for you to put forth any effort.

This is not the legacy of Islam. We have a long history of theologians and philosophers, concerned with political issues, going to the Qur'an to find solutions for present-day problems. We don't do this anymore. We find our solutions not in the Qur'an or in the *sunna*, but from digging up the understanding our ancestors had of the Qur'an and the *sunna*. And it doesn't work. Every generation needs to bring the sacred texts to bear on current problems and discover their own solutions. Today, to think something different from the conclusions our ancestors made is blasphemy, heresy, and apostasy.

This is where we Muslims find ourselves today. Our teaching institutions no longer function as places to debate ideas—one of the ways human beings go about the business of creating knowledge. Without new knowledge, new perspectives, a culture cannot go forward. When I contemplate Egypt's future, it causes me no small degree of anguish.

10 A Decent Return

Every Egyptian I know longs to be buried in Egypt's soil. I've told Ebtehal, though, that if I were to die while still in exile, not to return my body home for burial. As a result of having been officially declared an apostate by the Egyptian courts, I feel as though my mother has rejected me. How can I rest peacefully in her bosom after she has treated me so unjustly?

Shortly after going into exile, I visited an American university in the state of Washington. An Egyptian attending the symposium asked me, "Are you serious? Did you really tell Ebtehal not to return your body to Egypt for burial?"

"Yes," I answered.

"Every Egyptian must be furious with you," he said.

"You are thinking of Egypt as a graveyard," I immediately responded. "I think of Egypt as home."

I have never wavered from my initial position—not to return my body to Egypt should I die outside her borders. My decision was reinforced in 1998 when Nizâr Qappânî, one of the great Syrian poets, died. Although he died in London, he had been living in semi-exile for the last thirty years of his life in Beirut, Lebanon.

In 1998, the Muslim world was celebrating the eight hundredth anniversary of the death of Ibn Rushd (1126–1198), known as Averroes in the West. His books were burned and he suffered the indignities of being condemned as a heretic. I've always thought of Averroes as a man of enlightenment, a man who found fertile soil for his own growth in the West, not in the Muslim world. The first paper I published after leaving Egypt was about Averroes. To whom does Averroes belong? Who is his biological mother? My point was that he was born Muslim and perhaps he is the child we abandoned, having forced him into exile.

When Qappânî died, his body—as is the custom—was carried to the mosque for funeral rites, but the entourage was forced to a complete stop before they could enter the building. Islamists stood shoulder to shoulder just outside the mosque, blocking the way, not allowing his body inside the sacred space because he was declared *Kâfir*, or atheist.

Qappânî could perhaps be described as the quintessential poet. He wrote about love, about women, and about physical beauty. Because he wrote in the common, everyday language of the people, his poetry was easily understood by folks, and therefore widely read. A book of his poems could be found under the pillow of every girl—at least that's the popular legend. Some Muslims consider poetry to be antithetical to religion. For Islamists, poetry—especially Qappânî's poetry—is obscene.

When I saw all this commotion around Qappânî's death, it reinforced my decision not to have my body returned to Egypt should I die outside her borders. After all, Qappânî had been labeled an apostate. So had I. I would not want Ebtehal to face a situation similar to the circumstances surrounding Qappânî's burial. Of course, barring my body from the mosque may not be something that would even happen in Egypt, but somebody might write an article asking, "Why was the body of this man (Abu Zaid) allowed to return to Egypt? He is an atheist." I want to spare Ebtehal this indignity. I know how hurt she would be.

Even though Ebtehal has traveled freely back and forth between Egypt and the Netherlands ever since 1995, I have not been home at all—even for a brief visit—except just recently, a two-week period during December 2002 and January 2003.

Ironically, I am still a professor at Cairo University, having received the title of full professor two weeks before the final verdict that declared me an apostate. (In 1996, divorce proceedings were suspended by court order. My apostasy conviction remained.) So, officially, I am a professor in the Department of Arabic, Faculty of Arts, Cairo University. Every year, I renew my leave. Every year, I pay into my pension fund.

In spite of my official title giving me the status of full professor, all of my books have been removed from Cairo University's library. An Egyptian journalist contacted me, not long after I'd gone into exile, when he discovered that my books were missing from the library's shelves. "What do you make of this development?" he asked.

My response was one of disbelief. "I don't believe you. You are lying just to get some kind of statement from me. I don't believe that Cairo University would do this."

By accusing him of lying to me, I thought I had insulted the journalist. Fortunately, he did not take my initial, knee-jerk response to his probing personally. He actually seemed quite appreciative of my reaction, taking it all in stride, assuring me that he was grateful for such an honest response. As the story unfolded, he told me that he had gone to Cairo University specifically looking for my books in the library, but did not find them. His attempts to interview the dean of the faculty were unsuccessful. The journalist published the conversation he had with me. The title of his article was "Abu Zaid has full confidence in his university. His university has none in him."

Ebtehal was furious that my books had been removed from Cairo University's library. During her next visit to Egypt, she went to the university, insisted on a meeting with the dean of the faculty, and confronted him with the fact that my books were no longer available on the library's shelves. "What is going on here?" she asked.

"It's appalling, but I have no idea who did this," he lamely confessed.

"OK, you have no idea who did this, so you order an investigation," Ebtehal said.

The dean refused to order an investigation.

"Are you telling me," asked Ebtehal, "that even though you don't agree with such action, you refuse to order an investigation? If books are removed from the library, you shouldn't just say, 'I don't know who did this' and leave it at that." Ebtehal was not shy about applying some pressure.

"Let me tell you something about Abu Zaid," she continued. "We are not talking about my husband. We are talking about Professor Abu Zaid. Why don't you just fire all the professors that gave him his M.A. and Ph.D. degrees? And while you are at it, why don't you just shut down the department from which he graduated?"

The dean stared straight ahead. Silence filled the room.

Frankly, I was delighted that Ebtehal had engaged the dean in such a conversation. If I had phoned people at Cairo University about the disappearance of my books, I wouldn't have known how to say what I wanted to convey. Ebtehal succinctly got to the point.

My books were removed from Cairo University's library in 1995. Even though my books are not banned in Egypt—you can easily purchase them in any number of bookstores—they remain out of circulation at Cairo University, and officially, nobody knows anything about how my books disappeared into thin air.

A few years ago, some intellectuals started to write letters and articles in the newspaper asking questions such as "When will Abu Zaid be back?" And then adding, "We need someone like Abu Zaid. Censoring him like Cairo University did is a crime against the institution." This renewed effort by the people to incorporate me back into the academy came after I had been on a number of TV programs in Lebanon as well as in Egypt. The Egyptian people were beginning to question the charges leveled against me. Apparently, on TV I did not come off like an apostate at all.

Reporters from newspapers and periodicals interviewed me as well. My colleagues and friends would often say, "We need you. Why don't you come back to Egypt?" I responded to this renewed interest in my case in a published interview.[1]

"I'm ready to go back," I remember telling Ebtehal, "but I need to make a decent return." I explained to the Egyptian people that my first visit back to Egypt after such an extended absence didn't warrant any fanfare, nor was I asking for a change in the court's ruling. That was beyond anybody's authority at Cairo University. But why couldn't I be invited to be a member of the jury to evaluate the M.A. and Ph.D. theses of students whom I had supervised? This would be an official recognition that I am still a professor of Arabic and Islamic Studies at Cairo University. I needed the university to act in a way that reflected this reality.

I have many friends in the Department of Philosophy at Cairo University. I told them, "I am willing to pay my own way. If you invite me to participate in some official function, I will come. All I need is twenty-four hours' notice. Just make my first visit back something that will make me proud to say that my university invited me to take part in an important public function. After this first visit, then we'll see. But isn't it time to break the ice?"

Four years have passed since I made this offer. I know there was some effort on the part of certain people within my department to re-connect me with the university. Nothing came of this effort. The hard truth that I need to face is that Cairo University doesn't want me. Certain individuals within the department, of course, have been friendly and supportive. The present chairman of the department is a close friend. We recently spoke on the phone. He told me, "We have extended your leave." This is the eighth year that I've been given an extension. According to the law, five years is the limit.

"Yes, yes, this is all very nice, thank you very much," I offered.

He continued by telling me how appreciative many Egyptian people are of my refusal to keep silent about the effects of corruption running rampant throughout the government—especially as that corruption evidences itself at the university level. "We are so pleased with all of your accomplishments while in exile."

"OK, I understand," I said. "But why is it impossible to invite me to be a jury member of a thesis committee?"

"No, it is not impossible," he quickly asserted. "It just so happens that there is no thesis that belongs to your field."

"Is that right?" I asked. "One of my students just graduated two weeks ago."

He acted shocked. "Really?"

"Yes, really," I replied. She had recently contacted me—even sent me her thesis, telling me, "I am very ashamed to send you my thesis. It is not the thesis I was hoping to write, but you were not there. Let's pretend it is a draft. I'm ready to rewrite it."

I said to the chairman of the department, "This is my student. The least the department could have done is to invite the ex-supervisor—me—to be a member of the jury. This is the normal academic tradition. I realize that it would be difficult to have me come to Cairo right now, but you are telling me that it is not impossible. I would like you to be up-front and honest with me. Don't make things look nice to me because we are friends."

My friend replied, "I'm sorry. This is a terrible university. This is a terrible department. You should be very happy that you are not here."

I get weary and frustrated when people obfuscate the truth. Be honest with me. Don't give me excuses. Don't give me this nonsense, saying, "There are security precautions and it is not possible for you to return to the university at this time." Ebtehal travels to Cairo every couple of months. Sometimes she visits her mother, but she also takes part in symposia and conferences at Cairo University as well as sitting as a jury member evaluating M.A. theses. It makes me sad to look down the road and see what seems to be an inevitable truth. I will never set foot again on Cairo University's campus unless it is absolutely necessary for administrative reasons—signing documents, for instance. I've stopped thinking that I'll ever have a decent invitation to take part in some aspect of academic life at Cairo University. After all, I'm sixty years old, the age most Egyptians are when they retire and start receiving their pensions.

As time goes by, I find myself more and more angry. Cairo University, an academic institution—one of whose purposes is to discuss and debate ideas—has failed in its mission. This sacred space no longer exists. It has evaporated, steamed away by a corrupt system of government. As a result, the Egyptian people suffer.

I've always guarded against playing a victim's role. So I was surprised to realize, not too long ago, that I'd been slipping little by little—imperceptibly—into the role of victim. I found myself depressed. I was waiting for Leiden University to decide whether or not it would offer me a permanent chair. I was waiting for Cairo University to incorporate me back into its academic life. Waiting . . . just waiting. And then it dawned on me. All this waiting around was siphoning off huge amounts of psychic energy—energy I could put to better use regaining a sense of control over my life. It was high time to maneuver a U-turn and begin to reclaim that power which I had allowed to slowly ebb away.

During June 2002, Ebtehal and I traveled to Istanbul to attend a workshop. It felt good to get away from the routine of work. Ebtehal asked me how I would like to celebrate my birthday. (My birthday is in July.) "I don't want anything, no present, nothing," I answered, surprising myself with my own irritability. But Ebtehal wouldn't take no for an answer, and I quickly wearied of her persistence. "Don't you understand? I don't want a present," I lashed out. Immediately, I felt ashamed. Here she was, trying to do something nice for me, and I reacted in such a foolish and stubborn manner.

"What is wrong with you?" Ebtehal asked.

"I'm not sure. I'm fed up with things. The future looks bleak. I feel as though my life is not in my hands. Ever since turning fourteen, I've felt as though I had a degree of control over my life. Not anymore. What has happened?" It all came pouring out of me. I had never spoken such words aloud before.

"Look at it this way," Ebtehal said. "You are angry because Leiden University has not given you a permanent chair, but you are a professor. You are known all over the world. Didn't you see the joy on the faces of the people you just spoke to in the workshop? Open your eyes. You are making yourself a victim. We are doing well. Your health is good. You've lost weight. Things are going well for us. Why are you so angry? You used to be somebody who accepted his life."

I had to admit that I felt as though the circumstances in my life had been pushing me around. "I need to be making decisions about what to do with my own life," I said. In spite of that assertion, I felt myself spiraling down into the vortex of a deep depression. After returning to the Netherlands from Istanbul, Ebtehal went to Egypt, returning a month later with her mother. Soon after that, Ebtehal headed off to Cairo University to teach for the fall semester. After she left, I became scattered—even desperate. I kept looking for the strong man I used to be. I grew fearful, afraid to be alone and sure that death stalked me at every turn. I went to the doctor and told him as much. I called Ebtehal two or three times every day.

"You are waiting for someone to take over your life," she said, "and you are the one who needs to take back your own life."

Yes, of course, that was it. It was time—time for me to take the proverbial bull by its horns. I would start by planning my own decent return to Egypt. The idea had begun to take root even before Ebtehal left for her semester of teaching in August. Why had I waited around, stewing about it, for so long?

In spite of having taken hold of the bull's horns, I vacillated with my decision to visit Egypt throughout the fall of 2002. Esther e-mailed me in December—the day before I was scheduled to leave for Egypt—sending me a draft of this book. I responded immediately, telling her about my travel plans. "I am leaving tomorrow for Egypt, and I am quite nervous." Besides Ebtehal and my immediate family, nobody knew. Telling Esther helped give me the courage I needed to follow through.

I did not wait for Cairo University's invitation for a decent return after all. What a relief to act on my own and plan the shape of my first visit to Egypt since going into exile in 1995. My initial visit to Egypt has renewed my strength, allowing me to better focus on the present. I returned in July 2003 to claim my pension and other rights my Egyptian citizenship entitles me to.

Living in exile has been debilitating—it's as though one of my veins had been slit. I've lost a lot of blood. I was unable to keep abreast with the children in the same way as if I had been in Egypt watching them blossom into maturity and middle age. But this visit did reconnect my slit vein with the circulatory system. The leaking has stopped.

My last evening in Cairo, I attended a dinner with many other guests, one of whom is a government official with considerable status. After talking with this official, it became quite clear to me that Cairo University will never invite me back to participate in the academic culture. I did have a reunion with some of my close friends, colleagues of mine. Visiting them has helped to connect me with the life I left eight years ago. Next time, I'll be able to see more of my friends. This was a short visit. I spent three days in my boyhood village, Quhafa; five or six days alone with Ebtehal along Egypt's northern coast; one day with her family in Cairo; and two evenings at semi-official dinners.

I wanted to be alone when I visited Quhafa. I didn't know it at the time, but Ebtehal was terrified when I left for Quhafa, leaving her behind in Cairo. When I returned to Cairo three days later, Ebtehal let it all out. "For the past two years, you have been talking almost nonstop about death. Then you decide it's time to visit Egypt. Once in Egypt, you of course want to visit Quhafa, but without me! What should I think? The only answer I could come up with is that you wanted to die in peace in your home village." She was visibly shaken.

"No," I assured her, sorry that she had gone through a wringer of sorts. "You came to an inaccurate conclusion. I just wanted to visit my village in peace—alone. That's all."

I had hoped to visit my elderly cousin, Sayyid. He's the man who became a father figure to me when my own father died. I didn't arrive home in time. Sayyid died on September 9, 2002. Ebtehal was in Egypt, about to start her semester of teaching at the time. She called me in Leiden the next day. I knew by the sound of her voice that whatever news she had to tell me was not good. "I hate to tell you this, but Sayyid passed away yesterday morning." Ebtehal became concerned when I didn't respond immediately. "Are you OK?" she asked.

"Yes, I suppose," I responded. And I left for my office at Leiden University. Later, well past midnight, I phoned Ebtehal. "I'm tired." That was all I could manage.

"I'll come back to Leiden. I've not started work yet," she said.

No, I couldn't ask her to do that, but something had happened to me. "I miss you very much," I told Ebtehal.

"Nasr, it's not that you are missing me so much. There's something more going on here. You've been orphaned for a second time," she said.

After I hung up the phone, I realized she was right. Here I was, a grown man, pushing retirement age, and feeling deep inside like an orphan. Anger tinged the sadness I felt—anger toward my mother, Egypt. If she had not abandoned me, perhaps I would have been able to help Sayyid as he helped me (and my family) so many years ago. Sayyid's daughter told me on my recent visit, "Don't feel sorry. His last days were filled with pain. If you could have seen him, you would feel nothing but relief that he had finally been released from his suffering." It was small comfort.

I did visit with my brothers and sisters (my children) in Quhafa. We had set this up to be a private reunion—no spouses; even Ebtehal was absent. I just felt as though I wanted to gather the children around me like a mother hen with her chicks, hold them in my arms, stroke them, and begin to fill in the gaping holes caused by our long separation. I was especially moved by Ayat and her ongoing marital difficulties—difficulties I knew nothing about until this recent visit.

Ayat married in 1981—not long after I returned to Egypt from the States. She and her husband soon had three children. Two of them are currently studying in the university. Once Ayat and her husband decided to marry, they pushed full steam ahead. I remember suggesting to Ayat that they wait: "Let's see how things develop between the two of you." Neither one of them, though, wanted to dillydally. They went forward with their plans enthusiastically—that's how it seemed to me. Frankly, though, I was uneasy with Ayat's choice. I felt that her soon-to-be husband insisted on having his own way all too often; he orchestrated every aspect of their lives. I remember telling myself at the time, "Don't judge your brother-in-law by your own standards."

So here I was in Egypt after an extended absence. Almost immediately, Ayat began to pour out her heart while crying on my shoulder. "On my first vacation back to Egypt from Saudi Arabia [Ayat's husband worked for years in Saudi Arabia], I really thought about divorce." Ayat returned to Egypt in 1982, some time after our mother died. Although I phoned her husband in Saudi Arabia, asking him to tell Ayat about our mother's death before they arrived back in Egypt that summer, he never found a way to convey the message. So she was not aware that our mother had passed away when her plane landed. As we sped away from the airport in the taxi, she asked me, "How is my mother?"

"Ayat," I said. "Your mother was very, very sick. She died." I took her in my arms while in the taxi as she wept.

As Ayat continued with her story, she told me she felt she could not follow through with her wish to divorce her husband back in 1982 because her mother had just died. "Where could I have gone?" she wailed.

Ayat returned to Egypt from Saudi Arabia for good some years ago, and her husband stayed on in the Arabian Peninsula to continue his work. She wanted the children to attend Egyptian schools. She felt uneasy with how intolerant Saudi schools were toward non-Muslims. After moving back to Egypt, her son came home from his first day of school terrified. "What has happened?" Ayat asked.

Her son had sat next to a Coptic child. In Saudi Arabia, a catechism is taught to children in school, beginning with the question and answer, "Who is your God? My God is Allah." Ayat's son had asked his new seatmate, the Coptic child, "Who is your God?" The child answered, "My God is Jesus." In Saudi Arabia, of course, this is blasphemy. So, Ayat's son didn't want to go back to school, telling his mother, "I sit next to a *kâfir*, an atheist."

As I reflect on it all, it seems to me that Ayat used her desire to have her children educated in Egyptian schools as an excuse to get away from her husband. She could not bring herself to directly tell her husband how disappointed and dissatisfied she was with their marriage. Ironically, he left Saudi Arabia soon after Ayat brought the children to Egypt because of the country's policy of Saudi-ization—the official push toward incorporating Saudi citizens into the many jobs that foreigners have filled since oil began spouting up through the sand.

Ayat, at this point, cannot see her way clear to break free from what she perceives to be the shackles that bind her to her husband. As a result, she feels helpless and desperate. I'm encouraging her to come back to the family and exercise a little more independence—not necessarily to get divorced. I let her know that we are ready to support her, whatever she decides to do. I think that ultimately she needs to make some space for herself and learn to rely on herself. That's what I have in mind when I encourage her to be a little more independent. Her husband continuously hovers over her. I had no idea how miserable she'd been for so many years.

I was glad I had insisted on meeting alone with the children. They all had their stories to tell. As I listened, I began to feel more in touch with what has happened in their lives. Ayat's story, though, touched me in a vulnerable place. I could identify with my sister's feelings of helplessness and despair. Wasn't I going through a similar period myself? Didn't I feel as if I had no control over where my life was going? By telling Ayat about the importance of taking responsibility for the direction her life took, I was in fact telling myself.

Shereen, the daughter who chose me, didn't seem all that pleased when she realized that I had met with the children alone in the village. "What was the wisdom in going at this alone?" she demanded. "Why didn't you take Ebtehal? And would the meeting have included me if I had been there? I get the feeling that you are treating me like a metaphor. Remember that I am still your daughter—a real flesh-and-blood daughter, like it or not."

Shereen had wanted to meet me on my arrival at the airport. With the exception of Ebtehal, I wanted nobody there to welcome me home. I wasn't sure how the whole scene would play out after my eight-year absence. "This has nothing to do with metaphor," I assured Shereen. "Of course, you are my daughter. I wouldn't have it any other way."

Arriving at Cairo airport felt rather odd. As soon as the plane landed, it seemed as though I had left Egypt only the day before. Surprisingly, I experienced no strong emotions of any kind. In spite of Egypt's reputation for bureaucracy, going through passport control and customs took only a few minutes. A customs official asked me, "Do you have anything to declare?" I simply answered no. He then produced a hint of a smile before saying, "Welcome back, Professor." I liked the sound of it.

I do believe that one day I'll be back in Egypt for good. I'll probably work at my home, receiving students who would like to communicate with me. I certainly do not foresee working in tandem with Cairo University in any capacity. I think I'll find it difficult even to have a friendly chat with some of my former colleagues.

But my recent trip home was all I had hoped it to be—a decent return.

11 The Nexus of Theory and Practice

When I do research as an Islamic Studies scholar, I painstakingly look for those things initiated by the Qur'an—ways of being and doing that did not exist before Muhammad received the revelation. When I find such phenomena, I take note. I delve into the text at this point, using this juncture to develop and steer Islamic thought. In so doing, I would say that I am moving in the same direction as the Word of God. I'm convinced that folks who think that everything mentioned in the Qur'an is binding, should be obeyed, and should be followed literally are going against God's Word.

It's important for me to have a handle on the direction my research takes. So, for example, with regard to punishment for crime, the destination we are after is justice. In order to establish justice, a society needs to punish people who commit crimes against that society. But the form of punishment mentioned in the Qur'an is a historical expression of punishment carried out by a specific society in a specific time and place—it is not a divine directive. Punishment for crime is a principle that, when carried out, establishes justice. Justice is a principle reflected in the divine, universal Word of God. Punishment is part of constructing a just society, but the form punishment takes is historically determined—it is not fixed.

Reading classical Islamic thought should be a critical exercise. What did our ancestors accomplish? What can we add or develop as a result of their accomplishments? Through my research and study, I've concluded that the Qur'anic objectives that jurists long ago agreed upon were deduced from the penal code alive and well during the seventh century on the Arabian Peninsula. The objectives were not deduced from looking at the paradigm of the entire Qur'an.

The first objective—protection of life—emerged from the penal code's prohibition of illegal killing. Retaliation, according to the Qur'an, is sanctioned only to maintain life itself. Protection of sanity was deduced from the Qur'an's directive to abstain from alcohol. Protection of property was lifted from the penal code's condemnation of theft and then incorporated into the Qur'an. Protection of progeny can be traced to sanctions already in place against committing adultery. Regarding the protection of religion, the Qur'an doles out no earthly punishment for people who turn their backs on Islam. Those who reject the faith after once accepting it, and remain defiant, will suffer in the life hereafter. Later on, the death penalty for turning one's back on Islam became established as a way to maintain political authority in a region.

The Qur'an contains the penal code. We call it the *hudûd*—all the verses that indicate specific punishment for certain crimes. I came to the conclusion that we need another reading of the Qur'an in order to make this particular manifestation of the Word of God meaningful in our present-day circumstances. If we look at the *hudûd* in a historical context, we find that these particular passages reflect a historical reality. They do not reflect Divine imperatives. For example, the killing for killing, the eye for an eye, stoning for adultery, the amputation of the hand for stealing, and death for changing religion—all this was in effect either before the Qur'an came along or instituted after Qur'anic revelation. The Qur'an did not establish this kind of punishment. If the Qur'an did not initially establish a punishment, we cannot consider it to be Qur'anic. The Qur'an adopted particular forms of punishment from pre-Islamic cultures in order to have credibility with the contemporary civilization.

Punishment for crime is a Qur'anic principle, but should a form of punishment, integrated into the body of the text from another source, be considered Qur'anic and therefore binding on the community of believers? We can say that the Qur'an leads us to understand that those who commit crimes should be punished. True enough, but the Qur'an contextualizes itself within accepted practices during a particular time. Contemporary society has every right—even an obligation—to institute more humane punishment for crimes. To do so in no way violates God's Word.

The Qur'an took a particular shape so that people in seventh-century Arabia would "get it." If we elevate historical aspects of the Qur'an to divine status, we violate the Word of God. God's Word becomes twisted when we freeze it in a specific time and space. The absolute Word of God goes beyond its historical context—this is what we want to get hold of. If anything spoken about in the Qur'an has a precedent in pre-Islamic tradition—whether Jewish, Roman, or anything else—we need to understand that its being mentioned in the Qur'an does not automatically make it Qur'anic, and therefore binding on Muslims.

What about slavery? Slavery as a socioeconomic system is mentioned in the Qur'an—it's a historical reality. Human beings have developed their thinking since the seventh century. Slavery is no longer an acceptable socioeconomic system in most parts of the world. How can we use the Word of God to legitimate a heinous system that human beings no longer generally practice? If we do legitimate such a thing, we freeze God's Word in history—but the Word of God reaches way beyond historical reality. Slavery is something that is not Qur'anic. Jurists, those folks in the Islamic world responsible for developing law, need to apply a healthy dose of critical thinking to their job as they go about the business of forming a just society—one that moves in the direction of the Word of God.

Another thing I have in mind when I do my research deals with discovering just what the ultimate objectives of the Qur'an really are. We learn, of course, from our ancestors. How did they go about deducing the meaning of the Qur'an? How did they read a text? To their accomplishments we add our modern disciplines of textual analysis, historical analysis, and hermeneutics.

Let's dig deeper into the subject of justice. This concept infiltrates all the passages of the Qur'an. "Just" is one of God's beautiful names. The Qur'an, when it admonishes people to avoid fraudulent practices, uses the image of a scale as a metaphor for justice. "Woe betide the unjust who, when others measure for them, exact in full, but when they measure or weigh for others, defraud them! Do they not think they will be raised to life upon a fateful day, the day when all mankind will stand before the Lord of the Universe?" (Sura 83:1–6).

Even the paradigms of the life hereafter are based on the concept of justice. The entire universe, the whole cosmos, is built on justice: "We shall set up just scales on the Day of Resurrection, so that no man shall in the least be wronged. Actions as small as a grain of mustard seed shall be weighed out. Our reckoning shall suffice" (Sura 21:47). Keeping things balanced—establishing justice—is spoken about over and over again throughout the Qur'an. Every story and each commandment are there with the intention to establish justice in a society. Justice easily emerges as one of the major objectives of the Qur'an.

The Qur'an took shape within Meccan society—an unjust society in many ways—where wealthy people oppressed poor people by charging them *ribâ* (usury). Why did the language condemning usurious practice have to be so strong? Mecca was smack dab in the middle of trade routes between the southern tip of the Arabian Peninsula and northern destinations such as Egypt, Jordan, Syria, and Turkey. Meccan citizens who enjoyed privilege and status became extremely wealthy as a result of trade. If poor citizens could not pay their debts, they were forced to borrow money from the wealthy (through usury) in order to save their own skins. There are many stories showing how the wealthy took advantage of the vulnerable in cities that dotted the trade routes in the Middle East. The Qur'an as a text emerged from the midst of this concrete and harsh reality. Usury, within the context of this particular reality, was used as an instrument that perpetuated injustice.

Why is the Qur'an so concerned about the orphans, the weak, and the poor? Muhammad himself was an orphan and poor. His father died before he was born. His uncle took him in after his grandfather died. He lost his mother when he was six years old. Because his uncle was so poor, Muhammad went to work early in his life. He belonged to the class of "have-nots" in a society where the "haves" flaunted their wealth, not caring an iota about the lives of people living on the brink or, as we say in more modern times, falling through the cracks.

The opposition to and harsh criticism in the Qur'an of the practice of *ribâ* stand in sharp contrast to the giving of alms—something the Qur'an commands as a path toward achieving socioeconomic justice. The two issues, alms and usury, are connected. The Qur'an gives us a nice image of those who give charitably, providing for needy folks without exposing them to embarrassment. This image stands in juxtaposition to the image of those who practice *ribâ*.

> God has laid his curse on usury and blessed almsgiving with increase. God bears no love for the impious and the sinful. Those that have faith and do good works, attend to their prayers and render the alms levy, will be rewarded by their Lord and will have

nothing to fear or to regret. Believers, have fear of God and waive what is still due to you from usury, if your faith be true; or war shall be declared against you by God and His apostle. If you repent, you may retain your principal, suffering no loss and causing loss to none. If your debtor be in straits, grant him a delay until he can discharge his debt; but if you waive the sum as alms it will be better for you, if you but knew it. (Sura 2:276–280)

During the past three decades, Islamic banks have been established all over the world, claiming to run on an economic system that practices no *ribâ*. But when it comes right down to it, these banks don't operate any differently than the existing banking system based on charging interest.

Many jurists (those responsible for enacting Islamic law) have ignored the circumstances surrounding the prohibition of usury. By ignoring the context of the Qur'anic position, the debate about *ribâ* has taken on a wooden character. The question has become focused on whether or not the financial transaction in the modern banking system, based on a fixed interest rate on both savings and loans, is actually *ribâ*. This misses the point. The Qur'an forbade *ribâ* because it was used to oppress the poor. *Ribâ* has entered aspects of Islamic law as an acceptable practice under some circumstances. Modern Muslim scholars do not consider interest, used today by the modern banking system, to be *ribâ*. Jurists who tightly grasp those solutions more appropriate to another age (seventh-century Meccan society) believe that interest of any sort is *ribâ,* and therefore inherently wrong.

No matter what subject the Qur'an talks about—the universe, the cosmos, nature, God and His activities, social life, or the life hereafter—justice is at its core. Justice gives shape to all of them. In light of the Qur'an's emphasis on justice, it's surprising to me that the principle of justice is absent from the list of agreed-upon objectives in classical Islam. Justice should be right there on top. If there were to be a conflict between justice and freedom, justice ought to prevail. I think that's why we find the principle of freedom in the Qur'an somewhat limited. Even with our more modern understanding of freedom, freedom as a Qur'anic objective must be couched within the primary objective of justice.[1]

Jâhiliyyah is commonly known as the Age of Ignorance in the West. The phrase "the Age of Ignorance" does not convey an accurate meaning of the term. *Jâhiliyyah* specifically refers to the pre-Islamic period, a time before Muhammad received Divine revelation. It refers to behavior based on the tribal code. The Qur'an condemns this code, a code insisting that members of the tribe comply with the group no matter what. (It's similar to the American expression "My country, right or wrong.") According to the tribal code of conduct, the individual has no voice. The individual is expected to follow the leader and obey blindly. The Qur'an condemns this, admonishing us to follow our own conscience, built not on the tribal code but on right and wrong, just and unjust, good and bad. Here we see the Qur'an coming up with something different, something in contradiction to the tribal code.

The Qur'an's language in reference to the Bedouin (tribal people who inhabited the Arabian Peninsula) is harsh. The word "Arab" is not even used in the Qur'an—just the word a'râb—a word synonymous with "Bedouin" and always used negatively. We can conclude from this that the Qur'an espouses a set of values and rules that is in direct contradiction to the Bedouin tribal code; therefore, the Qur'an considers the Bedouin tribal code jâhiliyyah.

Qur'anic values are built on the concepts of freedom and justice— freedom of thought in order to bring about a just society. So your tribe's going to war is no reason to think that you, the individual, must automatically go with them. In this way, Islam established a community, not a tribe—a community that went beyond the strictures of the tribal system. This was part of Islam: to establish a sense of community based on another set of values, another code. In order to establish this community, freedom is understood as a way to get out from under the stultifying practice of blindly following tradition, copying the past.

If you look at Arab and Muslim societies, you will see that most of the time no government has come to power by the choice of the people. You'll often find a military system in place, an archaic royal family at the nation's helm, or somebody who inherits power from his predecessor. Sometimes the new governing body takes a new name and puts on a modern appearance, but all you have to do is scratch the surface and you'll see it's the same old thing underneath. The tribal mentality is alive and well. The code is obedience. All our institutions— political, social, economic, and academic—have an authoritarian structure. Intellectuals have their own form of tribal behavior. You either belong to the right or belong to the left—you'd better not disobey the code of whatever intellectual tribe you belong to. It's a terrible situation.

For example, when the peace talks which led to the Oslo Accords began in 1992–1993, many intellectuals were in favor of establishing communication and cooperation between the Palestinian territories and Israel. People from the intellectual tribe—both the left and the right—

said they were in favor of peace. But, when two groups say they are in favor of peace, does that mean that both groups have identical views about a situation? Not necessarily. In spite of that, some members of the intellectual tribe believed that here was an opportunity to speak from a united front. No way did this happen. The group in favor of the Oslo talks called those folks who expressed some reticence about the talks stupid, retarded, and belonging to the old world. The reticent group shot back by calling their accusers traitors, using peace as a way to conspire with the "enemy" in order to wield influence and power. I was appalled. What kind of discourse is this? If we all claim that we are looking for peace and we, those of us within the intellectual tribe, are not able to tolerate different opinions among ourselves—well, it's very easy to despair.

I was about to write against this kind of tribal code of discourse—it was just before the Supreme Court decided on a verdict in the case where I was accused of apostasy. Mona, my lawyer, advised me, "I am not going to censor you. I know you are against any kind of censorship. You certainly have the right to write anything you want, but if you write something that has a political opinion, let me first have a look. I don't want anything to be used against you in court."

'Ali Shalaqani, Mona's husband, an intellectual Communist, thought it best if I not publish my article. He had gone through a lot of misery after he became a supporter of the peace accord. With the use of political language, he endured the accusation of political apostasy hurled at him from those in the political arena, no different in principle from being accused of apostasy in the religious sphere. If you disagree with the tribe, you are expelled from the tribe. I called Mona when all of this was happening to and around her husband.

"Look, Mona," I said, "I am not defending your husband or any member of his group in my writing. I am defending the integrity of our intellectual life. I may or may not agree with your husband or his group, but I cannot condemn them as political apostates. So I'll send you an article on this kind of crazy goings-on in the intellectual community."

"Listen," she said, "you are already condemned as pro-Western. Are you sure you want to make yourself even more vulnerable to name-calling?"

I think it was somebody in Jordan who said, "If you look to this man [Nasr Abu Zaid], maybe you'll find that his mother was Jewish."

I replied to this "accusation" with a huge amount of indignation. "You do not know what a mother is. Even if my mother had been

Jewish, she is still my mother. There is nothing wrong with being Jewish, but there is everything in the world wrong with being a stupid Muslim."

I refuse to play the tribal game. Consequently, I am one of those marginalized Arab intellectuals. Frankly, I take some comfort in being marginalized. I don't try to vote with the center because it's only from the margins that I feel I am able to threaten the center. If I were to be integrated into the center, I would not have much impact on the development of Islamic thought, and God knows, the Arab and Muslim world desperately needs to see the relevance of modern scholarship on individual lives and on societies.

When I applied my critical scholarship to the subject of women, I saw how well this subject nestled into the concepts of justice and freedom, two essential objectives of the Qur'an. The fourth chapter of the Qur'an is simply titled "Women." The opening verse tells us that God created a human being from one single soul, and from this one single soul, God created its mate, and from there, God created all humanity. "You people! Have fear of your Lord, who created you from a single soul. From that soul, He created its spouse, and through them He bestrewed [scattered] the earth with countless men and women" (Sura 4:1).

From this verse, we see the unity of human beings, of the human race. Male and female are created from one single soul. The Christian understanding of Eve, created from Adam's rib, has been integrated into Islamic thought—into the exegesis of the Qur'an—and so it became part of Islam. I am aware that Genesis gives two accounts of the creation of humanity, one of them being more in line with Qur'anic understanding (not the account where Eve emerges as a product of Adam's rib). But in the Qur'an, the chapter on women begins by establishing the unity and equality of human beings. There was one soul, and this one soul God divided into two, and from them, the whole human race came forth.

Let's consider polygamy, a subject not well understood even by most Muslims. Polygamy, historically speaking, was a popular practice in human societies long before the advent of Islam. It is a mistake to think of polygamy as part of the Islamic revelation. Yes, the Qur'an does address the issue of polygamy, but the verse so often used to legitimate polygamy is really addressing the issue of orphans who needed protection and custody after losing their parents in the battle of Uhud (625). Muslims lost ten percent of the army—seventy warriors—leaving many children orphaned. The historical context, as well as textual analysis, shows that permission was granted to marry a widow or a female orphan so that she would be protected and provided for in this particular society, a society that preyed upon widows and female orphans—often stealing their inheritance from them. Therefore, the Qur'an admonishes:

> Give orphans the property which belongs to them. Do not exchange their valuables for worthless things or cheat them of their possessions; for this would surely be a grievous sin. If you fear that you cannot treat orphans with fairness [giving them their inheritance], then you may marry other women who seem good to you: two, three, or four of them. But if you fear that you cannot maintain equality among them [within a marital relationship], marry one only or any slave-girls you may own. This will make it easier for you to avoid injustice. (Sura 4:3)

The syntax of the third sentence is conditional—if you are not sure that you'll be able to treat orphans with fairness, then you are allowed to marry two, three—even up to four other women. What is the text talking about? Justice is the goal, and the means to reach that goal in these particular circumstances comes through the practice of polygamy. Polygamy is used as a solution to establish justice. The plural "orphans" here is feminine. The focus is on doing justice for orphans. If that is not possible, there is a solution. Where does the solution come from? From pre-Islamic practice.

The Arabs living in the Arabian Peninsula of the seventh century mistreated orphans, denying them their rights. They took the orphans' inheritances and made them virtual slaves in the household. This was common practice. So the Qur'an asks, "OK, if you Arabs are so greedy, why don't you marry them?" Marriage brings about a whole new relationship. Marriage would be a means to bring about a more just society. The solution established by the Qur'an is not the same thing as establishing polygamy. It is using polygamy as a solution to a real problem in the seventh century, the problem of orphans. Polygamy was widely practiced already. So we cannot say that polygamy is Qur'anic law. It is not a law. It is a practical solution to a pressing, historical problem. Justice is the broader issue.

I've concluded through my research that the Qur'an does not favor polygamy. The Qur'an, in its attempt to establish justice, realizes that even if the Arabs chose the path of marrying orphans, the goal of justice remained out of reach. I don't believe I can conclude that the Qur'an is against polygamy—that would be jumping over history. The Qur'an recommends polygamy as a solution to a social problem. Since the Qur'an is not in favor of the practice, jurists in the business of establishing modern law would be wise to put tight restrictions around its use. This way, Islam will be developing societies in the same direction the Word of God takes: establishment of justice.

Given our present-day social circumstances, polygamy is insulting to women as well as to the children born into the family. I'm appalled that there is no discussion in modern Islamic thought about what effects polygamy might have on children. The questions have remained the same over centuries: Is polygamy allowed in the Qur'an? Is it legal? It's time we asked, "What about the children? What impact does the practice have on them?" We have to consider this first and foremost: The Qur'an is all about establishing justice in society.

When we look at other verses in the Qur'an about women, we should envelop them in the same context—justice. If certain practices in the Qur'an appear to be contrary to this concept, the context can usually explain it. For example, the beating of wives. It is mentioned in the Qur'an—it cannot be ignored. So the thinking goes like this: If beating is mentioned in the Qur'an, I have the right to beat my wife. I remember hearing a professor from the Islamic University in Rotterdam say in an interview that the Qur'an allowed a husband to discipline his wife by beating her. It's not only the fundamentalist or radical people who think like this. Somehow, if something is mentioned in the Qur'an, people think it is permissible.

It is possible to state from a supposedly academic position that the Qur'an allows a husband to beat his wife in order to discipline her. If everything mentioned in the Qur'an is to be literally followed as a divine law, Muslims should be consistent and reinstitute slavery as a socioeconomic system. It's mentioned in the Qur'an, isn't it?

When we speak of something being Qur'anic, we are talking about that which was initiated by the Qur'an and therefore is binding on Muslims. There is a distinction between the historicity of the Qur'an and the Word of God in its absolute form. We're back at the double nature of the Qur'an, human and divine. (According to Christian doctrine, not everything that Jesus said was said as the Son of God. Sometimes Jesus behaved just as a man.) The Qur'an is a mode of communication between God and humanity. When we take the historical aspect of that communication as divine, we lock God's Word in time and space. We limit the meaning of the Qur'an to a specific time in history. Far better—and more faithful to the Word of God—to ferret out that dynamic within the Qur'an which has been able to shape the lives of Muslims over centuries as they have wrestled with the question "How can I be a good Muslim in a changing world?"

Why is it, then, that when we read passages in the Qur'an dealing with women, the reading has concentrated on the historical aspect, not on the objective of establishing justice? Going back to the subject of polygamy, the Qur'an tells us, "Try as you may, you cannot treat all your wives impartially" (Sura 4:129). If you think that you will not be able to be fair with your wives, this verse confirms that fear. The problem comes as pre-Islamic social traditions have mixed with Islamic jurisprudence. This mixture has found itself woven into the fabric of Muslim societies, and then enforced there.

The name of the chapter—"Women"—is itself misleading. Muslims titled it according to its subject matter rather than the larger principle it encompasses, justice. The subject matter is women. The subject could just as easily have been war or the poor. Justice is the larger issue under which pressing social issues can easily be subsumed.

A problematic verse reads:

> Men have authority over women because God has made the one superior to the other, and because they spend their wealth to maintain them. Good women are obedient. They guard their unseen parts because God has guarded them. As for those from whom you fear disobedience, admonish them, forsake them in beds apart, and beat them. Then if they obey you, take no further action against them. Surely God is high, supreme. (Sura 4:34)

The English translation of this verse needs to be addressed. The Arabic word *qawwâmûn* is translated in some English texts as "protectors." Muslims generally understand this word to mean "superiors," meaning that men are financially responsible to maintain their families. The question comes down to this: Is the Qur'an here descriptive, merely describing what is going on, or prescriptive, admonishing believers to carry on the practice? Many folks argue that it is prescriptive. Going to the context, though, gives us amazing insight. A woman came to Prophet Muhammad, complaining that her husband had slashed her face. Muhammad simply said, "Slash him back."[2] What we note here is that Muhammad is going beyond the historical restraints placed upon women. (This anecdote always creates a lot of negative reaction from Muslim men.)

The Word of God continuously emphasizes equality between women and men. There is no distinction made regarding the rewards or punishments both women and men reap in the life hereafter. If there is equality in the spiritual realm, does it make sense that God would smile upon inequality in societies in the here and now? There is equality in creation itself and equality when Muslims perform religious duties and rites. We have seen how the Qur'an does not favor polygamy and how the entire thrust of the Qur'an is toward justice. How do we understand the Qur'an's directives regarding financial support, wife-beating, and inheritance?

Men have a superiority over women because of their contribution to the expenses of life. It has nothing to do with human worth. Human societies, though, have equated financial wealth with human worth, and this has shifted the balance of power between women and men unfairly. Men, as a rule in patriarchal societies, have more earning power than women. I understand this superiority that the Qur'an refers to as responsibility. This same term—responsibility—is a word used about God in relation to God's work in holding the universe together. Power is certainly involved, but the emphasis is on responsible action. We talk about God as being qayyûn in regard to the heavens and earth. He keeps watch. He keeps things in order. He keeps the world from destruction. The Qur'an uses the same word with regard to men—they are qawwâmûn. They are responsible for the family— they keep the family in order. It has more to do with responsibility than authority. Of course, responsibility could imply some authority.

In modern times, because of the changes that have affected all our social institutions, and therefore our social structure, women can be considered qawwâmûn. If the woman is the major source of family income, then she is superior. Textual analysis shows that God considers some people to be superior (responsible), depending on their financial contribution. The pronoun used could refer to either women or men. It keeps open the possibility of interpretation, but certainly if the woman is the only source of income, and therefore responsible to protect the family, then she is definitely qawwâm.

The context of wife-beating revolves around instances where a wife's behavior threatens the stability of the family, and therefore the survival of the community. The expression *nushûz*, means "going way out of bounds." The Qur'an says that if a woman goes way beyond the boundaries, she should first be admonished about her behavior. If this is not successful, she opens herself up to punishment. Her husband may refuse to share their bed or may beat her. (The Qur'an also mentions a case where a husband goes beyond the boundaries—in the mode of *nushûz*.) Again, are these particular punishments mentioned the Word of God or do they only reflect history? I believe these punishments were a historical solution to current social problems.

Of course it is entirely possible that some women would not have considered desertion from the marital bed to be punishment. We are dealing with the Qur'an, a historical text, coming into existence at a time when patriarchy was well established in cultures throughout the world. Patriarchy, literally meaning "rule by the fathers," is a social system with "domination over" somebody or something (men over women, masters over slaves, kings or queens over subjects, elite over commoners, human beings over nature) at its core. A patriarchal perspective sees things through a male-centered lens, and even though women can (and do) replicate the patriarchal order as their lives unfold, the gender roles that a society enforces on both women and men ensure that a male perspective remains dominant. Products of any given culture (and the Qur'an is a product of a specific culture) reflect the way things are in a society. The language of the text situates itself within a specific material reality—one that expresses itself through a patriarchal bent. Nevertheless, the absolute Word of God transcends the text. Part of my research has to do with distinguishing between the human and divine aspects of the Qur'an.

Before Islam made its appearance on the Arabian Peninsula in the seventh century, women inherited nothing. The eldest son received everything. Islam changed this.

> God has thus enjoined you concerning your children: A male shall inherit twice as much as a female. If there be more than two girls, they shall have two-thirds of the inheritance; but if there be one only, she shall inherit the half. Parents shall inherit a sixth each, if the deceased ha[s] a child; but if he leave[s] no child and his parents be his heirs, his mother shall have a third. If he ha[s] brothers, his mother shall have a sixth after payment of any legacy he may be bequeathed or any debt he may have owed. You may wonder whether your parents or your children are more beneficial to you [nearer to you in benefit]. But this is the law of God; surely God is all-knowing and wise. (Sura 4:11)

If you accept the reading that this verse establishes change—women have a right to be included in inheritance—and stop at that level, that's OK. The direction is toward justice. However, a deeper reading shows that this text is not about establishing the rights of women—it is about limiting the rights of men. The Qur'an here is moving in the direction of equality between women and men. It's a step in the right direction. Women should have a share in an inheritance just as men do.

"A male shall inherit twice as much as a female." The structure of the verse concentrates on the share of the male, not the share of the female. Suppose the structure were different? Suppose the text read, "A female shall inherit half of what a male inherits"? This gives us a different semantic reading. If the Qur'anic verse began, "A female shall inherit," we would know that the Qur'an is busy defining the share of the female. But it begins, "A male shall inherit." We see that the Qur'an busies itself defining just what the male's share is to be.

Remember that before Islam, the male received all of the inheritance. The Qur'an here is limiting the share of the male, not defining the share of the female. I believe the Qur'an's intention is limitation—it's the semantic focus of the text. Placing a limitation on what the male receives is not absolutely defining what he should get, but by saying "no more than this," it leaves open the good possibility that he could receive less.

Men should not go beyond that which the Qur'an entitles them to. Grammatically speaking, the Qur'an limits the share that men inherit. The Qur'an does not give an absolute share to either women or men. The structure of the Qur'an clears the way for societies to enact inheritance laws that reflect equality between the sexes. Its structure doesn't box us into absolute numerical amounts.

How should we understand "You may wonder whether your parents or your children are more beneficial to you"? Just because the context reflects the *jâhiliyyah* code of behavior, this does not necessarily imply that the Qur'an is trying to guide the believers to go beyond the blood bonds on which the inheritance passages rest. Nonetheless, reading the whole Qur'an in terms of its strong opposition to the tribal code would suggest such an implication. If we add the fact that Prophet Muhammad clearly indicated that his inheritance was to be distributed for charity, we can suggest that the whole inheritance system is really historically determined.

Much work begs to be done in the field of Islamic Studies. The nineteenth century saw a movement of revivalism in the Arab and

Muslim world that for a variety of reasons lost its momentum. The process of reforming Islamic thought by looking at the Qur'an and trying to differentiate between what is history and what is the absolute Word of God has continued since then in spite of that loss of momentum. I do not consider my work exceptional. I do not come out of a vacuum. I count myself among those few who have been trying to keep the Qur'an relevant to life in the modern age. We experience heavy resistance.

There are reasons for this resistance. One of the reasons stems from the absence of what I call a "free market of ideas." The acceptance of the economic free market in Muslim societies does not include the acceptance of this free market of ideas. In the Arab and Muslim world, the media are totally controlled by the government. There is no space for free thinking to flourish. Yûsuf Idrîs, one of our contemporary Egyptian writers (playwright and novelist), said that all the freedom in the Muslim and Arab world is not enough for a single person. I agree with him. Political authority in Egypt is oppressive authority.

On my recent visit to Egypt, I spoke with a male lawyer—one with considerable standing and clout in Egyptian society—about the recent appointment of a woman judge, Tahani El-Gebali, to the Supreme Court. "You know I'm really liberal," he noted, "but I'm not happy at all about a woman being appointed as a judge."

I looked at him askance. "Why not?"

"Because a judge must be somebody with experience—a judge needs to go from state to state and into the villages, examining evidence—it could be dangerous. You know the routine."

I'd heard it all before. Under the guise of protecting women, we restrict their activities, a climate that perpetuates inequality between the sexes. Many Muslims are liberal and open-minded, but when it comes to the subject of women, they take refuge in an outdated ideology. With the advent of cloning, the possibility exists that one single woman can reproduce life on her own. Men—especially Arab men—feel threatened. Many Muslims point to the verse that shows life springing forth from a pair, and then refuse to discuss the issue further, claiming that the Qur'an settled that issue long ago.

Democracy, rationalism, and freedom are not instilled in our consciousness. All too often, as in the case of the lawyer who is unhappy with the recent appointment of Tahani El-Gebali to Egypt's Supreme Court, these concepts skim along the surface of our understanding. We have not incorporated these values into the way we go about living our lives. That's why it's easy to find refined, intellectual men talking about women and the rights of women, but treating their own wives with scorn and contempt.

An acquaintance of mine invited me to his home to have dinner with his wife and family. I had just met him and felt somewhat uncomfortable with the invitation. So I said, "You cannot just surprise your wife by bringing home a guest for dinner."

"No, no, don't worry about it," he assured me. "My wife is gracious and hospitable."

I still was uncomfortable with the situation. I wouldn't surprise Ebtehal in this way. I reluctantly accepted his invitation, thinking that perhaps he and his wife had some sort of understanding about bringing guests home for dinner. When we entered his home, his wife graciously received us. The husband took off his jacket; flung it across the room, not caring where it landed; and then clapped his hands three times as a signal to his wife that he wanted some service. "Cigarettes, get me my cigarettes." His cigarettes were in his jacket pocket—the same jacket that he had just thrown across the room.

What kind of freedom is this? Where is the respect, especially in front of a guest? Perhaps a man might behave like this when he is alone with his family, showing how spoiled he is—but to do this in front of a guest?! But the man was not staging a scene. This was ordinary, everyday behavior. This showed me what a wide gap exists between people's talk about freedom and justice; all that talk has yet to make a dent on the way many people live. Clearly, we have not integrated our talk into our walk. Or, to put it in academic terms, theory has not made its way into practice.

12 Looking Ahead

As I watched with sickening horror that sad sight of the Twin Towers going up in smoke against New York's skyline on that bright and sunny September day in 2001, my immediate thought was "This must be a movie." The scene slowly began to sink in, and gradually it dawned on me. The world, because of this attack, was going to turn upside down. Reaction would be strong. This was white blood. Year after year, Palestinian carnage has continued—no big deal. Life goes on. Now, I'm certainly not without criticism of the Palestinian leadership. I'm convinced Yasser Arafat is at the helm of a corrupt system of government. But somehow, Palestinians who die day in and day out don't command the same kind of attention from the world that an attack on the Twin Towers and the Pentagon demands.

In the wake of September 11, 2001, I've been deeply concerned —even depressed—about the future of our world. I lost friends, both Americans and Muslims, trapped in the burning Twin Towers. Even in the middle of all the many crises I've lived through with my family, my university, and my country, I have never felt so down as I do these days.

A couple of years ago, a famous Egyptian actress, Su'âd Husny, committed suicide in London—at least it appeared that suicide was the cause of her death. She was popular when I was a youth; I remember her as a cultural icon of sorts. In Egypt, she was known as Cinderella. Recently Ebtehal and I were talking about Cinderella, and I asked her, "Do you think depression could lead somebody to commit suicide?"

There had been considerable speculation in the tabloids that Su'âd was depressed. She did have some health problems and was taking cortisone. She had gained a lot of weight and no longer looked like Cinderella. As a result, her career suffered.

Ebtehal took a long look at me. "Yes," she answered simply. Realizing that I was quite depressed, she added, "but there is no danger that you will go that deep."

"What makes you think that?" I asked.

"Because you love to be with people—even if you are sick or angry, you love talking with people. I believe this will protect you from sinking very deep," she assured me.

I know that isolating yourself from the company of other people can exacerbate depression. I'm not about to go into isolation. What I have noticed is that when I initiate some kind of change in my life, it works well as an antidote for depression. I find I'm always looking for ways to change this or make something else a little different. I recently shaved my beard. I'm presently trying to lose weight. If I lose some weight, I'll feel lighter. Who knows? This might revive my spirits. One of the reasons I decided to go to Berlin had to do with change.

During the fall of 2002, I worked at the Institute for Advanced Studies in Berlin. I had a fellowship—an honorary award—given to me in 1996. The hope was that I would be at the Institute in Berlin in 1997. The timing was somewhat awkward because the initial invitation extended by Leiden University after my exile was a three-year assignment—1995 (the first year of my exile) until 1998. I didn't think it appropriate to leave a three-year commitment in order to pursue a one-year fellowship in Berlin. The folks at the Institute in Berlin understood. From 1996 until the present, we've been in close contact. I've attended their symposia and conferences. In 2001, I joined the committee hard at work on a project about Islamic and Jewish hermeneutics. The project had taken off, and it seemed like the right time to go.

In spite of my discouragement about the world situation—specifically the way that situation has impacted on Islam—I plan to forge ahead with my work even though my optimism about the future has suffered a severe blow.

From the seventh century until the nineteenth century (when contact between Europe and the Islamic world began in earnest), the idea of Islam as a meld of religion and state (dîn wa dawla) was absent. This melding is a modern concept. Islam has always made a distinction between the ruler—for example, the sultan or caliph—and the law-

maker or *faqîh*. Beginning in the ninth century, though, literal interpretation of the Qur'an became the dominant trend throughout the
Muslim world. This was unfortunate. Literalism easily leads to a fundamentalism that manipulates religion in order to wield power, and we
see political leaders throughout much of our history doing just that. Of
course, using God to seize power is nothing new—this is a common
practice—but in spite of that, for most of our history, there was a clear
differentiation between political and religious authority. A sultan, a
ruler, a caliph, a king—these were not religious authorities.

What the Qur'an presents to Muslims is neither the Islamization
of life nor the absolute separation of religion from life. Separating religion from the state, though, is essential for protecting the integrity of
religion, but this does not mean relegating religion to a backseat in
society. The Qur'an, in the original text, gives us no political theory—
it espouses no political principles. Certainly, there are accounts of how
politics played out on the Arabian Peninsula during the seventh century. The Qur'an does give us some vivid, descriptive accounts of how
the new community of believers governed themselves, but the Qur'an
does not mandate any particular form of government. This is open to
Muslims to choose for themselves.

I firmly believe that separation of the state and religion is essential for protecting religion from political manipulation. When the state
identifies itself with a certain religion, folks who belong to another religious tradition inevitably are discriminated against. In addition, those
folks who belong to the religion officially sanctioned by the state, but
don't hold orthodox views (the right way to think about religion, according to those who have the power to say so), become subject to
persecution on the grounds of apostasy or heresy. A secular state—
one that gives no official sanction to any particular religion—gives religion the space it needs to meet the needs of the people. Otherwise,
religion easily becomes a weapon in the hands of those in power.

When Europe (and later the United States) flexed their muscles
in their attempt to conquer countries through colonization, a trap was
set. Europe was convinced that Islam was to blame for the backwardness of Muslim societies. Colonized countries reacted to this accusation in a variety of ways.

One reaction has been imitation. Thinking that the West's political system must be just as good as its technology, some non-Western
countries have superimposed an imported political system on their
people while at the same time using the West's technology to compete

in the world economy. Professor Senghaas, from the Institute for Inter-cultural and International Studies—the man with whom I dialogued in 1996—uggested that Korea best exemplifies this response to coloni-zation.

In the Arab world, we have Muhammad Ali, the founder of mod-ern Egypt. He attempted to imitate the West by setting up a modern state in Egypt during the mid-1800s which included developing a strong military. We ended up embracing the benefits of European technol-ogy without understanding the critical, scientific thinking that gave this technology its oomph. In fact, we didn't give two thoughts to that. We liked the fact that technology gave us more of a standing in the modern world while making our lives somewhat easier.

An intellectual response to the encroachment of modernity came from the Egyptian scholar Muhammad 'Abduh (1849–1905). His book *Islam Is the Religion of Science and Civilization*[1] spearheaded this in-tellectual movement. 'Abduh believed that people who wanted to rid themselves of their religious heritage misunderstood religion. If religious tradition had lost meaning for the people, then religion had to be un-derstood in a fresh way. This rational thinking about religion had been neglected in the Arab world for several centuries. 'Abduh's contempo-rary, Rashîd Rida (1865–1935), advocated a return to tradition and an Islamic state based on an updated understanding of *shari'a* law. This fresh understanding would pave the way for Muslims to become players in the modern world while still holding on to their identity as Muslims.

Another response to colonization, according to Professor Senghaas, has been for a culture to dress up or put a modern face on its traditional laws and policies—laws and policies that have long since stopped being useful. A supposed golden era in the distant past becomes the model. The Middle East tends to respond in this manner.

Sometimes the reaction of colonized people can be summed up like this: "Well, let's modernize in the technological/scientific field, but let's steer clear of anything foreign in the cultural sphere." This explains why in much of Muslim society, there is such animosity toward litera-ture (novels, poems) and the arts (paintings, films). There is this fear that religious commitment will somehow be compromised by import-ing these specific cultural artifacts.

Occasionally, the colonized respond with creativity and innova-tion. Social reform never happens in a straight line, though. Reform movements are messy. Many traditionalists today fear possible change in their society as a result of applying creative and innovative solutions to problems in their present circumstances, believing that Islam will be obliterated in the process. In addition, because Arab culture stresses obedience at the expense of critical thinking, when creative solutions do emerge as one way to go forward, all too often these movements are squelched. They're much too threatening to those who hold power. As a result, Muslim society stagnates.

Muslim identity, more often than not, wraps itself tightly around a narrow understanding of religion. It is the Muslim, though—not Islam—who resists modernization. This resistance has not been the case for most of Islamic history. Our ancestors did their best to think creatively, integrating available knowledge with Qur'anic principles and then applying appropriate solutions to modern problems.

When we look at what the Islamic Reformation Movement of the nineteenth century initiated and then follow its course up to the present, we can see some progress. I'm thinking specifically about what we presently call the dialogue of civilizations or the dialogue of cultures. We do have within Islamic discourse a liberal understanding—a liberal interpretation of the Qur'an based on modern knowledge. The essential part of this modern knowledge we owe to Europe's Enlightenment.

When the Arab world first encountered the West (Europe), it made a distinction between intellectual Europe with its ideas of progress and development and imperial Europe with its occupying forces that were resisted. The Islamic Reformation focused on incorporating Europe's ideas of progress and development within Arab society. We have this legacy. I place myself within this legacy. My research in the field of Islamic Studies is all about trying to find a way of incorporating modernity and progress into Islamic thought.

Ever since September 11, 2001, a large number of radical Islamic groups, most notably Osama bin Laden and his cohorts, have attempted to hijack Islam by claiming to be the representatives of Islam, speaking for all of Islam. Of course, other groups have tried to do so as well—the Wahhabis of Saudi Arabia, the Mahdis in Sudan, and the Sunusis in Libya. None of these groups with its specific ideology has succeeded in establishing itself as the only vision or understanding of Islam. Islam has always expressed itself in a variety of ways—ways that have been present, recognized, and respected since its inception.

It seems to me that in spite of an initial valiant attempt on the part of the Bush administration to differentiate between radical Islamic groups and Islam as it has been expressed in its various forms since the seventh century, America still perceives Islam as a monolithic enemy. Immediately following September 11, 2001, I heard President Bush talk about the need for the American people not to equate Islam—one of the major world religions—with radical groups within Islam. It gave me pleasure to hear him say this. I thought he was right on target. Fringe elements, powerful though they may be, ought not to be considered representative of Islam.

My initial pleasure evaporated quickly as Bush continued to talk. I am not an Islamist, but I felt completely excluded as Bush spoke about "our culture, our values, our freedoms, and our democratic ideals" as he juxtaposed "our" with "other," implying that the "other" is not civilized. I belong to this "uncivilized" world. I'm critical of my culture, to be sure, but I still belong to it. This categorization of "our" values and "other" values is merely a construct manufactured in the heads of people in the West and is taking shape in the heads of Islamists as well. It's the same exclusiveness—Bin Laden talking about infidels (Christians and Jews), and Bush talking about "our" culture, "our" values, "our" freedoms, and "our" democratic ideals. What does he mean by "our"? Freedom and democracy do not belong exclusively to one society. He's talking about human values—values we all share—and if Bush had addressed the devastation of September 11, 2001, keeping in mind that his society has no monopoly on freedom and democracy, I think he would have garnered much respect in the Arab world.

A rational and farsighted policy would have first found a way to separate and dissociate these radical, terrorist groups from the mainstream, thus leaving them without any kind of public support. I believe the political administration in the United States wanted to ease the emotional pain of the American people, many of whom had suffered painful losses. Revenge seemed the way to go. Without much understanding about how this strategy would be perceived throughout the Muslim world, bombs began exploding over Afghanistan. I understand, respect, and sympathize with the feelings of the American people. But should we carry out political strategies just to retaliate, or should we have a more measured strategy, one where we give more thought to what was an act of terror that affected the whole international community—including Muslims?

I think the decision to attack al-Qaeda was made in haste. This attack allowed Osama bin Laden, in a taped message, to just sit there and tell the whole world that he was defending Palestine. I was scandalized. Osama bin Laden, who had never spoken publicly about Palestine before this, was able to lay claim to this very thing. Of course, he got a lot of support from the Arab world because of this speech. The whole scene made me deeply depressed, and I cannot ignore the fact that all this was given to him on a silver platter by the United States because of its government's hasty, unstudied decision to retaliate. This decision was a pragmatic one—a political decision that, in my opinion, was not in the interest of the American people, although no doubt in the interest of the elite and powerful in the United States. Al-Qaeda remains in Afghanistan. We know this. Up until this point, Osama bin Laden had not been able to bend the meaning of Islam to suit his purposes. Suddenly, here it was—given to him as a gift. The effects are far-reaching.

Because a powerful country, the United States, fought against Afghanistan, an Islamic country, Osama bin Laden was able to reinforce to the young—teenagers from Pakistan to Palestine—that the American foreign policy toward Palestine is absolutely unjust. There is this sense in the Arab world that the West generally, and America in particular, is against Islam, and part of this being against Islam is being against the Palestinian people and in favor of Israel. As long as the Arab–Israeli issue remains unsolved, there is no way we can expect any further reformation in Islamic thought. Because resolution of the Arab–Israeli conflict has taken low priority on the agenda of Western political leaders, this feeling that Muslims have of being under attack continues. Frankly, it terrifies me.

It's as though the positive gains by the Islamic Reformation Movement of the nineteenth century came to a grinding halt in 1948. Systems of thought—especially those reflecting radical or fundamentalist ideology—remain alive and well because to a large extent they are claiming to solve the problem between Palestine and Israel. If any change is ever to come about in the Arab world, and therefore in the Islamic world—whether the subject is politics, democracy, human rights, or Islamic Reformation—solving the Palestinian–Israeli conflict has to come first. I'm not just talking about what the Arab world expects, I'm talking about establishing justice in this world of ours that over the past decades has become a small village.

Never before in my life have I been so determined to show my political affiliation as I am these days. Even though I have studied opinions about certain things, I've always taken the staid, intellectual route to protest what I perceive as injustice, not the route of public demonstration. I've undergone some kind of change—a change that began to happen even before September 11, 2001, as I watched

Palestinian children being killed for throwing rocks at Israeli tanks. These images appeared on the Cable News Network (CNN), the British Broadcasting Company (BBC), and the Dutch media—not just the Arab media, which might be criticized for exaggerating. Of course, children—for lots of reasons—ought not to be throwing rocks at tanks. But kill them for such activity?

The first Intifada (1987)—the effort by the Palestinians to shake free from Israeli occupation—led to the signing of the Oslo Peace Accord in 1993. Negotiations between Israel and Palestine put into motion concrete plans that had the potential to eventually bring peace between the two sides. The second Intifada (2000) should have led to further positive developments in the Middle East. What began to gnaw at me was that most of the world didn't care—all this fighting, killing, and dying fit right into the backdrop of people's lives.

Two or three years ago, I seriously considered packing my bags and heading back to Egypt. What am I doing here in Europe? Developing Islamic thought? That goal grows more and more elusive. Sometimes I feel as though all the effort Muhammad 'Abduh made in the direction of integrating Islam and the West has been wasted. We seem to be heading back toward exclusiveness—the West as the oppressor, the West as the invader, the West as the occupier. 'Abduh was able to make a distinction between the colonizing aims of the West and the beneficial values the West offered. He fought against the West's exploitation of Muslim people while embracing the useful and valuable parts of Western culture.

Today, this distinction is not being made. For the most part, the younger generation in the Arab world hates America. But it's a paradox. They hate America because they are excluded—they are not part of it. Most of these young people would jump at the opportunity to obtain a green card allowing them access to America. What does America mean? Is it paradise? No, of course not. But on some level, in the minds of these young people, America is a cursed paradise because they are excluded. There is some truth to the expression "They hate us because they envy us," but when America wraps all political, economic, and social problems between the Muslim world and the West in such a simplistic statement, its naïveté shows up big time.

So in going about my work (as part of a long line of reform), I was (and still am) growing increasingly frustrated. The press and even some intellectuals within the academy want me to parrot their ideas about Islam, which usually means casting Islam in a negative light. And then it dawned on me. I'm not supposed to say what I think. I'm supposed to say what people want to hear—here in the Netherlands, of all places. What difference, then, does it make where I am—Egypt, Syria, Saudi Arabia, or even Holland? If that's the case, I might as well pack my bags and head back to Egypt.

It was around this time that I had to prepare my lecture for the Chair in Law Responsibility, Freedom of Religion and Conscience at Leiden University—a chair named after Professor Cleveringa.

Professor Cleveringa (1894–1980) taught at Leiden University in 1940, a time when the Nazis occupied the Netherlands. The Nazis, in their attempt to leave all Jews unemployed, asked every Dutch person to declare his or her religion. The Dutch resisted, but in the end, all of them complied—including professors at the university. The Nazis then dismissed all Jews from their positions, and that included a Jewish professor at Leiden University, E. M. Meijers. On the day Mr. Meijers was to give one of his regular class lectures, Cleveringa took his place. During his beautiful and well-prepared speech, he spoke out against the Nazi decision to sack all Jews from their teaching posts at the university. Two minutes of silence followed his talk. Then clapping broke out in the audience, followed by a demonstration and protests. Cleveringa and others were arrested. Leiden University closed down until the end of the war, when Cleveringa returned and once again assumed his teaching responsibilities. After his death, Leiden University established a chair to be occupied every year by someone whose work furthers the cause of freedom and human rights.

Because of my writing, I occupied this chair in 2000–2001. As I was preparing my lecture, I found myself moved by Professor Cleveringa's stand. Using Cleveringa's speech as a backdrop, I brought the Palestinian situation before the public just as Cleveringa had brought the plight of the persecuted Jews living under Nazi occupation into public scrutiny. I introduced my talk by wrapping my subject in the cloak of justice as it is reflected in the Qur'an. What kind of justice do we see in this world of ours? I talked about Palestinian children in need of homes, schools, hospitals, and Palestinian children who are killed in cold blood.

Cleveringa, in his speech, spoke about the brutality of the Nazis. I spoke about the brutality of the Israeli military. Cleveringa suggested that the Dutch people put this Nazi decision under their feet, meaning to treat it as the nonsense it is, and to take heart from the radiant Jewish professor, E. M. Meijers. I suggested that we put the Israeli military under our feet and look up to the radiant Qur'an. The world's indifference to the suffering of those caught up in this conflict had gotten to me in such a way that I could no longer work only within the intellectual arena.

As somebody who identifies himself as a member of the oppressed—fighting against an oppressor—I feel ashamed to be living in this world. I agree with Chinua Achebe, the brilliant, contemporary Nigerian novelist, who said, "The world is not well arranged."[2] This sense of shame leads me to long for death at times. This is no exaggeration. What kind of world am I going to witness in the coming years? I believe that doing the right thing is quite clear at times. Sometimes, in order to gain political advantage, those with power blur the lines between right and wrong to the point that I feel I must learn all over again what justice and human rights mean.

In addition, the West (Europe and America) does not seem to see how the gains made as a result of the Enlightenment are threatened—all under the guise of security, protecting themselves against real or imagined dangers. The values we cherish (human rights, freedom, democracy), established since the seventeenth century, are melting away. If these values are already endangered in Europe and the United States, how can we expect them to be established in the world where they have never existed? How can anybody be optimistic in the face of this? It's easy to give in to despair. It's even difficult for me at this particular time to write a short article in Arabic—my mother tongue.

Never before, throughout my entire life, did I ever feel I had the luxury to be pessimistic about the future. I've used my critical scholarship to work on specific issues, trying to bring reformation to Islamic thought, to Islamic theology, to the concept of the Qur'an, and to Qur'anic interpretation. But when all is said and done, whatever I write is addressed to people within a context, and no thinker—no writer— would write just for the sake of writing. I have things to say and write about the Qur'an, about the meaning of the Qur'an, about the humanity of the Qur'an, and about the Prophet. I want them to be received.

Nowadays, though, when I try to show how relevant and important these topics are for the future of Islam and Muslim people, most Muslims frown at me and say, "What are you talking about? We have a lot of trouble right now. What does the textuality of the Qur'an have to do with us? This does not concern us."

They do not see that Islam has become an instrument in the hands of political pundits. Lack of application of critical scholarship to Islam has allowed these pundits to twist the words of the Qur'an to fit their own purposes—usually that purpose has to do with seizing power—and hold Muslims hostage. Muslims feel as though I want to strip them of their weapon—a wooden interpretation of Islam that gives threatened and oppressed people an illusory sense of control over their own lives—and expose them to their enemy. They either stare at me blankly or get hot under the collar when I tell them, "No, I am not taking your weapon. I am giving you another weapon—a far better one." Applying theological and critical scholarship to social, political, and economic problems does not seem relevant to Muslims at the present time. It's understandable. Many of them live in daily fear of annihilation. Their needs appear to be more immediate.

I have no doubt that reformation of religious thought was one of the reasons Europe and the United States progressed by leaps and bounds over the last three centuries. My goal, through my writing, has been to impact the Arab world with a new perspective, a perspective that ultimately will bring about reform of Islamic religious thought. But I see Europe and the United States taking a step backward, entrenching themselves in a fundamentalist mind-set—both religiously and politically. Well-known religious leaders in the United States have blatantly declared Islam an evil religion. In addition, Bush's declaration to the world in response to September 11, 2001, "You are either with us or against us," reflects simplistic political thinking which has had an enormous impact on America's foreign policy.

American foreign policy when it comes to Israel is not based just on political, economic, or even social expediencies. American foreign policy is based on mythology. I use "mythology" in a classic sense. Every culture has stories or myths that seep into the consciousness of people belonging to that culture. People live out these myths as they go about their day-to-day business, making decisions that emerge from having soaked up the truths inherently found in myths or stories. I'm convinced that the roots of American foreign policy toward Israel are firmly planted in the myth of Zionist Christianity.

The stories or mythology of a sacred text belong to a genre of literature or writing not intended to be read literally. Doing so invites disaster. A literal reading of sacred text gives myth the weight of fact, legitimizing the carrying out of acts just because they are recorded in sacred text.

Interestingly enough, whenever Jerusalem is mentioned, the understanding of the West, generally, is that Jerusalem belongs to the Jews—not even to the Christians, and certainly not to the Arabs. But let's look at the story. The Jews lived in Jerusalem. They built a temple. They left Jerusalem in the first century. They lived other places. Are the people who returned to Jerusalem the same Jewish people who left in the first place? If so, does that history entitle them to take over a specific piece of real estate, especially when that entails displacing people living there already?

The myth of Zionist Christianity says yes, but this response comes only by giving myth the weight of factual truth. According to the story, God promised the Land—a specific piece of real estate defined in the Bible—to the descendants of Abraham through his son Isaac. If the myth is given the weight of factual truth, Jews have every right—even a sacred duty—to reclaim that Land. And as the story is interpreted, we find that time becomes of the essence. There would be no redemption for the Jews until they settled this Land and then, through the redemption of Israel, the whole word would be redeemed. With this kind of vision, it is no wonder that Israel has gone about its task with such zeal.

Here in the Netherlands, it has become more difficult to speak about Israel in a critical context without feeling like a criminal. And I'm talking here about universities, about intellectuals—people whose very job is to wrestle with subjects within a critical context. Ordinary folks, the people in the street, may not be overtly religious; nevertheless, they have absorbed the Christian mythology that has shaped this European country. Many do not reflect on what gives their ideology its particular shape. It just seems right to them, having unreflectively absorbed the myths of their particular culture.

Because of all the upheaval present in the world, sometimes I feel like a fireman putting out fires here and there as I address and try to write about the political trajectory that both Western and Middle Eastern policy takes. It's a different kind of work than what I had been doing with the Qur'an. Putting out fires is not the same thing as creating knowledge.

Recently, I had a couple of interviews with a reporter from one of the Dutch newspapers. The editors weren't happy with one of the interviews, so the reporter called me to ask, "Can you do this over again?"

"No," I answered. The editor of the paper wanted simple answers to specific questions about Islam. The reporter had posed thoughtless questions in the first place—questions that I reformulated in order to give an intelligent response. What the newspaper was actually looking for, I came to understand, were statements I had made at one time about the deterioration and backwardness of the Muslim world. I remained firm. "No, I don't work for you. You are looking for a puppet. I'm not going to play the role."

More and more, I hear the media talking about Islam as something outdated. Western media seem to be focusing on Muslims—how dangerous they are; perhaps we'd better be rid of them. Even if the government were to get rid of every Muslim in this country, this would not solve the perceived problem of "the dangerous Muslim." Disruptive changes brought about by globalization have created social and economic problems that have nothing to do with Islam. But everybody needs a scapegoat. So the welcome mat for Muslims is being pulled away in more and more areas. I'm trying to sound the alarm. I am not Dutch, but I live in Holland. I'm concerned about what is going on around me. Folks seem to want to listen only when you talk about Islam in a negative sense. I refuse to play that game. And that's why I came down so hard on the editor of the newspaper.

Being critical has become increasingly difficult. I often get the sense that I am respected in many places in the world because I have been so critical of Islamic thought. I'm not looked upon favorably when folks perceive that I am critical of certain things within their particular culture. I spent six years living abroad—two years in the States and four years in Japan. In addition, I've lived eight years in exile. I've immersed myself in three cultures different from my own. I've acquired wonderful tools from each of those cultures, tools I consider gifts. They've broadened my worldview. How can I get across that I'm not critical of many of their values? I see those values—values that I love and respect—being threatened, and I cannot be silent.

Not too long ago, I met up with Muhammad Arkoun, a Muslim scholar, at a conference in Berlin. He currently lives in Paris, works at the Sorbonne, and is fluent in several languages. I spoke with him after he finished giving his lecture. He commented on my work as well as the work of Mr. Soroush, an Iranian scholar, who was also present at the conference. He criticized both of us for discussing outdated issues in our writing and specifically referred to what constitutes a large chunk of my work, the doctrine of the created Qur'an. Even though my Iranian friend kept silent, I felt I had to address Mr. Arkoun's criticism.

"Yes," I said, "I agree with you, I do focus on outdated discussion—outdated in European countries like France, places like the Sorbonne in particular, where you live and produce your discourse. But people die in our countries for lack of what you call outdated discussion. We can learn from you and the work you produce in your ivory tower, but that does not give you the right to undermine our work."

Mr. Arkoun apologized profusely. "I'm sorry, I didn't mean it."

"You didn't mean it, but you implicitly said it," I reminded him. "You are the scholar who taught me that discourse is saying something beyond intention. I am not talking about your intention. I'm talking about what you said—your discourse. I deal with fallout from issues you call outdated every day."

Muhammad Arkoun subsequently included a description of my work in an article published in *The Encyclopedia of the Qur'an*.

> Nasr Hamid Abu Za[i]d, the first Muslim scholar to face the Arabic world directly by writing in Arabic while teaching at Cairo University, tried to break the many taboos which prohibit the application of the most relevant achievements of contemporary linguistics to the Qur'an. Before him, Muhammad Khalafallah tried to apply literary criticism to narrative in the Qur'an, and in spite of its modest scientific span, his essay caused a major upheaval. The works of Abu Za[i]d contain nothing revolutionary if one places them within the scholarly production of the last twenty years, since they explain quite straightforwardly the conditions necessary for applying the rules of defining and analyzing a text to the Qur'an (*Mafhum al-nass*). Once more, the violent reaction to attempts intending only to popularize knowledge long since widely accepted, underlines the area in contemporary Islamic thought of what [many believe] cannot be and has not been thought.[3]

Mr. Arkoun and I met again several times at conferences and symposia. He surprised me when he started to evaluate my work positively. This has encouraged me to press forward. At the present time, Mr. Arkoun and I are involved with other Arab intellectuals in a fledgling organization called the Arab Foundation for Modernizing Arab Thought. Our goal is to bring modern scholarship to bear on Arab thought.

Not too long ago (1998), scholars from all over the Muslim world—Indonesia, Malaysia, Sudan, Egypt, Iran—as well as representatives from some Western countries gathered at Leiden University to discuss the future of Islam. A friend and colleague of mine, Dr. Nico J. G. Kaptein, and I organized this symposium, titled "Qur'anic Studies on the Eve of the 21st Century." My conclusion at that time was that any real reformation of Islamic thought was going to come from the periphery of the Muslim world. In the wake of September 11, 2001, I'm not so sure.

The Muslim world feels threatened by its perception that America is somehow against Islam. In order to preserve their identity as authentic Muslims, many have adopted what looks like extremism to outsiders. What they perceive as having worked well for their ancestors must be the answer. So there is a regression to "those good old days," and as a result, they go about implementing certain doctrines, certain dress, and specific ways of being in the world they feel connects them to the tried-and-true certainties of the past.

Iran is a good example. If you look at some of the changes in Iran that were happening before September 11, 2001, liberal thinkers, intent on bringing Iran along as a player in the modern world, were having more and more of an impact on Iranian society, gaining significant ground from those who resisted any kind of change. I felt optimistic that, under the umbrella of Islam, a budding democracy had begun to sprout. The authority of the *imam* began to dwindle. A theological revolution—the counterrevolution of Khomeini—also started to form.

One of the ways Khomeini was able to draw such a following was by establishing the authority of the *faqîh* or jurist, known as *wilayati faqîh*. Iranians, for the most part, belong to that branch of Islam known as Shi'i. Within Shi'i theological understanding, the Muslim community waits for the absent *imam* to bring about justice and make things right in the world. The Iranian people were beginning to challenge this concept of the *wilayati faqîh* as it moved into politics and eventually into policies that affected the people. So Iran was busy hammering away at this within its political structure. Free elections were looming in the not-too-distant future.

Then, when President Bush, in a post-September 11, 2001, speech, declared Iran one of the players in the trio of the "axis of evil" (North Korea and Iraq were the other two), the traditionalists—those against liberalizing Iran—immediately gained ground. It became easy for them to say, "You have been trying to open dialogue with the West and have been attempting to apply some democratic principles garnered from the

Enlightenment, and now look what happens. This is the West for you."
President Khatami was pressured to side with the traditionalists against
the United States.

I had been hoping for some time that something within Shi'i
theology would influence Sunni theological thought. We've seen how
the Khomeini revolution influenced fundamentalist groups within Sunni
Islam. Revolt in the name of God began to explode throughout the
world. Shi'i Islam had been coming up with some creative solutions
to the problems Muslims face in the modern world while still holding
on to the values inherent in their religious faith.

What direction can Muslims take in the wake of Bush's declaration? The path, to a large extent, has been blocked. And who bears
some of that responsibility? Countries who meddle in other countries'
affairs as a way to further their own interests. External interference
blocks the internal dynamics of a country, a dynamic that in Iran was
leaning toward openness, liberal thought, and reformation.

In spite of that, I'm convinced that we are lazy. I'm talking about
Muslims specifically. We are damn lazy. We think that what our ancestors accomplished is the be-all and end-all. This is absolute stupidity. Knowledge develops. As we study and learn from the world
in conjunction with our sacred text, the Qur'an, new knowledge
emerges. To glorify the past is to misunderstand the past. We block
the way forward as we freeze in our tracks when we attempt to defend and vindicate the past while criticizing the present. This gets us
nowhere fast.

Our propensity to stagnate is odd, given our heritage. Our sacred
text admonishes against *jāhiliyyah* (the tribal mentality of the pre-
Islamic era). This tribal mentality fosters fanaticism and narrow-
mindedness. Originally, the Muslim community found the principles
evident in the Qur'an to be a catalyst for intellectual growth, a growth
that challenged the existing culture. There is nothing sacred about our
history. Events came to pass as a result of social, economic, and political factors. Muslims—or anyone else, for that matter—have no pure
religious history, nor have they ever had a perfect political system in
place. Religion and politics have always influenced one another. It is
folly to think that any country exists where this has not been the case.
But many Muslims today believe that there is a pure form of Islam, one
that is apart from the influence of culture, geography, and history. The
sooner we understand that there is no such utopia, the more effective
we can be in the modern world.

Ever since September 11, 2001, the West (the United States in particular) has pressured the Islamic world to change the way it teaches Islam to its people. The critique of religious discourse has been the focus of my academic career. I'm not as concerned with the questions that come to us from outside the Muslim world as I am with questions that emerge from within our own experience—the stuff that comprises our own lives—questions we are reluctant to address.

We have a long history of defensiveness. We think we have to vindicate Islam. We do need to take a long, hard look at ourselves and ask the tough questions we've dodged over the last several centuries. It's the only way we'll ever move ahead. The Islamic Reformation Movement in the nineteenth century began a forward thrust. We need to pick up where that left off.

What is the nature of this renewal? Sheikh Amîn al-Khûlî, a twentieth-century reformist, defined it this way: "Renewal begins with a devastating enquiry into the past . . . ideas that [were once] forbidden . . . may later turn into a doctrine, a reform that takes life a step forward."[4] Reform or renewal happens this way in the political realm as well. In spite of what traditionalists would have us believe, renewal is not a leap into the dark, looking for some unknown entity. It starts with critically evaluating the past and proceeds from there to determine what is worth keeping from the past and what is best left behind. We must carefully study what we have inherited. In order to do this, we need a free public atmosphere where we can debate and discuss ideas. No idea or doctrine should be off limits. There can be no censorship if renewal and reform are to take place. Free societies do not stagnate.

Liberal Islam deals with words and reason. How can words and being reasonable bring justice, many Muslims ask, when Muslim people today feel so threatened by forces outside their borders? When folks perceive a threat, the easiest and safest thing to do is return to those ways of being and doing that seem to have worked well in the past. Liberal Islam has everything to do with exchanging views—dialoguing. Fighting does not require rational thinking and dialogue. Much American foreign policy as well as fundamentalist Islamic policy assumes a pugnacious stance rather than going about the laborious process of diplomacy that requires us to connect with each other.

I am not going to give up trying to bring about change through my writing. My weapon is my critical scholarship. But the climate at the moment is not one in which many Muslims are of a mind to hear me. "What is this man talking about?" they ask. "We are fighting against an enemy, and he is talking about things that have no relevance for us." It's difficult—if not impossible—to convince people ready to fight for what they perceive to be their own survival that what they really need is knowledge.

It's downright scary.

13 The Way Forward

Islam, like any religion, speaks on several levels and from more than one perspective. Religious thinking in Islam, above all, is human expression about metaphysical reality. Islamic scholarship attempts to give a comprehensive and coherent understanding to the Qur'an, God's speech revealed to Prophet Muhammad by the angel Gabriel. Islamic thinkers—scholars, jurists, and philosophers—have applied their own particular disciplines to the Qur'an in order to ferret out meaning from the text. Human effort, grounded in and informed by a particular historical and social setting, distilled (and continues to distill) the material of revelation into a precise intellectual form.

The Arab-Islamic Reform Movement, begun in the nineteenth century, has been sidetracked. Under the wider heading of justice, we had begun to address issues concerning human rights, women's rights, and the rights of minority groups. We also started to deal with issues such as education, freedom, democracy, and progress. Today we must not let ourselves be defined by a phony identity that manifests itself in terms of backwardness and resistance to progress, under the guise of defending Islam and our identity. Our aborted Renaissance looked to the future as it attempted to break free from outdated structures of thinking. It's high time for us to pick up the ball where it was dropped, and carry on. To carry on, we need an orderly way to talk about religion—a discourse.

Religious discourse is human discourse—it consists of people talking about religion. Therefore, religious discourse has the ability to stimulate progress or defend the status quo. Discourse that envisions progress will be inherently critical. This criticism will be aimed at the past along with the present, and will encompass other cultures as well. Critical examination of Islam digs deep. Pioneers of modern Islamic discourse, such as Muhammad 'Abduh, Tâhâ Husayn, and 'Ali Abdel Râziq, contextualized social and political issues within religious discourse, attacking the thoughtless imitation of the past as a way to move Islamic culture forward. These men called for religious renewal, yes, but their discourse integrated the whole public realm into their understanding of that religious renewal. How can we think of ourselves as good Muslims when injustice runs rampant? Why is there such disparity (economic, social, political) between the so-called elite and ordinary citizens?

Conservative discourse, on the other hand, most often resists criticism and looks for pragmatic solutions to problems in the modern world that uphold the status quo. The Egyptian market became glutted with books on Arab nationalism and Islamic socialism during the 1950s and 1960s in an attempt to superimpose a practical, political ideology on the Egyptian people. These books lacked any kind of critical analysis. In the 1970s, books abounded that denounced market-oriented policies. These authors tried to make a case that agrarian reform, inheritance taxes, and interest rates were un-Islamic practices. As a result, many citizens supported Islamic investment companies as alternative institutions to Westernized banks. These Islamic investment companies were later exposed as fraudulent pyramid schemes—too late for many Egyptian people, who by this time had been swindled out of their life savings. Conservative, pragmatic religious discourse can generate alternative ways of interacting in the modern world, but does so without grappling effectively with changing circumstances. Conservative Islamic discourse merely spreads itself like a veneer over problems that emerge from the changes we experience in the ebb and flow of a world that is in constant flux.

Oftentimes the phrase "religious discourse" becomes synonymous with sacred propaganda and the rhetoric of Friday sermons. That's certainly not what I have in mind when it comes to a conversation about religion. Religious discourse is not preaching—something in dire need of reform and modernization in the Muslim world—but consists of a process that engages the intellect while grappling with the question "How can I hold on to Qur'anic values in a changing world?" Referring to words uttered by somebody, somewhere, at some time or another and expecting those words to magically effect a solution just doesn't work.

It is imperative for us to understand that in order to create a society based on freedom and justice, we must change the way we think. A new religious discourse is part of the broader call for freedom. For any endeavor—such as creating a just society—ultimately to be successful, citizens must be able to think critically and express themselves freely. Unfortunately, most of the Arab world today remains shackled with chains of fear, chains that squelch free thinking and its expression.

For renewal of religious discourse to take root, we need to take a long, hard look at our own religious legacy. There can be no safe doctrinal havens or sacred cows inaccessible to critique. Safe havens and sacred cows restrict the process of renewal and, bottom line, amount to censorship. Censorship and stagnation go hand in hand. Because religious discourse is tied to public discourse, all facets of society deteriorate as a result of censorship. Only confident and free societies have an ability to repel stagnation and decay. Challenging the status quo opens the pathway to progress. People must be free to hold what other folks deem to be erroneous opinions. People must be free to challenge opinions in the marketplace of ideas. Islam must protect this right. It's the only way to move forward with integrity. It's the only way to establish a just and free society.

Just what is it that fuels nothing less than panic nowadays when Muslims critique established Islamic thought? Why does Islamic culture today consider critique of our historical past and orthodox religious expression to be a crime? What do we make of the fact that the fifteenth-century encyclopedist Jalal al-Din al-Suyûtî (d. 1505) forthrightly stated that Prophet Muhammad received revelation (the Qur'an) only in content, and that the actual phrasing of the Qur'an came from the Prophet himself? Today, such an idea cannot be discussed, nor even mentioned, publicly. People have lost their lives for speaking out in this manner.

What is it that offends so many people when historians speak of the failure of Prophet Muhammad's preaching to win over Meccan society, forcing him to flee with his small band of followers to Medina? Why is there such animosity toward the arts, particularly the performing arts? Are not Qur'anic recitals a form of vocal performing art? Isn't the Qur'an a work of literature? Why do we prohibit the personification of historic, religious figures, thus impoverishing even further our culture's theatrical expression? Are we not able to distinguish between the represented figure and the actor playing a part? Can we not sort out reality from fiction? More to the point, are we not able to find spiritual meaning for our lives through artistic expression? Is it possible that we are so dull? It is as though Islamic culture has become incarcerated by literal and concrete thinking. No distinction is made between language (a symbolic system) that a culture uses to express and create itself, and Divine reality.

This is an odd phenomenon, given our broad historic legacy—one based on the Qur'an, a book that opposes *jâhiliyyah* (pre-Islamic tribal code of behavior) while calling for the engagement of an individual's conscience in the quest for justice and freedom. Islam gave birth to intellectual and philosophical structures that challenged the ways of the past. Intellectual and philosophical structures, though, cannot by themselves transform a culture. People must integrate these structures into the way they live. This is difficult to do. A culture's familiar ways of going about living in a society carry a momentum, and those familiar ways of being and doing have staying power.

It is at this juncture (where thought and practice meet) that we can begin looking for those fault lines that have led to ignorance, injustice, and tyranny in much of the Muslim world. The faults lay within Islamic social history, not Islamic religious texts. Arab-Islamic culture, not Islam, showed no confidence or faith in democracy and critical thought. Islamic history is human history, a history based on social, political, and economic factors. Understanding the Qur'an and applying its message has developed through social, political, and economic forces. Religion does determine and shape social life, but religion gets its shape, to a great extent, from factors present in that society. There never has been any such thing as a pure, abstract Islam situated above the rough-and-tumble of geography and history. We cannot speak of any one manifestation as being the true Islam, whether that manifestation takes form in the shape of the al-Azhar of Egypt, the Taliban of Afghanistan, the Hawza in Iran, the Zaytûna of Tunisia, the Wahhabi of Saudi Arabia, or the Diyanat of Turkey.

We can, though, speak about two dimensions of Islam—the historical dimension that presents its particular teaching regarding belief and ethics in a seventh-century context, and the universal dimension that presents values transcending time and place. Some Muslim thinkers emphasize the historical dimension, considering this interpretation essential to Islam. The field of jurisprudence emphasizes the historical dimension. Jurists deal with practical actions of individuals within their society. A variety of political Islamist groups, known as fundamentalists, see the jurist view of the Qur'an as the only true and valid understanding of Islam. It follows then that *shari'a* law—human law derived largely from the foundational texts of Islam (the Qur'an and Prophetic Tradition) along with the consensus of earlier generations—must be implemented in an Islamic society. Throughout most of Islamic history, the jurists' understanding of religion has taken hold and often has been held in place by force.

Reading the Qur'an from a different perspective suggests more universal and inclusive objectives. For example, creating a community of believers, rather than relying on behavior that a tribal system of kinship dictates to the individual, ushered in what I call human rational conduct. Rational thought and conduct freed the individual from the mindless duty of submitting to the tribal code of conduct. One was expected to replace *jâhiliyyah* with human, rational understanding. Another example would be establishing the practice of almsgiving. Social justice became an important facet of religious expression. Freedom to act according to one's conscience and caring for the poor in a society go beyond specific geographical boundaries and take us into a more universal understanding of religion.

This broader, more universal understanding of Islam, representing basic human principles, remains politically and intellectually marginalized in the Muslim world. Modern Muslim intellectuals (and I consider myself in this category) who try to perpetuate this broader understanding of Islam through our writing and through public dialogue are in the minority. I'm convinced we need a broader understanding of Islam if we are to be effective in the modern world. The Mu'tazilites, whom we met earlier, produced a rational theology able to cope with the demands of modernity in the ninth century.

The Mu'tazilites established the principle that knowledge starts from this world. We can speak about the unseen world only on the basis of indications furnished by the evident reality of the seen world. God and His attributes can be known only by reflection and acquired knowledge, not necessarily by direct or revealed knowledge. Ibn Tufayl's twelfth-century allegory, *Hayy ibn Yaqzân*, illustrates this point well.

This is a story about two islands. No human being ever lived on one of the islands until a child, known as Hayy ibn Yaqzân, comes ashore one day, having floated there in a box. His name means The Alive, son of The Awake. A gazelle suckles him until her death, at which time he is left on his own to provide for his needs. His innate intelligence, feeble at first, develops. Through the tedious process of observation and reflection, he acquires knowledge of the physical universe. His thinking takes him into the realm of metaphysics, and the existence of an all-powerful Creator becomes obvious to him. Through ascetic discipline of his mind and body, he seeks union with this One Eternal Spirit—as he has come to understand the Creator. Ultimately, he arrives at a state of ecstasy where his intellect merges with the Active Intellect and he is able to apprehend those things which eye has not seen, nor ear heard. Without prophet or revelation, he achieves full knowledge and everlasting happiness in metaphysical union with God.

One day, while walking on his island, he's astonished to discover a creature like himself. It's none other than a holy man named Asâl, a recent arrival from the neighboring island, where the good king Salaman rules. Life on Asâl's island revolves around a conventional religious system that uses rewards and punishments to keep people in line. Asâl has reached a deep level of spirituality—deeper than his peers have been able to achieve—and has come to what he believes to be an uninhabited island in order to reach even more depth through asceticism and solitude.

Asâl teaches Hayy language, and Hayy is amazed to discover that the pure Truth he struggled to attain in solitude is the same Truth symbolized by the religion Asâl professes. When Hayy learns about the condition of people on the other island, he is moved with compassion, and vows to go and offer them the benefit of his knowledge. Asâl and Hayy set out on this mission together. However, the mission is an abysmal failure. Most of their audiences cannot grasp Hayy's exposition of the Truth. They call it a dangerous innovation and become hostile toward him. Because they are fettered by their senses, they can respond only to concrete imagery. Their moral nature responds only to a crude system of rewards and punishments. Hayy soon realizes that the Prophet Muhammad's way with them, as expressed in the Qur'an, is the only effective method for them. He apologizes for his intrusion, exhorts them to be faithful to their religion, and returns with Asâl to his home island.

The name of the hero of this allegory is suggestive. *Hayy* means "alive"; *ibn* means "son of"; *Yaqzân* means "awake." "The awakened" refers to the intellect. Human beings are alive only when their intellect becomes activated. With intellectual reflection, a human being can acquire knowledge of God. Divine knowledge need not depend on revelation, although revelation need not contradict knowledge obtained through human intellect. Enlightenment, however, is not purely an intellectual exercise. Our hero, Hayy, practicing asceticism in mind and body as well as developing his intellect, achieves union with God—something that happens only through this synthesis of rationalism and mysticism.

Ibn Rushd (1126–1198), known as Averroes in the West, influenced both Jewish and Christian philosophers (Maimonides, Thomas Aquinas, and Albertus Magnus) with his rationalistic thought. Averroes argued that real knowledge took shape in the form of philosophical, rational knowledge. Only a small, elite minority of society should be privy to this knowledge—knowledge he thought would harmfully affect the belief system of most people. We saw this illustrated in our allegory. Hayy felt compelled to withdraw his message and insights from the people living on the other island. Because they strictly followed religious teachings and adhered to their literal meaning, they were unable to apprehend Hayy's "higher" discourse.

Before Averroes, Abu Hâmid Muhammad al-Ghazâlî (d. 1111), a Sufi, wrote a book considered to be his masterpiece, *The Revival of the Religious Sciences (Ihyâ' 'ulûm al-Dîn)*.[1] This work became extremely popular—only the Qur'an and the *hâdith* (text based on the life of the Prophet) surpassed it in popularity. Al-Ghazâlî emphasized that mystical knowledge is not meant for the public. Simply stated, he believed sound knowledge (and to his way of thinking, sound knowledge took the shape of mystical understanding) is revealed to a chosen elite.

Despite their different philosophical orientations, Averroes and al-Ghazâlî agreed about the necessity to keep ordinary people distanced from true knowledge. This legacy has stayed with us in the Muslim world, especially since al-Ghazâlî's writings dominated Islamic discourse until the nineteenth century.

The nineteenth century ushered in a new age. The Muslim world felt threatened by European political aggression. Islam became identified not just as a nationality or an ethnicity, but as a repository of specific characteristics of the collective "self" (Muslim) opposed to the "other" (European). Intellectuals responded to this aggression by defending Islam and Islamic culture against those who simply pronounced Islam to be backward rather than looking at the social, economic, and political realities of the Arab world in order to understand why Arab societies took on a particular configuration. Islam was put on the defensive. It felt it had to explain and interpret itself as a religion that encourages progress, is rational as well as scientific, and accepts modern institutions.

I continuously struggle with where to place myself as I wrestle with creating a modern Islamic discourse. Does modern Islamic thought have to start with Averroes's philosophy and the rational understanding held by the Mu'tazilites? I used to think so. Today, I'm not so sure. The huge chasm that exists in Averroes' philosophy between the elite and the public will never help to achieve enlightenment—a free and just society.

According to Averroes, knowledge is not for everybody, it is not open to all—it is an elite privilege. Enlightenment, therefore, can never be institutionalized in society. Enlightenment has never been a public movement in any Muslim country. Our history is riddled with examples of how those who hold political authority have been able to impose their thinking on the majority through the force of inquisition. Ignoring the individual's intellectual freedom only perpetuates this thinking, and hence repressive societies abound. This notion of dividing people into the elite (knowledgeable) and the public (ignorant), the cultured and the commoner, and the statesman and the ordinary citizen dominates the Muslim world even though education is free and open to all.

The ideals of the Enlightenment—freedom of speech and freedom of thought—values that have become part of my academic research, are not fully embraced in the Muslim world. The fear, of course, is that Islamic values will be rendered null and void if freedoms, as envisioned by the Enlightenment, are unleashed. There is this sense that there should be security zones, places not accessible to intellectual discussion or academic investigation. Academic research, freedom of thought, and freedom of speech are guaranteed only as long as they do not impinge on what is known as absolute truth. Of course, truth is the interpretation given to the Qur'an by the orthodox, those who have the political power to enforce their views. Orthodox Islam, it should come as no surprise, emphasizes obedience as a religious, obligatory duty. Political rulers often combine political and religious authority and become known as God's authority on earth. (Christianity had this understanding for years, something known as the divine right of kings.)

Many Muslims are persuaded that freedom of thought and free-dom of speech are products of Western culture and European civiliza-tion—a culture and civilization seen as antithetical to the essence of Islamic culture and civilization. In order to avoid being swallowed, controlled, and manipulated by powers that once sought to conquer them, many Muslims believe it cannot be in their best interest to adopt values associated with the West.

Is there hope? Is it possible to envision Muslims embracing free-dom within a framework of democracy? Yes, of course. However, it is imperative that citizens in what are generally known as democratic nations understand how their countries' own economic and political interests often subvert the very thing (democracy) they purport to want established in Islamic states. It is also important to understand that it is not Islam that prevents Muslims from accepting democracy, but rather a religious and political dogmatic trend of thought, ever prevalent, which claims that Islam and modernity contradict one another.

Political regimes in the Muslim world to a large extent unfold in what I call modernity without rationality. Since democracy is not based solely on respect for the individual, but takes into account through free elections the individual's opinion, it seems that this lack of rationality found throughout the Muslim world blocks democracy at every turn. Turkey, the only Muslim country ever to claim to be a secular state, controls its so-called democracy through military cen-sorship. Iran's ayatollahs, upon seizing power, interestingly enough did not restore the caliphate, but established a republic. All the demo-cratic accoutrements—popular election, a constituent assembly, a parliament, a president, political factions, a constitution, and so forth—emerged. But can there be democracy when clerics wield au-thority? Can shari'a law as interpreted by the ayatollahs yield a demo-cratic society? Would a secular party be welcomed in Iran? Doubtful. Both countries, under different guises, reflect this idea of modernity without rationality.

The West places an inordinate amount of pressure on the Mus-lim world in order to protect the West's economic and political inter-ests. There have been a number of puppet political regimes in Muslim countries (Iran, Iraq, Afghanistan), held in place by Western powers against the will of the Muslim people. This is democracy? No way. In addition, how many times is Islam portrayed, especially by the Western media, as an inherently violent religion and antithetical to Western values? How is it that in many developing countries a wider and wider gap exists between the haves and the have-nots? Modernity, human rights, and democracy seem to be the domain of the privileged, who, more often than not, turn a deaf ear to underprivileged folks crying out for justice. This cry for justice, when it goes unheeded by those with privilege and power, easily turns violent. The seeds of violence are found at this juncture, not in Islam—or in any religion, for that matter.

How do we go forward? I trace the conflict between secular and religious forces that we experience within Muslim cultures to an absence of a public forum for debate and dialogue. Many ideas and opinions circulate among us. I believe that defending democracy unconditionally is the only way to crystallize these ideas and opinions. It is imperative that we defend a democracy that does not shunt aside any of those opinions coming from our perceived enemies.

The developed world navigated this ideological terrain by agreeing to organize its disagreements through the mechanism of democracy, relying heavily on freedom of speech—the ability to express one's opinion. It's high time that we in the Arab world began to organize our disagreements. The saying "I may disagree with you, but I am ready to give my life to defend your right to express your opinion" needs to seep into the marrow of our collective bones. Those who are afraid of disagreement should look again at our history. When did Arabs ever agree with each other about anything? Historically, there has always been a difference of opinion among us.

In modern history, Muslims have managed to present a united front in their struggle against Western imperialism and Zionism. These two threats have managed to squelch the establishment of civil, democratic society based on multiplicity, diversity, and the peaceful circulation of power.

At the same time, I believe that those democratic countries that have inherited the values of the Enlightenment—freedom of thought, freedom of expression—need to reclaim those freedoms and apply those eroding values in their own societies. The West badly needs to put its own house back in order.

Muslims need to focus on creating just and equitable societies based on creatively formulating and integrating thoughtful religious and political discourse into daily life. Seeing in a new way—an act that enables us to create a better society based on a fresh perspective—then becomes useful in the modern world. It's high time we shed this *jâhiliyyah,* blind obedience to the echoes of our ancestor's voices.

Appendix

On this eighth day of June 2002, the Franklin Delano Roosevelt Freedom of Worship Medal is awarded to Nasr H. Abu Zaid, who holds the prestigious Cleveringa Chair at Leiden University, as a defender of freedom of thought and conscience. Like Leiden Professor Cleveringa, who in 1940 spoke out against the dismissal of all Jewish professors by the Nazis, you—as a professor of Islamic Studies—have attacked both the Islamists who advocate intolerance for those within the Muslim diaspora who do not accept their views, and those in the West who in their ignorance and cultural arrogance equate Islam with terrorism. At great personal cost, you have spoken the truth eloquently and forcefully, a champion of intellectual freedom for professor and pupil, cleric and layman. Through it all you have remained firm in your commitment to the principle that "man is alive only when his intellect is activated."

For this courageous, if lonely, position you were exiled from Egypt by a civil court in 1995. The court pronounced you a heretic and apostate, declaring that you were no longer entitled to be married to your dear wife, Dr. Ebtehal Younes. Now living in the Netherlands, a land that in the seventeenth century was a refuge for religious exiles from England on their way to the New World, and that continues to embody the humanist spirit of free inquiry of the great Erasmus of Rotterdam, you are in the right place to speak to the world.

A hermeneutic scholar of the Qur'an, who understands with clarity the evolution, since the seventh century, of the major interpretations of Islamic scripture, you have embraced the rational dimension of an enlightened tradition in Islam as well as the mystical tradition. Critical of those militant anti-secularists—in America we call them fundamentalists—who justify their righteousness and aggressive actions in the name of God, you both locate and affirm the spirit of tolerance, of nonviolence, and indeed of equality among both men and women in the Qur'an.

Growing up a peasant boy in Quhafa, a village in the Nile Delta, you had memorized the Qur'an by the age of eight, but, diverted from your love of such study by your father, you went on to become a technician, an interlude which allowed you to become intimately acquainted with the Muslim Brothers before returning to your Qur'anic studies. While fascinated by the Muslim Brothers' commitments, you came to distrust the merger in their ideology of Islam and the state, a recent development in Islamic history, and one which you regard as leading inexorably toward totalitarian dictatorship, the worst kind of despotism because it presumes to exercise authority on Earth in the name of a higher authority. A serious scholar of Islam and of Arabic, you studied in Philadelphia and Osaka, as well as in Cairo. While in Japan, you wrote *The Concept of the Text*, interpreting the Qur'an in its historical context, a major if fundamentally controversial approach in the eye of fundamentalist Islamists.

At the dawn of our new century, when religious intolerance looms as the most dangerous source of conflict—indeed of terrorism—among human beings, your courageous independence of thought, devotion to Islam, clarity of vision, and keen understanding of western European philosophy and religion, including modernism, as well as your Erasmian belief in humanity, makes your voice indispensable in the cross-cultural conversations so desperately needed to foster mutual respect and understanding. May this Freedom of Worship Medal, cast in the spirit of Franklin D. Roosevelt, give you renewed strength to persevere in your quest for true enlightenment among and between men and women of all religious faiths and classes, and an expanded audience for your wise teaching.

FREEDOM OF WORSHIP AWARD SPEECH—NASR ABU ZAID

Besmi 'Allahi 'Rahman 'Rahim
In the Name of God, the Compassionate, the Merciful
Your Majesty,
Your Royal Highness,
Miss Elizabeth Roosevelt,
Miss Margaret Roosevelt,
Ambassador William J. Vanden Heuvel,
Mr. Van Gelder, the Queen's Commissioner in Zeeland,
Your Excellencies,
Ladies and Gentlemen,
Al-Salamu 'alaykum wa rahmatu 'Allahi wa Barakatuh
May peace and the mercy of God and His blessings be upon you.

It is a great honor to receive the medal of Freedom of Worship this year. This great honor implies a great responsibility. The history of Islam, as the last of the Abrahamic religions, has made it very possible to acknowledge and respect all previous religions and to establish "freedom of faith and freedom of worship" as an essential component of the faith. Even the traditional concept, identifying non-Muslims as the "protected people," reflects the existence of a sphere of freedom within the framework of traditional Islamic thought.

Reality, however, does not always reflect the ideal. Hence comes the responsibility of the intellectuals, the writers and the scholars in all cultures. The "four freedoms"—freedom of speech and expression, freedom of worship, freedom from want, and freedom from fear—are meant for every human being everywhere in the world. The dream of Franklin Delano Roosevelt has not yet, unfortunately, become true. Our world of the third millennium is still a world of fear, want, oppression, and injustice. Destruction of houses of worship by religious fanatics, military intrusion to altars by politicians, genocide of others because they belong to another faith, are still worldwide phenomena. This makes the receiving of this great honor a very heavy responsibility.

As a Muslim and a scholar of Islamic Studies, the first Muslim to receive such an honorary award, I feel obliged to explicate what I think [is] the double message implied in awarding me the medal of Freedom of Worship. The message is to address both the Western world and the Muslim world as such. Islam is not static, nondynamic, or a fixed set of rules. It is not a violent terrorist religion by nature. Any religion could be misused, politicized, and manipulated to serve certain ideology. The Qur'an, the holy book of Muslims, is silent; it does not speak by itself but people speak it out. As the Word of God to man, its understanding and interpretation reflect the human dimension of religion. It is then unacceptable to ascribe to Islam whatever problems Muslims might have in their sociohistorical existence.

Let me take this extremely exceptional occasion to greet the great man of our time, Mr. Nelson Mandela, the man who suffered the utmost of human suffering for about thirty years to bring peace and equality in his country. More than that, when he triumphed, he did not follow the public emotional reaction of revenge; he insisted on propagating forgiveness and peacefully healing the wounds of the past. He also willingly stepped down [from] his political office to fight in another front, the front of human need all over the world.

Dear Mr. Mandela,

I hope the lessons you taught the world will not be forgotten. It is also a great honor to me to have my name mentioned alongside your great name.

God bless you all, *wa al-salam 'alaykum wa rahmatu 'Allahi wa baraktuh.*

Notes

PREFACE

1. Mary Anne Weaver, "Revolution by Stealth," *The New Yorker* (June 8, 1998): 40.
2. Mark 16:15–16, Authorized King James Version.

CHAPTER 1

1. Fauzi M. Najjar, "Islamic Fundamentalism and the Intellectuals: The Case of Nasr Hamid Abu Za[i]d," *British Journal of Middle Eastern Studies* 27, no. 2 (2000): 179.
2. Nasr Abu Zaid, *Critique of Islamic Discourse* (in Arabic) (Cairo: Madbouli Press, 1992).
3. Nasr Abu Zaid, "Inquisition Trial in Egypt," *Recht van de Islam* 15 (1998): 52.
4. Najjar, "Islamic Fundamentalism and the Intellectuals, " 194.
5. Ibid., 193–194.
6. Ibid., 194–195.
7. Ibid., 195.
8. Ibid., 196.
9. Weaver, "Revolution by Stealth," 44.
10. Ayman Bakr and Elliott Colla, interview with Nasr Hamid Abu Za[i]d about ideology, interpretation, and political authority. "Silencing Is at the Heart of My Case," *Middle East Report* (November–December 1993): 29.

al-Sabur Shahin, *My Father Adam: The Story of Creation Between nd Truth* (in Arabic) (Cairo: Dar al-Nasr for Islamic Publication, 1998). ar, "Islamic Fundamentalism and the Intellectuals," 199.

CHAPTER 4

1. 'Alî Abdel-Râziq, *Islam and the Foundation of Political Authority* (in Arabic) (Cairo: Egyptian Public Organization for Books, 1925).
2. Tâhâ Husayn, *Pre-Islamic Poetry* (in Arabic) (Cairo: Dar al-Ma'arif, 1926).
3. Tâhâ Husayn, *Pre-Islamic Literature* (in Arabic) (Cairo: Dar al-Ma'arif, 1927).
4. Nasr Abu Zaid, *The Trend of Rational Exegesis of the Qur'an: A Study of the Mu'tazilite's Concept of Qur'anic Metaphor* (in Arabic) (Beirut: The Arabic Cultural Center, 1982).
5. Ibn 'Arabî, *The Meccan Revelation* (in Arabic) (Cairo: Bulaq, 1858).
6. Nasr Abu Zaid, *The Philosophy of Hermeneutics* (in Arabic) (Beirut: The Arabic Cultural Center, 1983).
7. Nasr Abu Zaid, *The Concept of the Text: A Reinvestigation of Classical Qur'anic Disciplines* (in Arabic) (Cairo: Egyptian Public Organization for Books, 1990).

CHAPTER 5

1. Lawrence Wright, "The Man behind Bin Laden," *The New Yorker* (September 6, 2002): 62.
2. Ibid.
3. Nasr Abu Zaid, *Circles of Fear: Analysis of the Discourse about Women* (in Arabic) (Beirut: The Arabic Cultural Center, 1999).
4. The speeches of Anna Eleanor Roosevelt and Nasr Abu Zaid, given at the Franklin D. Roosevelt Four Freedoms Award Ceremony in June 2002, are in the appendix.

CHAPTER 7

1. Inazo Nitobe, *Bushido—The Way of the Samurai* (New York: G. P. Putnam, 1905).

2. Nasr Abu Zaid, *The Concept of the Text: A Study of the Sciences of the Qur'an* (in Arabic) (Cairo: Egyptian Public Organization for Books, 1990).

3. Nasr Abu Zaid, *Critique of Islamic Discourse* (in Arabic) (Cairo: Dar Sina, 1992).

4. Dieter Senghaas and Nasr Abu Zaid, "The Islamic World and the Modern Age" in *Development, Cultural Diversity and Peace: Visions for a New World Order* (Bonn: Development and Peace Foundation, 1996).

CHAPTER 8

1. Nasr Abu Zaid, *The Concept of the Text: A Study of the Sciences of the Qur'an* (in Arabic) (Cairo: Egyptian Public Organization for Books, 1990).

CHAPTER 9

1. Nasr Abu Zaid, *Critique of Islamic Discourse* (in Arabic) (Cairo: Madbouli, 1992).

CHAPTER 10

1. Interview with Fathi Amer. Originally published in the Cairo newspaper *al-Arabi* (November 7, 14, and 21, 1999). Available at www.geocities.com/lrrs.geo/Zaid/zaidarabiinterview.htm.

CHAPTER 11

1. For a fuller treatment and development of the concept of justice, see Nasr Abu Zaid, "The Qur'anic Concept of Justice," *Forum for Intercultural Philosophizing* 2 (2001): 1–43. Also available at www.polylog.org/them/2/fcs8-en.htm.

2. Jalal al-Din Suyûtî, *Occasions of Revelations* (in Arabic) (Cairo: Dar al-Tahrir, reprint edition 1989).

CHAPTER 12

1. Muhammad 'Abduh, *Islam Is the Religion of Science and Civilization* (in Arabic) (Cairo: Dar al-Manar, 1923).

2. *Chinua Achebe,* prod. and dir. Gail Pellett, Public Affairs Television, 1994, videocassette.

3. Jane Dammen McAuliffe, ed., *The Encyclopedia of the Qur'an*, vol. 1 (Leiden: Brill, 2001), 426.

4. Nasr Abu Zaid, "Heaven Which Way?" *Al-Ahram Weekly Online* no. 603 (September 12–18, 2002): 3.

CHAPTER 13

All quotations from the Qur'an taken from *The Koran*. Translated with notes by N. J. Dawood. (London: Penguin Books, Reprinted 1999.)

1. Abu Hâmid al-Ghazâlî, *The Revival of the Religious Sciences* (in Arabic) (Cairo: Al-Halabi, n.d.).

Index

About the Authors

NASR ABU ZAID is Professor of Arabic and Islamic Studies at Leiden University in the Netherlands. He has published several books in Arabic and many articles in English. In 2002 he was awarded the Freedom of Worship Medal by the Franklin and Eleanor Roosevelt Institute.

ESTHER R. NELSON is Professor of Religious Studies at Virginia Commonwealth University. She is also a freelance writer and has published her work in a variety of mainstream publications.

CPSIA information can be obtained at www.ICGtesting.com
Printed in the USA
BVOW03*0949100214

344009BV00009BA/651/P